Dark Matter in Breaking Cyphers

Dark Matter in Breaking Cyphers

The Life of Africanist Aesthetics in Global Hip Hop

IMANI KAI JOHNSON

OXFORD
UNIVERSITY PRESS

Oxford University Press is a department of the University of Oxford. It furthers
the University's objective of excellence in research, scholarship, and education
by publishing worldwide. Oxford is a registered trade mark of Oxford University
Press in the UK and certain other countries.

Published in the United States of America by Oxford University Press
198 Madison Avenue, New York, NY 10016, United States of America.

© Oxford University Press 2023

All rights reserved. No part of this publication may be reproduced, stored in
a retrieval system, or transmitted, in any form or by any means, without the
prior permission in writing of Oxford University Press, or as expressly permitted
by law, by license, or under terms agreed with the appropriate reproduction
rights organization. Inquiries concerning reproduction outside the scope of the
above should be sent to the Rights Department, Oxford University Press, at the
address above.

You must not circulate this work in any other form
and you must impose this same condition on any acquirer.

Library of Congress Cataloging-in-Publication Data
Names: Johnson, Imani Kai, author.
Title: Dark matter in breaking cyphers : the life of Africanist aesthetics
in global hip hop / by Imani Kai Johnson, Ph.D., Assistant Professor,
Critical Dance Studies, University of California Riverside.
Description: New York : Oxford University Press, [2023] |
Includes bibliographical references and index.
Identifiers: LCCN 2022005170 (print) | LCCN 2022005171 (ebook) |
ISBN 9780190856700 (Paperback) | ISBN 9780190856694 (hardback) |
ISBN 9780190856724 (ePub)
Subjects: LCSH: Hip-hop dance. | African American aesthetics.
Classification: LCC GV1796.H57 J65 2022 (print) | LCC GV1796.H57
(ebook) | DDC 793.3—dc23/eng/20220321
LC record available at https://lccn.loc.gov/2022005170
LC ebook record available at https://lccn.loc.gov/2022005171

DOI: 10.1093/oso/9780190856694.001.0001

Paperback printed by Integrated Books International, United States of America
Hardback printed by Bridgeport National Bindery, Inc., United States of America

Portions of chapter 4 were previously published as "B-Boying and Battling in a Global Context:
The Discursive Life of Difference," *Alif: Journal of Comparative Poetics*, n.31 (2011): 173–195.
Portions of chapter 2 were previously published as "Battling in the Bronx: Social Choreography &
Outlaw Culture Among Early Hip Hop Streetdancers in New York City," *Dance Research Journal* 50.2
(August 2018): 62–75.

> Try to think bigger than you ever have
> or had courage enough to do:
> that blackness is not where whiteness
> wanders off to die: but that it is
> like the dark matter
> between stars and galaxies in
> the Universe
> that ultimately
> holds it all
> together.
>
> —Alice Walker, "Here It Is" (2016)

Contents

Being There	ix
Preface	xiii
Introduction: Dark Matter, Breaking, Cyphers	1
Dark Matter	25
1. Dark Matter and Diaspora: Cyphers in an Africanist Context	29
Superheroes Among Us	59
2. Battling in the Bronx: Social Choreography and Outlaw Culture	63
Crossing the Line	95
3. Badass B-Girls Dancing the Dissonance of a Breaking Sociality	99
Circles or Cyphers	127
4. Dancing Global Hip Hop: Negotiating Difference and Tradition in Cyphers	131
Coda: Cyber Cyphers and Africanist Aesthetics	164
Acknowledgments	173
Notes	177
Selected Bibliography	221
Index	229

Being There

US-Battle of the Year in Hollywood, California, 20 August 2006
It is nearing one o'clock in the afternoon, and the doors will open in an hour. I sit in a darkened corner attending to my brand new mini-DV camera and watching the scene unfold before me. As hundreds of breakers line up outside along the Hollywood Walk of Fame, I prepare myself for the day's undertakings. US-Battle of the Year (BOTY) is a regional preliminary to International BOTY in Germany. In it, crews of eight to ten perform a five-minute choreographed show for the stage, from which the top four crews then battle for a variety of cash and prizes, including a trip to Germany to battle for worldwide recognition. For me, attending battles usually begins by taking in all of the fashion choices of those in the line: colorful, athletic, and strategically coordinated outfits that are functional yet fresh. Before the doors open, the space is bare save for a handful of people practicing on the stage or scurrying about to ensure the bar is well stocked with bottled water. When the doors open, the lights are predictably low as it's time for open cyphering, my main motivation for coming. This event's organizer, Poe One, is known for making cyphers "a priority."[1]

Two hours later, there are wall-to-wall cyphers and it seems like there is always something to see. Each cypher borders on multiple others such that at one point, all I have to do is slightly pivot around and I am on the outskirts of another circle. The low lighting summons a focus from spectators and dancers alike, but outbursts from the enthusiastic crowds across the room constantly pull my attention "over there." At this point in my research, I am well rehearsed in being an active nondancer in the circle, so I transition with ease.

Over time and with experience I have learned that I am as much a part of the unfolding scene as I am an observer of it. My early attempts for impartial and even distant observation, as academic convention, made me feel like an intruder who was just taking up space. Cypher spectators are <u>in</u> it—listening, watching, feeling, responding. There are unspoken rules for the nondancer in the cypher. Personally, I have seven:

1. It is imperative that you express yourself. If you really like something, if it looks painful, if this is <u>your</u> song, it needs to come out. Your reactions matter because you're part of the energy exchange.
2. The shorter you are, the less you'll see. Accept it; I have.
3. Getting on the floor or climbing to higher ground for a better view may be good ideas. Risking getting stepped on or losing your balance can be worth it.
4. Stay anchored. Don't let people push you around and only move as far as you must to keep your spot (if it's good). If you don't, you will quickly find yourself in the very back, only able to see the flailing legs of someone's power moves.
5. Clearly then, "rude" is flexible. It is not wrong to take advantage of an open space by stepping directly in front of someone else.
6. With that said, dancers have priority over spectators. They will and should step in front of you if it's convenient for them. In that same vein, children and crew members will do the same. In this case, it is in poor taste to ask them to get out of your way or to step in front of them if you're not dancing. (Lesson learned.)
7. Lastly, don't get hit. Footwork or sloppy power moves are quick and unpredictable, which can hurt if you're not careful and observant. If you get hit, shake it off because unless you're bleeding you may not get any sympathy or attention anyway. In other words, it's not about you.

I remember how I learned some of these lessons, but the rest I just absorbed over time. I suppose after being pushed to the back, stepped on, kicked, and criticized, eventually I learned to adjust. Breaking is deliciously erratic, with dramatic changes in direction and proximity that, even when anticipated, does not make the dance predictable. My rules are ad hoc, unwritten until now, and matter as much as my equipment. Poe One asked me to tape the event so my camera (one of the few) makes it easier to finagle my way into inner circles or to shoo people from blocking my view. Yet I still have to raise it overhead at times and shoot beyond my own line of sight.

The camera can also make me feel like I'm not a part of it. The two-inch LCD screen makes it seem as if I'm watching TV. And prioritizing the dancer on my screen can mean cutting the crowd off at the knees. There's always some move, a gesture from an onlooker, a back story to a battle that I am unaware of that fuels the performance. By subordinating the crowd's reaction, I lose sight of the dynamic between dancers and spectators, which is fundamental to the ritual.

To focus on one means missing some part of the other, which means I cannot take in everything. This is true whether I have a camera or not. Rule 7 feels especially palpable as I avoid the occasional foot flying near my head. I hope the recording takes in more than my eyes miss but resign myself to the footage's inevitable incompleteness.

At the same time, it is impossible to feel entirely separate from the moment. The speakers belt out the urgent beats of Mongo Santamaria's '69 rendition of The Temptations' 1968 hit "Cloud 9." I tap into a musical groove, imagining my parents as teens dancing to this song or the original when it came out. This cross-generational connection flows through the speakers and I ride that feeling, becoming a part of the cypher's many conversations. I start to put the camera away, battery drained. Someone walks up and asks me if I have footage of them in the cypher I have just left, and I honestly cannot remember. I go to plug in my camera in an off-limits room and return to rejoin the cyphers.

Each circle has its own life. Some are intense and tight-knit. Others never find their rhythm, dispersing before they ever really begin. From a bird's-eye view, the continual formation and dispersal of each cypher has the pattern of pebbles dropped in a pond, rippling endlessly into new tidal flows. After several hours, my sense of time begins to falter when I melt into the collective. There is no "personal space." I feel the b-girl next to me taking in gulps of air as she rises from the floor drenched in sweat. I can feel the chest of the man behind me as he presses forward in an attempt to look overhead, and when he shifts the tickle of air tells me he's left a sweat spot on my shirt. I can smell the breath of the kid next to me every time he cries out in excitement or disappointment. And I am leaning on someone I don't know. My locs brush across another's shoulder each time I move for a better view. More so than anything, a heat emanates from our bodies, confounded by pungent smell of the whole room. A steamy funk rises. The club feels like a sauna with the aroma of a gym, and I am part of it.

The circle begins to close in on itself. The more into it we are, the closer we have to get, as if proximity is praise. Whatever space is available becomes something to fill, but that feeling never lasts. While the tipping point is unclear, sometime during a cypher's peak intensity is also the moment of its demise. The more densely formed they are, the less those in the back can see to the point where they stop trying and simply walk away. As people depart, whatever accumulated in our dense circle begins to fade as well. The hot, sweaty, cramped cypher seems to inhale fresh air as we relax into our individual selves again. I move from one circle to another and these moments blend together, becoming one extended cypher.

The next thing I know, I am scooped up by a swarm of people rushing toward the center of the room. I know a fight has (almost?) broken out, but why and who is involved? I want to see, but in the seconds it takes me to regain steady footing and discern the activity, it's over. I am there in time to see two heated young men being held back by friends as they are pushed and pulled into neutral corners. They are familiar faces, and this fight is a carryover from last night's pre-party with members of the Zulu Kings. The backstory is lost on me save for the other crew's adopted name: Zulu Killers. It is not the only near-fight of the evening. Soon after I witness the tail end of what I can only describe as a young woman taking swings at a man and bouncers threatening to escort her out. I know even less about this fight. Despite these interruptions, it does not take long for cyphers to resume. People's priorities are clear, and the evening proceeds as if uninterrupted.

By 11:00 p.m., my body tells me in no uncertain terms that I have been standing, squatting, angling, reaching, and sitting crossed legged for over nine hours! I am suddenly and overwhelmingly exhausted. Whatever daze I had fallen into lifts. My energy reserves depleted. I am dog tired, though now I need to actually speak to people, introduce or reintroduce myself, make appointments, and the like. People walk around literally dripping with sweat and smiling from ear to ear, energized by their exertions. Some change into the spare clothes they bring in anticipation of the cold air outside. Others opt instead to just take off their shirts altogether, coincidentally showing off sweaty and well toned bare-chested or sports bra-topped torsos. The lights come up fully. Cypher-time is done.

Preface

I grew up among the first generation of youth for whom Hip Hop was always part of pop culture. I could feel Hip Hop's influence on TV commercials, in fashion, videography, in movies, in the R&B and New Jack swing that sampled the same beats. By the late 1980s, classic Hip Hop movies like *Beat Street*, the *Breakin'* series, and *Krush Groove* were on regular rotation on basic cable TV, in all of their eighties cheesiness, and I was captivated. Watching kids dance on flattened, discarded cardboard boxes on crowded street corners, or in the park, or local basketball courts felt like some version of Neverland: a world of Black and Brown youth, run by kids for kids. Since I attended predominantly white schools in Northern California, this was exciting and very different. I taught myself what I could glean from movies, a six-step and a backspin, though I doubt either amounted to very much. I would eventually let it go, as many had by 1986. As Hip Hop music grew in popularity, "breakdancing" was treated as a passing fad. This book was a chance to delve into a culture that has always thrilled and awed me. While I never developed the skills to competently battle in a cypher (*I took my first breaking class at thirty!*), my research offered a chance to learn from those who rocked cyphers of all kinds, not just battles. In doing so, I came to recognize the force of cyphering's aesthetic imperatives.

Dark Matter in Breaking Cyphers: The Life of Africanist Aesthetics in Global Hip Hop focuses on the Africanist aesthetics of Hip Hop that are evident in its cypher rituals and that ultimately hold together a global culture. It makes the case that, rather than prioritizing dance technique alone, they teach alternative knowledges, values, and forms of sociality. Cyphers teach participants about Hip Hop through Africanist aesthetics (call and response, polyrhythms, improvisation, etc.), influences that have been de-emphasized or erased altogether in popular understandings of Hip Hop as a global cultural signifier.

In the context of breaking in the first quarter of the twenty-first century, the period of my research, I explore these aesthetics, traditions, and legacies in contexts not necessarily comprised of Black people. What happens to Africanist aesthetics when Black or African diasporic people no longer dominate the culture? What changes, or gets lost, discarded, or adopted, and what persists? What do we enable by thinking about Africanist aesthetics in the context of global Hip Hop today? Might the adoption of Africanist aesthetics by non-African diasporans model forms of cross-cultural exchange *through* Black aesthetics rather than the antiblackness of cultural erasure and appropriation? However aspirational this last question may seem, the possibility nonetheless persists.

Cyphering encapsulates an entire constellation of diasporic elements and sensibilities that Hip Hop did not invent but rather rebirthed.[1] What I refer to as the dark matter in breaking cyphers are those invisibilized Africanist aesthetics. As Alice Walker reminds us, blackness does not cut off Hip Hop, breaking, and cyphers from the world; blackness opens Hip Hop up to the world in distinct ways. When we look at cyphers, know that they are enacting more than a combination of acrobatics and tricks. The capacity to groove to the music in a playful exchange with others means, at its core, activating a constellation of aesthetic elements that give way to cyphering's epistemological possibilities. To miss the dark matter of cyphers is to miss all the things that make nine hours feel like minutes.

Introduction

Dark Matter, Breaking, Cyphers

Breaking is a culture unto itself, a form of living with its own set of cultural codes, communicative styles, fashions, and social priorities. Within that culture and circulating as that culture are cyphers, deceptively simple practices with layers of meaning. In the simplest terms, a cypher is a dance circle: a crowd of engaged participants (comprised of both active spectators and potential dancers) surrounding breakers who take turns, one at a time typically, dancing in the center. Cloaked as a series of individual acts of dance, cyphers are actually collective enactments wherein dancers and nondancers are both "in it," providing instantaneous support and critique, studying someone else's style, and vibing with each other. The feeling and atmosphere cultivated by these exchanges are extraordinary. I have attended events that lasted more than eight hours; and I have watched breakers cypher for the duration of that time. In the orb of surrounding energy cultivated by the collectivity, those hours sometimes passed like minutes, reminding me that the ritual itself is a powerful force that can shift our experiences of space and time. What may be less obvious, or perhaps gets taken for granted, is that cyphers are also ritual practices that evoke a constellation of Africanist aesthetics in global Hip Hop, teaching lessons in cultural values, sociality, musical history, and spiritual expression through physical practice. In this chapter I lay some groundwork that will allow us to play in the cypher-chapters to come.

The term "Africanist aesthetics" refers to aesthetic imperatives and expressive principles that are evident within and across African and African diasporic cultures. I build on Brenda Dixon Gottschild's use in *Digging the Africanist Presence in American Performance: Dance & Other Contexts*, wherein she employs "Africanist" to "signify the African and African American resonances and presences, trends, and phenomena."[1] The meaningfulness of Africanist aesthetics extends beyond the fact of them as "survivals" or "retentions"—that case has been well established by earlier generations of scholars, and should be understood as *living* cultural resources.[2] Gottschild uses the term "invisibilized" to get at how their influences have been rendered invisible by racism, segregation, and discrimination in the context of a racially stratified US.[3] African Americans have been historically disarticulated from their own cultural production once that expressive practice has achieved mass commercial appeal. Rock 'n' roll and jazz are examples. Oftentimes, those forms are repackaged as genres whose openness is disarticulated from the Africanist dimensions that shape the terms of that openness. Hip Hop dances are embroiled in their own version of this process when read as simply American, invisibilizing its unnamed Africanist dimensions. As a dance scholar, I continue in the path carved out by Gottschild and others like Halifu Osumare, whose book *The Africanist Aesthetics in Global Hip-Hop: Power Moves* brings Africanist aesthetics to bear on Hip Hop dance and non-Black practitioners of global Hip Hop culture. Osumare's work in fact inspired the subtitle to this book, and I extend her analytic focus on breaking's Africanist aesthetics to a focus on ritual circles specifically. My research deals with living cultural resources, often invisibilized by the global reach of antiblackness, revealing otherwise unrecognized layers of meaning within cyphers. Ultimately, Africanist aesthetics are on-the-ground expressive resources with epistemological lessons embedded in them.

This book also extends from work on the Black radical tradition. In *Black Marxism: The Making of the Black Radical Tradition*, Black studies scholar and political philosopher Cedric Robinson describes the Black radical tradition as "a collective consciousness informed by the historical struggles for liberation and motivated by the shared sense of obligation to preserve the collective being, the ontological totality."[4] Rooting his argument in histories of escape, marronage, and revolt, Robinson directs us to a consciousness that prioritized its own metaphysics, and the preservation of what he calls the ontological totality, or one's existence as inclusive of the soul, one's cosmologies, and whole ways of life that refused the social death imposed on the enslaved. This tradition was not, as Robinson articulates, "a variant of Western radicalism whose proponents happen to be Black. Rather, it is a specifically African response to an oppression emergent from the immediate determinants of European development in the modern era and framed by orders of human exploitation woven into the interstices of European social life from the inception of Western civilization."[5] Building on Robinson's examination, Fred Moten's *In the*

Break: The Aesthetics of the Black Radical Tradition looks to "the aesthetic genealogy" of the Black radical tradition, disrupting conventional notions of radicality by examining its sonic extension in avant-garde Black music and performance.[6] Such works pave the way for this project precisely because the Africanist aesthetics I write about are of the same collective consciousness and traditions noted, taking on new life and expression today in Hip Hop. This book shifts perspective from the genealogy of that tradition to the life of those aesthetics when such practices are channeled through a culture whose Black practitioners are now in the minority.

As well, my research operates within the vein of other Hip Hop scholars like Su'ad Abdul Khabeer, Nitasha Sharma, Marc Lamont Hill, and H. Samy Alim, who have written about Hip Hop epistemologies and the ways they challenge sanctioned forms of knowledge, thereby possessing the potential to cultivate counterhegemonic discourses, especially in rap music.[7] Breakers also cultivate inexact, unofficial, and not-entirely-Western forms of knowledge about how to move through and act in and on the world, thereby linking (often marginalized) people in particular to each other across various forms of difference and through a shared dance culture (akin to Osumare's notion of "connective marginalities."[8]

Dark Matter in Breaking Cyphers argues for epistemological qualities (qualities that indicate deeper systems of knowledge) that act as ingredients for an alternative sensibility informed by Africanist aesthetics and embedded in Hip Hop through the ritual cypher. This is not a history of those aesthetics nor of cyphers, but instead a study of a taken-for-granted ritual practice in Hip Hop and the Africanist aesthetics that inform them. And while a wholesale cypher theory might have some appeal, I echo African American literary feminist scholar Barbara Christian's argument in "The Race for Theory" that to produce a singular, all-encompassing cypher theory both assumes I occupy a position to do so (I do not), and misrepresents cyphers as containable to one theory.[9] As well, linear histories tend to foreground the great men, like DJ Kool Herc (credited as "the father of Hip Hop" who began to extend the break of a song) while losing sight of the collective of dancers who inspired him. Or as Hip Hop and Latinx feminist scholar Jessica Pabón-Colón so poignantly writes, "The static Hip Hop icon silences the dynamic Hip Hop community."[10] Ultimately, I take a multipronged approach because cyphers demanded just that.

Methodological Mixtape

I employ ethnography, oral histories, performance and movement analysis, and archival research. My field sites followed a circuit of breaking and Hip Hop events in multiple North American cities and three European cities from 2005 to 2012. I conducted formal interviews with over seventy practitioners, primarily breakers but also poppers, lockers, house dancers, two DJs, three MCs, and several event organizers, with some people overlapping in these categories. Informal conversations (unrecorded, casual, spontaneous) also inform my research. The circuit of breaking events ranged from small local battles with one hundred or so attendees, to large-scale international and corporate-sponsored competitions with ten thousand or more attendees. Additionally, I conducted archival research on early representations of Hip Hop in popular and niche market print media in the early 1980s at the Lincoln Center for the Performing Arts Library, Cornell University's Hip Hop Collection, the Schomburg Center for Research in Black Culture, the Center for Puerto Rican Studies at Hunter College (El Centro Archives), and the Harvard Hip Hop Archives.[11]

While my research approach casts a wide net, my focus has been on oral histories and the cyphering practices themselves. Since breakers are practice-based experts in the field, I refer to them by their (sometimes multiple) names as practitioners,[12] and prioritize extended quotes to allow the reader access to as much of their insights and the context of our exchanges as possible. Performance itself is its own kind of epistemology, one wherein embodied practices are ways of knowing the world.[13] Performance studies scholar Diana Taylor argues just that in *The Archive and the Repertoire*, wherein she looks to repertoire as the vehicle of memory, sociocultural knowledge, history, and a sense of identity.[14] In the repertoire, live performance is a necessary component of producing and transmitting knowledge, resisting standards that overvalue the retention and replication of recorded or written things in archives. In this work movement is a source for political praxis, debate, spiritual and communal connection, and alternative sensibilities that disrupt a mind-body split. Dance warrants particular attention because it forces us to think about the cultural impact of embodied practices whose epistemologies are drilled into the body through hours of physical training. Moreover, the cypher orients its practitioners into its epistemological lessons. I seek to be in conversation with experts of all kinds, and add to an understanding of breaking, cyphers, Hip Hop, and especially Africanist aesthetics.

I lacked personal connections at the beginning of the research; thus competitions were the most accessible way for me to enter this subculture. I organized my research around following a circuit of breaking events, some of which I found online and others that I learned of while attending events, either via word of mouth or hard-copy fliers. From 2006 to 2008, when I was half in New York City and half in Los Angeles, and later between 2009 and 2012 while based in New York, I traveled to as many competitions as I could attend along the East Coast of the US. When based in Los Angeles, I attended events and conducted oral histories throughout California. I also took multiple short trips to Europe at different points in my research to attend battles, showcases, and workshops. I attended events in San Francisco, Oakland, San Diego, Los Angeles, San Jose, Philadelphia, New York City, Boston, Chicago, Minneapolis, Fort Lauderdale, London, Thun in Switzerland, Braunschweig in Germany, and Toronto, Canada. These public events typically had reasonable entrance fees or were occasionally free. They provided opportunities for me to meet people, learn the environment, witness firsthand the new directions of the dance, and purchase merchandise (including DVDs, hats, and sneakers) otherwise unavailable to me outside of these spaces. My efforts to travel to as many breaking events in as many cities as I could afford to go shaped my findings in that most of my sites were US-based, and thus my analyses carry that bias. At the same time, following breaking circuits exposed me to multiple scenes rather than one place. This meant that I encountered dancers from all over the world, and especially became acquainted with breakers who travel these same circuits as part of their practice.

While events differ in size, breaking competitions share certain qualities that give an idea of my research sites. Such events usually last six to ten hours a day, spanning from single-day events to weeklong programming. They include prearranged battles (one-on-ones, duos, and crew battles of five to ten members), where practitioners compete in front of a panel of judges and an audience of spectators until a winner is declared. Sometimes these battles happen on stage, occasionally on concrete (see Fig. I.1), and often in large venues (gyms, clubs, etc.) with spectators and dancers sitting or standing around the competitors in a wide circle. Breaking competitions typically begin with preliminary battles that lead up to the finals, occasionally interspersed with live entertainment. My attention was largely, though not solely, on the time in between the staged battles, time devoted entirely to cyphering.

Since I traveled to events rather than anchoring my research in a single place, I did not always get a clear sense of the contours of specific local scenes,

Figure I.1 B-boy after round in a Concrete Battle, Rock Steady Crew Anniversary 2007 (26 July 2007). The mix of blood and concentrated study in this picture is a striking demonstration of the commitment it takes to break on concrete.

nor did I have immediate or sustained exposure to those dancers who did not attend competitions or had no interest in battling events. Yet my approach afforded me the opportunity to meet particular groups of breakers who also traveled to events around the world. The first was an older group (ranging in age from thirties to early fifties) who made names for themselves as teachers and oral historians. They were breaking celebrities who were flown worldwide on a regular basis to teach workshops, speak on panels, and judge competitions. I became a familiar face (and perhaps a nuisance) to this group. The other was a smaller contingent of traveling breakers—usually from the same crew from a shared city or country—who saved their money for the express purpose of traveling abroad to compete in circuits of regional breaking events (usually in Europe, North America, or Asia) for periods lasting from two weeks to as long as an entire summer. For them it was an opportunity to become known in different countries, meet with local crews, learn about other scenes, and meet the people and be exposed to the environments at the center of breaking's history. These two groups play a big part in fostering a global Hip Hop community.

Breaking is a culture that spans generations, and those generations continue to dance together today. Thus, my interviewees are diverse. The youngest interviewee was about nineteen at the time; my oldest was over fifty. (I did not have Institutional Review Board approval to interview minors who were almost always present.) I conducted interviews with breakers ranging from "pioneers" or "OGs"[15] who had been breaking since the seventies, to new practitioners only breaking for six months. "Hanging out" as a method made me privy to the social life of breakers beyond the event itself, including training sessions, social gatherings, and day-to-day living as artists attempting to make a living through dance or folks who worked day jobs and whose souls were revived of breaking. Approximately 30 percent of the interviews are with women, 20 percent are dancers not US born or based, and over 90 percent are people of color. Interviews revolved around people telling me their stories, family responses, memories of epic battles, nuanced insights about the state of the culture, history, debates, experiences of global Hip Hop, and personal testaments to how breaking has changed or shaped their lives—all with cyphers as the linchpin.[16] Interviews were held at competitions, private residences, restaurants and cafes, parks, and performance and practice venues.

I often started interviews by asking, "Do you remember your first cypher?" both to get them to tell me a story and to orient the research participant to their earliest or most memorable cyphering experiences. I asked questions about cypher etiquette, topical debates around race and gender, and family life (e.g., "Did you grow up with music in the house?" or "What did your parents think of your dancing?"), allowing unstated assumptions embedded in the question (e.g., that both parents were there) to prompt clarification and self-guided divulgences of personal information to the degree that they were comfortable. Interviews lasted anywhere from twenty minutes to three hours, and a handful of people were interviewed multiple times as opportunities arose. Overall, these interviews offer material evidence of an understanding or an interpretation *at that time*, something I emphasize since many interviews were recorded in the earliest stages of my research in 2006. It goes without saying that I also spent time with these interviews to best understand their nuances.

In an effort to convey the fullness of my own experiences and amplify my sense of the vast possibilities of cyphering beyond my analysis, I have interspersed between chapters cypher stories, thick descriptive narratives of particular experiences in the course of my fieldwork, like the opening story "Being There." Telling stories opens up the scope and nature of my field research. I have written them in present tense to portray the feeling of participation in the moment, and communicate the sensibilities that I write about in a hopefully more accessible way. Each story is purposefully juxtaposed before a chapter that elaborates on some of its themes to equip readers with fuller insights on cyphering in general, beyond my particular analyses. My hope is that these stories allow breaking's pleasures, contradictions, tensions, and possibilities to become more evident across the text as a whole. I contend that cyphers are sites whose particularities cannot be fully contained by any overarching theory or analysis, and these stories allow me to interject that sentiment alongside my own interventions.

Breaking, B-Boying, and B-Girling

To move through this work, you first need to understand the titular key terms: breaking, cyphering, Africanist aesthetics, and dark matter. These terms act as points of entry into underexplored dimensions of Hip Hop culture beyond commercial rap music, which too often is overdetermined as *all* of Hip Hop.[17] This book offers an alternative perspective on Hip Hop by foregrounding the dance element.

As a politics around naming changes over time, the terms breaking, breakdancing, b-boying, and b-girling warrant clarification. Take "breaking," which is sometimes interchangeable with "b-boying" or "b-girling" and sometimes not. For example, at the 2007 "Unity and Respect" battle in Boston (hosted by local popping OGs Megatron and Shallow), documentarian and locker Moncell "Ill Kosby" Durden and I interviewed Trac2, a 1970s breaker from Star Child LaRock crew. Moncell and I tag teamed on questions in an effort to compel this natural storyteller to keep it going. Despite my efforts to remain inconspicuous to the camera and Trac2's flow, I briefly became the center of attention as he made a point to correct my choice of terminology: "*B-boying*, honey. B-boying. Not breaking." More flustered by the public critique than bothered by the patronizing tone, the experience stuck with me, and for a while I was very committed to almost exclusively using the term b-boying. Fast-forward ten years and the stakes have changed as more b-girls brought the culture to task about its gendered language, and

Ogs began to openly speak to the social construct of "b-boying" as a seemingly more authentic term than breakdancing.[18]

Regardless of which term, breaking, b-boying, and b-girling roughly refer to the same genre of dance. The dance began in the early 1970s among Black diasporic youth in poor and working-class areas of New York City's outer boroughs, especially the South Bronx. The roots of the dance were a potent combination of footwork stylings and movement practices that borrowed heavily from icons like James Brown and the Nicholas Brothers, past social dances like mambo and the lindy hop, local current street styles like the rock dance (sometimes referred to as uprock), and whatever kids at the time were most drawn to, from gymnastics to martial arts, from movies and to cartoons. As the dynamics of the dance attracted attention among young people in surrounding neighborhoods, it did not take long for the scene to further diversify. Early Puerto Rican breakers acknowledge that, though in the seventies it was still seen as a Black dance, they eventually brought their own flavor and contributed to expanding breaking's core repertoire.[19]

In the early 1970s, the developing dance had a variety of terms: going off, rocking, burning, or boi-yoing (like the boing of a bounce or spring).[20] As it became a genre of its own, "break" stood at the intersection of multiple meanings. The musical connection is an obvious starting point. The break refers to the moment in a funk song when most of the instrumentation falls out and the drums are emphasized.[21] This is the point in a record that famed DJ Kool Herc recognized as the part where people danced with greater intensity, and he began to innovate ways to isolate and loop or repeat that section of the song to encourage the most frenzied dancing.[22] As a street term, "break" had other meanings.[23] In the documentary *The Freshest Kids*, graffiti artist Phase 2 argued, "I can tell you straight up, the terminology 'breakin'' comes from the street terminology. The people used to say, 'Why you breakin' on me?' 'Why's my moms breakin' on me?' 'Why you actin' crazy?' It really just meant doing shit above normal." Herc adds, "It didn't come from breaks on a record. It comes from this man, he broke. He went to a point, a breaking point. You know what I'm saying? So we just used that exaggeration of that term to the dancing."[24] Breaking as a dance genre encapsulates these various meanings—the drums in the break of a song tap into the most frenzied dancing, which resonates with notions of "doing shit above normal" or a dance that exaggerates the idea of being at a breaking point.

By the early 1980s a burgeoning culture inclusive of various creative practices—graffiti, rap, beatboxing, and breaking—spread out of the boroughs and hit the mainstream with a force that captured the imaginations of kids and marketers alike. Breaking was among the first Hip Hop elements to garner large-scale commercial appeal through film and television.[25] Documentaries and independent art-house films coming out roughly at the same time—like *Style Wars* (1982) and *Wild Style* (1983) —showcased Hip Hop as a multipronged culture, but it was the commercial success of 1983's *Flashdance*, with its one-minute feature of members of Rock Steady, that catapulted breaking to international audiences.[26] Movies featuring "breakdancing" rapidly flooded the market. Between 1981 and 1985, there were upwards of twenty movies about or featuring scenes showcasing elements of Hip Hop street dances under the label of breakdancing.[27] (This does not include TV shows and commercials that did the same.) Whether they actually showed people breaking did not seem to matter. For example, *Breakin'* and *Breakin' 2: Electric Boogaloo* (both released in 1984) had little actual breaking in it, and prominently featured locker Adolfo "Shabadoo" Quiñones, popper Michael "Boogaloo Shrimp" Chambers, and modern dance-trained actress Lucinda Dickey as their main characters.[28] Media attention brought about a new term, breakdancing, and used it as an umbrella for multiple street dances, which overshadowed specific histories and even names.

By repackaging street dances into a broad and commodifiable term, "breakdancing" always lacked specificity and roots in communal contexts. At the beginning of my research in 2006, "b-boying" was rigorously promoted by US breakers to counter the nearly impenetrable familiarity of the term "breakdancing." Today practitioners have begun to grapple more seriously with gendered language, reviving "breaking" as gender neutral. Especially to American or US-based breakers, "breakdancing" is associated with the commodification of Hip Hop. Many American breakers that I have interviewed use "breakdancer" to refer to someone unschooled in breaking history or one who exploits it for financial gain without respect for the culture. It is worth stating, though, that in my experiences outside of the US, the term circulated a bit more commonly across language barriers and national borders. As well, those who circulated in commercial and professional dance networks accepted that it is a term that still offers legibility in those settings. Breakdancing remains a more familiar term than breaking in countries around the world.

By no stretch of the imagination, then, are these debates settled, and there are those who would still argue with my decision, but I use "breaking" in this book. After consulting many different types of breakers—of different generations, genders, races, regions, and nationalities—the multitude of their voices informs my decision.

Cyphering

Dark Matter in Breaking Cyphers fills in the blanks on one of the most ubiquitous of Hip Hop rituals: the cypher. There is no single, all-encompassing definition of cyphers in breaking culture. The practice, like the word itself, has both concrete and abstract meanings, attesting to their multidimensionality. I share them by way of a definition with multiple parts, not unlike any word in the dictionary.

> [1] **cypher** [sī′·fer]: *n.* at least two practitioners, some spectators, and a music source (Jihad, Third Sight); a self-contained space, where there's no escape for the energy (Krazy Kujo, Soul Patrol); a cypher is when people get together, take turns, and the music's playing nonstop (Triple7, Street Masters Crew); the stage where you go to show off or the battleground (Brooklyn Terry, Elite Force Crew); the imaginary space or circle a b-boy creates in his mind to battle his opponent (Trac2, Star Child La Rock).

> [2] **cypher:** *n.* the heart of breaking (Ana, Fraggle Rock Crew); a meeting of souls, getting together as one, and taking over (Aby, TBB Crew); it's spiritual, going back to the motherland, you know, whether it was to communicate with gods or for better crops or something (Ness4, Zulu Kings); energy, spirit, emotion, confronting fears, confronting your own demons, self-testing, and self-release that can make or break you.... There's a whole circle and we're channeling this energy (Poe One, Style Elements).

> [3] **cypher, to:** *-ing v.* you got to listen and know the music and also know how to break to the music where everything you are doing is to the beat (Leanski, Floor Lords); it must entail a rawness and a powerful energy of respect, competitiveness and love and passion for what you're doing or what your counterpart is doing (Genesis, Flowzaic); there's always drama of some sort (Slinga, KR3Ts).[29]

The range of meanings for cypher comes directly from practitioners themselves, most of whom are breakers but also inclusive of a popper, a house dancer, and two MCs. As in the first set of descriptions, cyphers have practical elements: a music source, multiple people, a designated space, and sometimes a battle. The more spiritual affective and inexplicable qualities that make cyphers special are apparent in the second set of descriptions. These points pay attention to the nature of the collective experience and the invisible force of their exchange. The third definition, the verb, reminds us that cyphers are not things but acts. They are created through the practice of breaking together while negotiating the music, other dancers, past dramas, and more.

Cyphers are communal rituals fueled by a distinct understanding of competition, and operating within an aural-kinesthetic setting wherein dancers take turns in the center while building on and responding to the offerings of preceding dancers. That call-and-response exchange among practitioners and with the DJ cultivates an energy or vibe distinct to that cypher. The language of ritual lends itself to this analysis because it speaks both to that which is enabled by performance and a continuity of practices that transmit knowledge. Danced rituals communicate much of their history nonverbally. As anthropologist Yvonne Daniel argues in *Dancing Wisdom: Embodied Knowledge in Haitian Vodou, Cuban Yoruba, and Bahian Candomblé*: "Participants learn from observation, witnessing, modeling, and active participation.... And as they continue to perform in ceremonial repetition over time, in the process of music-making and dance performance, embodied knowledge is accumulated and constantly consulted."[30] While every cypher is unique, ritual cyphers teach participants social and individual responsibilities within the collective.

The term itself is also not how people "originally" referred to the ritual dance circle. Earlier, it was simply called the circle. When nonpractitioners hear this word, I imagine that they most likely land on "cipher," a mathematics term referring to encrypted or coded writing for which one needs a key. Etymologically, "cipher" is rooted in the Arabic word *çifr*, meaning "empty" or "void," and in mathematics it came to refer to zero.[31] A cipher, as a zero, is not empty but instead full in indeterminate and incalculable ways. Evident in the etymology of the word "cipher" is a relationship between law and chance, between the measurable and the incalculable that also characterizes cyphering practices, perhaps capturing what W.E.B. Du Bois names as the "paradox" of humanity: "1. The evident rhythm of human action; 2. The evident incalculability in human action."[32]

"Cypher" did not come into common use within Hip Hop until the late 1980s and early 1990s, adopted more directly from the Nation of Gods and Earths (NGE), whose lessons had grown in popularity in New York and among MCs, and whose terminology had come into common use outside of the organization. Also known as Five Percenters, the NGE formed in the early 1960s after splintering off from the Nation of Islam, articulating themselves as a way of life rather than a religion.[33] They bring together a complex set of lessons informed by a combination of numerology, Freemasonry rites and signs, Islamic beliefs, and Black nationalist politics. Ciphering among the NGE referred to their own ritual circles of "building" with others schooled in their Lost-Found lessons, which incorporate a coded use of numbers and letters that carry religio-cultural meaning with political import.[34] Their 360-degree circle is not empty but an enactment of 120 degrees of knowledge, 120 degrees of wisdom, and 120 degrees of understanding, all of which carry particular meaning in their philosophy.[35]

New York–based MCs schooled in the lessons of the NGE began incorporating more of this terminology into their rhymes, helping to popularize the NGE's discourse through Hip Hop music.[36] Just as MCs used the word to refer to their own improvisational rhyme circles, so too did breakers find the term appropriate for their circle practices.[37] While the legacy of the NGE is evident in the lyrical content of MCs, it is less so in breaking. Yet the knowledge, wisdom, and understanding evident in breaking cyphers are embodied and kinesthetic, taught through repetition of practice, and full of the possibility of the incalculable. In an effort to tap into that quality, I do not use "cypher" interchangeably with "circle," so as to invoke this meaningful depth. Moreover, I spell "cypher" with a *y* rather than an *i* to distinguish it in Hip Hop terms versus that of math and the NGE.

Cyphering is a multisensorial, collective experience cloaked as an individual one (see Fig. I.2). There is more going on than a mere competitive back and forth. For example, the type of competition that characterizes cyphering is wrapped up in how dancers often try to improve upon *their* last time in the cypher, which is to say that at minimum, people are always competing with themselves to maintain or build on the energy in the circle. Cyphering's competitiveness is not always about a battle. As a consequence, competitiveness can also fuel innovative movement,[38] which is then *gifted* to the culture as a whole. Moreover, cyphering's ritual quality actively affirms them as communal acts, even when they seem individualistic.

Figure I.2 Battle cypher, Mighty 4 Birthday Bash, San Francisco, CA (21 March 2009)

Cyphers are also very much a product of the sonic landscape that 1960s and 1970s soul, funk, and rock and eighties and nineties rap left to dancers as a treasure chest full of sonic possibilities that continue to thrive at breaking events alongside some newer music. While the aesthetic imperatives of what would become Hip Hop musical production were still in the making (Hip Hop scholars Tricia Rose and Joseph Schloss write about bricolage, repetition, flow, among other aesthetics),[39] the musical terrain itself fostered a kinesthetic experience where dancers had a lot to play with on the dance floor. When practitioners began to stay down on the ground with increasingly energetic, punchy, and acrobatic moves in the seventies, it coincided with multiple DJ's experimentations with already complex music, stimulating intelligences throughout the body.[40] Cyphers remind us that the simultaneity of music-movement is essential to understanding the space. Or as Cleis Abeni writes, "Black vernacular music and dance are conceptual and experiential partners that feed on the same processes for invention."[41] Even my participation as a nondancer is part of this call and response, as it includes gestures of appreciation, of musical recognition, and adding to the sonic arena though verbal and physical demonstrations of involvement. As American dance historian Jacqui Malone puts it, to "dance the song" is in the tradition of African dance cultures.[42]

In a piece called "Music Meant to Make You Move: Considering the Aural Kinesthetic," I introduced a concept called the aural kinesthetic, in reference to the simultaneity of music and movement. I wrote, "I am looking to engage more than just the sensory response of moving to what one hears. Aural kinesthetics recognize that social dance practices are kinesthetic forms within the all-encompassing aurality of an environment. I use spatial terms to acknowledge sound's omni-directionality, coming at you from all sides and helping to actually produce the social dance place."[43] "Aural kinesthetic" is a term concerned with Western epistemes that treat music and dance as separate categories of study. While the term is new, the concept itself is not original. It shares concerns expressed by scholars of music, movement, ritual, and expressive practices in the African diaspora. In his 1974 book *The Music of Africa*, J. H. Kwabena Nketia writes about music and movement as interrelated, though he does not name this interrelationship in a singular way.[44] In 1985 composer and music scholar Olly Wilson discusses more specifically the interrelationship between music-making and rhythmic movement.[45] Both explore performance practices and practices of everyday life to illustrate this interrelationship, in contrast to notions of musical accompaniment to dance or the reverse. "Aural kinesthetic" is my attempt to name this phenomenon, joining the list of terms employed by those who further unpack how a movement-sonic simultaneity can play out in practice.

For example, both social critic and philosopher Cornel West and ethnomusicologist Kyra Gaunt use West's term "kinetic orality" to talk about Black folks' expressive aesthetic arsenals of performative and performance-based oral practices, whose potency is wrapped up in the simultaneity of sound and motion. West focuses on kinetic orality as a "dynamic repertoire and energetic rhetorical styles that form communities." He aligns it with two other overlapping concepts—passionate physicality and combative spirituality—to describe mediums of collective responses to institutionalized terrorism.[46] In *The Games Black Girls Play: Learning the Ropes from Double-Dutch to Hip-Hop*, Gaunt expands on kinetic orality as a means of carrying intergenerational and translocal embodied archives about raced and gendered Black life. Embodied musical gestures like handclapping games transmit "musical ideals and social memories," particularly as they get "passed on through the musical practices of girls."[47] Both use kinetic orality to emphasize community formations through practice. Kinetic orality also resonates with dance scholar Thomas DeFrantz's term "corporeal orature." Perhaps as the opposite side of the same coin, corporeal orature is about the way Black dancing bodies "speak" to Black audiences who understand the hidden cultural transcripts embedded in Black social dances.[48]

More recently, religion and Black studies scholar Ashon Crawley coined the term "choreosonic" to amend the categorical distinction between the choreographic and the sonic, where sound and motion are one and the same. In a chapter on shouting traditions in *Blackpentecostal Breath: The Aesthetics of Possibility*, Crawley further articulates the choreosonic as an episteme in itself, where the sonic and the choreographic are irreducible to each other, and wherein noise is embraced, and there is a different orientation to space and time.[49] In doing so he highlights how choreosonic practices (like the ring shout) combat philosophical and theological traditions that misrecognize Black worshiping practices as pathology or primitivity.[50] The "collective, improvisational, choreosonic performance of blackness" is the "ontological totality" to which Cedric Robinson speaks.[51] They are the enactment of what Crawley calls "otherwise worlds."[52]

All of these authors, myself included, are writing about an African diasporic sensibility that is evident in various Black expressive cultures and needs to be named precisely because, within a Western academic framework, music and sound are treated separately from movement and kinesthesia. Moreover, all of these categories are rendered into discourses of a mind-body split, where intellectualism is applauded but the body as an instrument of knowledge on its own terms is downplayed if not ignored. Both kinetic orality and the choreosonic capture particular ways of interpreting this simultaneity, adding philosophical weight to the music-movement of Black diasporic expressive practices. The aural kinesthetic is a conceptually simple reference to music (broadly defined) *and* movement at once, where the sonic and the choreographic are mutually shaping or constituting forms. In cyphers, danced exchanges happen in the context of often culturally meaningful music that activates a live call-and-response experience with the DJ and other dancers.[53] Cyphers bring together disparate groups, competing interests, and artistic innovation into a shared cultural space where these elements commingle and sometimes clash. This book explores what might otherwise be thought of as incalculable forces, extraphenomenal experiences, and other unseen influences and possibilities. By understanding the force of the invisible, we can begin to understand the connections that cyphering fosters.

Dark Matter and Africanist Aesthetics

Finally, this book pays particular attention to the role Africanist aesthetics play in the things we do not see that nonetheless matter. Aesthetics are typically defined as a branch of philosophy concerned with beauty. As bell hooks elaborates, "Aesthetics then is more than a philosophy or theory of art and beauty; it is a way of inhabiting space, a particular location, a way of looking and becoming.... This historical aesthetic legacy has proved so powerful that consumer capitalism has not been able to completely destroy artistic production in underclass black communities."[54] Africanist aesthetics are born from the people, cultures, and sensibilities of the African diaspora. I am especially drawn to dance scholar Brenda Dixon Gottschild's definition, which highlights "African and African American resonances and presences, trends and phenomena,"[55] and acknowledges them as living cultural resources tied to Black life and forms of living. Recognizing Africanist aesthetics in action and centering the layers of information they carry is a means of combating their invisibilization.

While Gottschild names five elements of Africanist aesthetics evident in American concert dance, and adds an additional six qualities that she sees across Caribbean dances, other scholars have developed lists that speak to oral and literary traditions, theater, sports, martial arts, spiritual expressions, music and dance forms, everyday expressive practices, and more.[56] Sometimes their assessments are specific to a US-African American context, others speak to specific sites within the African diaspora, and still others are thinking through and across the diaspora or on the continent of Africa. Table I.1 lists a number of qualities especially relevant to breaking cyphers. I have compiled it from multiple sources, and roughly organized it around dance, spirit, and conversational elements. I chose to organize these elements into a chart for the sake of clarity, with explicit caution against treating it as a static list, exhaustive of all dimensions of Africanist aesthetics. It is not. If it is treated as a checklist, one misses the point.

While many of these qualities are likely evident in other cultural paradigms, Africanist aesthetics are discernible by the layered and mutually activating quality of each element. For example, aural kinesthetics is an Africanist aesthetic whose meaningfulness gets activated when it is part of a call-and-response exchange with the DJ and among dancers; where people are expected and encouraged to move improvisationally and originally; where polyrhythmic music is met with a bent-knee stance that allows for

Table I.1 Africanist Aesthetics Relevant to Breaking Cyphers

Conversational Elements	Dance Elements
Call and response (antiphonal exchange)	Groundedness (bent posture, butt out, "get low" stance)
Battles, ritual derision, insult games, mockery	Buck, wing, and jig movements
To be on the one, metronomic sense	Improvisation, play
Repetition	Isolations
Signifyin' (trickster qualities, irony, subtext)	Dancing apart
Circles (multifocality, spatial awareness, active participation)	Individual originality
	Polycentric movement
Hidden transcripts (coded or cultural insider knowledge, corporeal orature)	Aural kinesthetic, kinetic orality, Choreosonic
Versioning	Marathoning
Poly- and cross-rhythms	High-affect juxtaposition
Deification of accident (or the anticipation of disruption, engaging risk)	Aesthetic of cool
	Loose audience/performer divide
Spiritual Elements	Asymmetry as balance
Sense of spirit, energy, vibe, possession, Gettin' happy, axé, soul focal moments	Vital aliveness, youthful energy, kinesthetic Intensity, ephebism
Loose sacred/secular divide	Percussive movement
Communion with God and/or community	Dimensional awareness
Sense of liberation, freedom, healing	

polycentric movement. When organized within a ritual circle, each quality activates a constellation of others that work together. The epistemological possibilities of Africanist aesthetics becomes evident in their mutual interaction. Within all of it are layers of meaning not meant for everyone to understand or interpret equally. Those more exposed to the subterranean meaning of these practices know the body speaks multiple tongues. (Dance scholar Thomas DeFrantz's concept of corporeal orature captures this latter quality.) Gottschild reaffirms these connections, noting that "they are 'intratextual,' so to speak, and do not appear as separate entities in practice."[57] Gottschild also reminds us that though always already active in new and syncretic forms, Africanist aesthetics are "invisibilized" as a function of power and antiblack ideologies that erase histories of African peoples in the Americas.[58]

Although the Africanist aesthetics of the cypher are often invisibilized, in this book the physics concept of dark matter returns me to them and their continued relevance (as material forces, as something that matters) in global

Hip Hop culture regardless of whether folks know it or not.[59] In trying to understand cyphering practices on a deeper level, I realized that they are essentially about force, matter, energy, speed—all of which brought me to physics. Dark matter is a physics concept describing nonluminous matter, believed to comprise the majority of the universe. Unlike a black hole, where light cannot escape, dark matter *is* matter, a different kind of matter altogether with no visible light, though luminous matter interacts with it. Dark matter is "seen" and understood by way of its gravitational influence on surrounding visible matter. Thought to be five times more prominent than visible matter and over six times its density, dark matter is powerful enough to hold together galaxies and connect distant ones.[60] In my use, the term elaborates on the substantive presence of things unseen.

Dark matter is the very presence of possibility in the universe. Though there are clues as to what it is and is not, a stable theory has yet to take hold, which has left many theoretical physicists fascinated by what could be. Some speculate that there could be other dark elements or dark chemistry.[61] There is also speculation that dark matter, while difficult to detect, is nothing particularly special or mysterious at all, but simply "missing in the current models of particle physics."[62] That range means it runs the spectrum of possibility. I am drawn to dark matter precisely because it both captures a presence that cannot be conventionally marked or measured, and because it inspires a speculative response, recognizing an *extra*ordinary and powerful force beyond what is readily visible to us. Ultimately, dark matter is all about what else matter *could* be, and by extension the untapped knowledge of the known world. As a metaphor, it also speaks to the unseen and unknown within Western approaches to knowledge production. By using the language of the hard sciences to speak to embodied experiences, the dark matter metaphor troubles a hierarchy of knowledge that devalues and delegitimizes embodied knowledges.[63]

It is fitting then that I came to the speculative possibilities of dark matter after initial inspiration from a work of speculative fiction about Africanist circle rituals: Henry Dumas's Afrosurrealist, Afrofuturist short story "Will the Circle Be Unbroken." It follows the lethal encounter between "three white people" (depicted as self-righteous interlopers) who breach the Sound Barrier Club doors despite warnings of it being dangerous to enter and "for Brothers and Sisters only."[64] It is also the story of Probe, an enigmatic jazz musician whose most recent musical excursions involve an unnamable "new sound," a "lethal vibration" generated out of the collectivity formed in a jazz circle, and via an ancient Afro-horn.[65] When Magwa's rhythms and Probe's horn elevate the energy of the jazz circle to its zenith, the new sound gives birth to an energetic material force, an actual baby.

A seeming metaphor with symbolic appeal to the (re)productive or generative capacity of the circle, Dumas shifts from metaphor to the literal. Rhythm, in the story, envelops everyone in a kind of womb-like atmosphere, then the collectivity of diasporan Blacks begin to twitch like an embryo. Dumas ends when an actual child "grow[s] out of the circle of the womb, searching with fingers and then with motive."[66] The word "motive" repeats in the story as Probe gets "deeper into motives," calls for them, recognizing how "motives" can easily "tear the building down"—alluding to its overlapping meaning as motive and motif.[67] Both words share roots in fourteenth-century French, meaning "something brought forward." And this sums up the child of the circle; it is something brought forward through the collectivity, the bridges of sound produced by the musicians and the Afro-horn connection. Thinking of the literal child as that which has been brought forth in a ritual circle suggests that diasporic circle rituals operate outside of Western sensibilities and bring forth different possibilities. This realization made me consider *all* aspects of cypher enactments, especially their extraphenomenal qualities. And along those lines, I began to search for my own metaphor, something that helped me bring forth a deeper understanding of cyphers.

Physics also intervenes in my concern over language. This is where I turn to dark matter, not to replace practitioners' language but to contextualize their words through a relation to Africanist aesthetics. Translating the force of such experiences into a scientific discourse gets at both the nature of the experience—or its substantive materiality—and the real matter of African diasporic social dancing, which always seems to come back to energy, force, spirit, and connection to the whole. And while these elements usually fall out of the purview of physics, my use of *that* language troubles the intellectual disarticulation that haunts comparisons between spirit and matter, or between dance and physics.[68] I use the dark matter metaphor to also capture varied, on-the-ground experience of cyphers that often lack a clear explanation. It is conceptually open enough to engage meaningfully without succumbing to the academic pressure to prescribe a singular interpretation of people's extraphenomenal cyphering experiences.

Dark matter reasserts its usefulness in other ways. As a concept of ongoing discovery in physics, it symbolizes possibility that moves away from a definitive or fixed theory of cyphering (even as some of the ideas encapsulated in the metaphor echo aspects of other theories).[69] This book also adds to the varied iterations of dark matter in recent Black studies scholarship.[70]

Dark Matter in Breaking Cyphers joins other works that recognize how blackness and physics, when thought together, produce new analytic tools.[71] Since the "dark" in dark matter is more akin to invisible matter rather than its literal darkness, some physicists bristle at its use as a metaphor for blackness. Undoubtedly its repeated invocation in Black studies is prompted by the way that "dark" connotes both color and character: something evil, invoking the racist undertones in Western symbolism around the color black; and something surreptitious or hidden, which echoes Black people's survival responses to living in racist societies. As well, blackness speaks to a racialization that is both hypervisible and invisible (in an Ellisonian sense). I too am drawn to the slippage between dark and invisible, especially because Africanist aesthetics are invisibilized for antiblack reasons.

Dark matter is a metaphor that carries the traces of all of these different meanings, resonating distinctly with Africanist aesthetics as potent but invisibilized forces in global Hip Hop that I argue act as the glue holding together global Hip Hop. The dark matter of cyphers ultimately refers to the possibilities enabled by Africanist aesthetics, and the conditions that invisibilize any kind of common-sense understanding of their ongoing importance to global Hip Hop, a culture that overlaps with but extends beyond the African diaspora.

Chapter Breakdown

Similar to my pivoting between cyphers as described in the opening story, each chapter pivots to cyphers occupied by particular groups of practitioners or organized around key themes, often centering the key Africanist aesthetics that matter to them. Conceptually, this approach plays out in chapters that are organized around spiritual and liberatory experiences, 1970s and 1980s breakers in the South Bronx, b-girls from around the world, those negotiating differences in global framework, and a brief meditation on the internet.

Chapter 1 goes through a comparative look at multiple African diasporic circle practices, drawing attention to their extraphenomenal, spiritual, and liberatory feelings and experiences, articulated differently by practitioners in each form. In this chapter, I bring cyphers into conversation with other circle practices in the diaspora, namely African American ring shouts, Brazilian capoeira rings, and Puerto Rican bomba circles. My main interlocutors—including Float, Silky Jones, Poe One, Triple7, Miss Little, Aby, Pia, and Jaekwon —discuss this little-recognized dimension of the cypher. By amplifying Africanist aesthetics, we can better understand breakers' broad articulations of overlapping experiences of spirit and liberation. I further explore the epistemic violence involved in invisibilizing Africanist aesthetics.

While chapter 1 situates breaking and Hip Hop within a diasporic framework, chapter 2 recognizes the imprint of New York City and specifically the South Bronx on breaking. Hip Hop's quintessential qualities, captured in the warrior aesthetics of breaking, are also wrapped up in life and living in New York City during the 1970s. I deploy the term "outlaw culture" to capture that imprint specifically on breaking's battling culture, and how it gets lived by practitioners and shaped by their corporealities. My focus on battling principles, as introduced by Trac2, are elaborated on in oral histories from Aby, Cartoon, Baby Love, and Kwikstep. I draw attention to the possibilities enabled by an outlaw sensibility, which I argue developed from the margins of society and intersects with Africanist aesthetics. Those sensibilities helped early practitioners navigate battle cyphers and everyday life in the Bronx.

Chapter 3 pivots to the possibilities of cyphers primarily comprised of b-girls. Through a focus on two Africanist aesthetics (rituals of derision and the imperative for originality) and a reconsideration of badass femininity, I explore how b-girls embody battling imperatives through burns and playing in the profane, contending with normative notions of femininity whether they intend to or not. At the same time, their practice cannot be reduced to an assessment of gender, and, as they bring their whole selves to their identities as b-girls, they enact a mode of relationality that fosters a competing sensibility on sociality, one that makes breaking a more inclusive space for future b-girls. The chapter focuses on Emiko, Black Pearl, Rokafella, and Hanifa Queen, and puts their oral histories in conversation with recent scholarship on b-girls to expand a comparative analysis.

Chapter 4 draws our attention to the ways that difference is dealt with discursively—displaced onto conversations about moves—and gets negotiated alongside tradition or "foundation" among breakers from all over the world. In contrast to an idealized multiculturalism that elides difference, their own articulations of their relationship to breaking and Hip Hop hearken back to the culture's Africanist qualities, which helps to bring breaking's transnational scenes "on the one." With insights from Q Rock, Frostalino,

Hanifa Queen, Profo Won, and Rokafella, this chapter explores how the everyday ways that breakers negotiate differences in race, ethnicity, gender, and nationality can tell us something about coalitional political projects that operate across similar sets of differences.

The coda pivots to cyphers online or activated in social media. Rather than look at literal online footage of cyphers, the conclusion explores how a cypher quality is activated online, amplifying cyphers as speculative projects, and offering questions that demonstrate how this research can continue on.

Ultimately, *Dark Matter in Breaking Cyphers* is about the blackness of Hip Hop, the parts that often go undetected, unacknowledged, or simply misunderstood. If we know that Hip Hop matters to how we understand power, politics, and culture on a global stage, then that means naming Africanist aesthetics. I hope that this book demonstrates how foregrounding Africanist aesthetics gets at Hip Hop's most quintessential and mesmerizing qualities.

Dark Matter

2008 US-Battle of the Year, Hollywood, CA
This is my second time at US-Battle of the Year, held at the same club in Hollywood, and full of breakers I admire (see Fig. 1.1). When I arrive, the mood is casual. Some stretch in corners, and others converse with friends. I seek out familiar faces as I walk the perimeter of the room trying to decide where I'm going to focus my attention. I see b-boy Viazeen and head toward his circle nearest the stage. When I get there, I see struggle on his furrowed brow.

I have seen Viazeen break before. At his best, he brings a combination of intellectual curiosity and creative intensity to the floor, attacking it with a clean diligence as he crafts new angles and shapes with the traces of his footwork. A transplant to Los Angeles from Philadelphia, his fans and friends multiply with each event. Viazeen is a thoughtful breaker, but when he cannot quite get into his groove, he tends to look increasingly

pensive if not outright frustrated. He stands slightly removed from this circle, watching others dance while making only the occasional effort to join in. He starts and stops his toprock, but does not do a full run in the circle. (He tells me later that he could not figure out why he struggled. He could not get out of his head, and perhaps was not feeling the music the DJ played.)

I pivot left to a different circle. No one appears to be struggling, though they are distracted in a different way. People watch with varying degrees of interest, very few bother to dance, and instead they chat and laugh among themselves. If cyphers are distinguished by the energy of the exchange between the solo and the collective or the dancer and the DJ, then it occurs to me that circles are often like this: barely engaged, paying little attention to the dancer on the floor, everyone on the cusp of walking away. There are lulls between each dancer's turn. Someone finishes . . . pause . . . pause . . . someone else enters. Each set is short—ten to fifteen seconds in a circle versus twenty-five to thirty in more high-spirited cyphers. My own interest begins to wane as I consider moving again to a possibly "better" circle. Yet I know that regardless of which one I occupy, lackluster moments are inevitable and changing circles is not always for the better. Besides, if

Figure 1.1 Flyer for the US Preliminaries of Battle of the Year 2008, Los Angeles, CA. Features a rendering of Poe One, esteemed b-boy and event organizer.

I leave I might miss something, so I stay. It feels like waiting . . . for . . . something to break the monotony. And then it happens.

B-boy Smurf jumps in the circle in a precarious, twisting-drop to the floor. His body moves in full revolutions, suddenly halts for a second, and then swiftly propels in the opposite direction. He ends with quick footwork and an unwavering freeze. Smurf moves so quickly that when he finishes his set, my brain is still trying to register where he came in from. I see everything yet remember nothing in particular, but I know his style. It is a compelling mix of easy strength in tumbling and power moves, coupled with fluid and frenzied footwork that glides his body along the floor as if it were an oil-slick surface rather than hard wood underneath his rubber-soled Converse. Better still, Smurf dances with a flavor all his own. The only real comparative that I can think of for Smurf's style is "The Three Stooges."[1] One moment he looks like an angry Moe with an intense glare and his lips cutting a line across the lower half of his face. The next he embodies Curly, whose enthusiasm bursts out in erratic twitches of hyper fidgetiness. Smurf plays with restlessness, constantly changing gestures, characters, and movement as if on the brink of losing control over his own body while artfully maintaining the upper hand. Though small in stature, he is an eruption of kinetic energy; a whirlwind that leaves me thrilled.

I'm not the only one who notices. The mood changes instantaneously. People are suddenly alert. Smurf barely has time to step out of the circle before another b-boy jumps in. They become, as Ness4 would characterize them, "hungry dancers," anxious for their turns to ravenously feast on this newfound intensity.[2] With no more lulls, the pace quickens—a b-girl enters on the heels of the breaker before her as the half dozen of us move in closer. Each breaker wants a turn and they have to <u>take</u> it; anyone who hesitates loses out. In this way, they accept Smurf's unspoken challenge to step up their game. It is not a battle, but they cannot be out-danced.

More than a mere chain reaction, the circle's initial casualness births something at once shared and transmitted, first by Smurf and then by the whole of the circle. Or maybe it's something channeled, making Smurf a kind of shaman who's brought forth a force at this moment, compelling a new focus from those of us surrounding him. The goings-on of the rest of the club fall away, and the intimacy of our little cypher becomes its own world. Funnily, Smurf doesn't even stick around to notice what he helps manifest, perhaps moving on to revive some other circle with his magic. Regardless, the contrast from before Smurf to after is palpable, and the cypher starts to find its groove.

Yet, as quickly as it begins, the music stops and the cypher is cut. One of the event's hosts comes on the mic: "Ok y'all, we're about the start the shows. Check-in with me if your crew still needs to sign up."

A low grumble echoes throughout the venue, suggesting that this cypher was not the only one to end prematurely. Given cyphers' potent vitality, it is no wonder that breakers refer to these abrupt endings as "killing the cypher." These deaths happen repeatedly throughout the night. As we shift our focus to the stage, I am conscious of the fleeting nature of a perfect moment. I bask in the lingering exhilaration of being swept up in the unexpected pull of Smurf's playful and rousing performance. Though more cyphers will come later, that one is gone forever.

1
Dark Matter and Diaspora
Cyphers in an Africanist Context

> I saw the circle before I saw the kid in the middle. I was nine years old, the summer of 1978 . . . I wandered up to something I'd never seen before: a cipher—but I wouldn't have called it that; no one would've back then. It was just a circle of scrappy, ashy, skinny Brooklyn kids laughing and clapping their hands, their eyes trained on the center . . . I shouldered through the crowd toward the middle . . . but it felt like gravity pulling me into that swirl of kids, no bullshit, like a planet pulled into orbit by a star. His name was Slate and he was a kid I used to see around the neighborhood, an older kid who barely made an impression. In the circle, though, he was transformed, like the church ladies touched by the spirit, and everyone was mesmerized.
> —Jay-Z, *Decoded*[1]

The pull of a cypher is undeniable. The transformation that Jay-Z witnessed in Slate carries a number of key qualities that are experienced kinesthetically in breaking cyphers, and are not always readily visible. The gravitational pull, the touch of the spirit, and the impact of the memory itself all demonstrate the capacity for cyphers to move people in ways that are more embodied than visual. In this chapter I pivot to cyphers animated by what I refer to as their extraphenomenal capacities, those enigmatic and ineffable qualities that pull you in and keep you there. The difficulty of explaining it in a believable way ("no bullshit") is a challenge. To echo Nathaniel Mackey, "Words don't go there," at least not fully.[2] By looking at the Africanist aesthetics of various African diasporic circle practices and focusing on their extraphenomenal dimensions, I seek to make these experiences legible.

Cyphers are rituals at the heart of breaking's sociality that teach participants how to be in community with one another. Breakers often refer to it as an "energy exchange." B-boy Ness4 characterized the dynamism of exchanges between dancers and spectator-dancers as a mutual focus channeled entirely to the center.[3] Whoever dances in that focal point imbibes the energy of everyone else's single-minded attention, all while putting their own energy into themselves and onto the floor. Everyone has an opportunity to feed off each other. It is cyclical and recycled, constantly flowing in and out the circle, back and forth between spectators and dancers, because, according to b-girl Emiko, giving and receiving go hand in hand.[4] She suggested that if one does not give energy back, then there is little point to being there in the first place. To that end, Krazy Kujo stated that if he cannot build on the cypher, he would rather not enter at all.[5] As Dark Marc notes, "You just use each other's energy to do your thing."[6] People bring different kinds of energy to circles, though. During an interview with b-boy Machine, he suggested that some people know better than others how to channel their emotions in a productive way that helps create a mutually inspiring vibe in the cypher.[7] For those that do, they open themselves up and surrender themselves to a potentially profound experience, lest they risk destroying it altogether.[8]

While "energy exchange" was a relatively common phrase among breakers in the mid-2000s and the early 2010s, it does not fully encapsulate the extraphenomenal experiences at the heart of their references. It is ultimately in the ways that breakers' experiences resonate with circle practices throughout the African diaspora that Hip Hop's aesthetic commonalities to those circles becomes more pronounced. What follows is a small comparative sample of African diasporic circle practices whose parallels to cyphers provide specific insight on the extraphenomenal.

Cyphers in Diasporic Continuum

Breaking cyphers sent me to African diasporic circle practices that preceded Hip Hop. There are circle dance practices in many cultures around the world; however, as dance scholar Brenda Dixon Gottschild writes, circles "reign" in the constellation of Africanist elements.[9] Circle rituals are ubiquitous in the African diaspora, and a brief exploration of them—specifically Brazilian capoeira, bomba circles in Puerto Rico, and the ring shout among African Americans—reveals an overlapping ensemble of Africanist aesthetics.

On their surface, there are clear things worth mentioning that evidence a range of Africanist aesthetics at work. Diasporic circles often look one of two ways. The first is a ring comprised of people moving collectively like a wheel, often in a counterclockwise direction. Ring shouts, a Black American ritual associated with Christianity, are an example of this version of circle practices. The second version consists of overlapping positionalities as musicians, singers, dancers, and spectators who form a relatively stationary circle, while practitioners take turns in the center. Cyphers, the Brazilian martial art of capoeira and their *rodas* (Portuguese for "wheel"), and the music and dance practices of street bomba circles in Puerto Rican culture are examples of these types of circles. Both approaches enact communal experiences. The former emphasizes a communal act that all participate in as a group, while the latter encourages performances by individuals or pairs (depending on the genre) in the center, though *still* as a collective practice.

Among the other common Africanist aesthetics in circles are qualities like multiple overlapping rhythms, improvisational play, and call and response.[10] Circles are multifocal,[11] necessitating that one project their energy in all directions, because the audience is all around. Spectators are themselves potential participants, blurring the lines between audience and performer. Marathoning, or ceaseless dancing over extended periods of time, is also common and likely contributes to experiences of catharsis. Battling, signifyin', ritual derision, and competitive exchanges are also common in Africanist circles, though they often overshadow cyphering's more extraphenomenal qualities. Most importantly though, cyphers encapsulate more than moves and style. Cyphers possess epistemological elements of not-entirely-Western modes of doing and being, and teach those lessons in the context of literal practices. In this chapter, my analysis centers call and response and spirit specifically, which act as salient points of overlap with subsequent firsthand accounts of cyphering experiences from breakers Silky Jones, Float, Poe One, Triple7, Miss Little, Aby, Pia, and Jaekwon.

Call and Response in Aural-Kinesthetic Environments

Though all of these practices are related aesthetically, how that relation plays out in any specific comparison depends on the practices being compared. What any two practices may share in common will likely differ, at least in part, from the features between another pairing; there are also evident Africanist sensibilities that clearly relate them all to each other. Africanist aesthetics offer a perspective on how to think about that relation. For example, the often-cited likeness between breaking and capoeira frequently takes the form of people arguing that breaking "comes from" capoeira, in many ways discrediting New York City youth of their innovations.[12] What these two practices share—combative moves to music in a circle, inverted positions and acrobatics in a warrior practice—is more meaningful when read through their overlapping Africanist aesthetics.

Consider, for example, call and response, which is rooted in a conversational or dialogic exchange between a soloist and an ensemble. The Western musical term for call and response, "antiphonal," refers to sounding (*-phonal*) in response (*anti-*). This term carries an implied distinction between music and movement in its emphasis on sounded responses as independent from kinesthetic ones. In the practices that follow, though, from a dancer's perspective, sound is "one element of an entire experience."[13] By talking about them separately, one masks the multiple bodily responses to a call, which can be sung or spoken as well as danced, clapped, nodded, pantomimed, and otherwise gestured. Thus, when linguistic anthropologist and Hip Hop education scholar H. Samy Alim notes that there are "multiple levels of call and multiple levels of response occurring simultaneously and synergistically," that synergy occurs in the context of an aural-kinesthetic experience.[14] The levels of call and response also then feed off of and into each other.

Bomba, an Afro–Puerto Rican music and dance dating back to the seventeenth century, is a practice that captures call and response as an organizing principle that informs the exchanges at the foundations of the entire scene. Songs are sung in a call-and-response manner, and drummers engage in another level of exchange. Part of the circle consists of multiple percussionists who play foundational rhythms, and a primary drummer who follows the center dancer's rhythmic and percussive movement; the dancer performs the rhythm and the drummer must keep up. Dance scholar Jade Power-Sotomayor refers to bomba as a "danced sounding practice," where "the dancer's moves are marked with rhythmic synchronicity by the lead drum."[15] In her article "Corporeal Sounding: Listening to Bomba Dance, Listening to puertorriqueñxs," Power-Sotomayor emphasizes that within a call-and-response exchange, successful participation requires "acute attention and listening," reading others' cues, and trusting in one's own "kinesthetic intuition"—all while playing one's part. At the heart of bomba's call and response is a complex, multidirectional exchange that, for the dancer, produces "the sounding that ripples out and around their movement choices."[16] Power-Sotomayor activates Ashon

Crawley's choreosonic,[17] to capture the "unprecedented musical and aural responsibility and agency, upending gendered hierarchies about music-making versus dance-making."[18]

Call-and-response exchanges within capoeira rodas offer another way of thinking about call and response in an aural-kinesthetic environment.[19] Dance scholar Cristina Rosa notes a standard sequence of events in a capoeira roda, consequently illustrating the martial art's aural kinesthetic qualities: practitioners enter the circle first by paying respect to the drummers; praise songs (called *ladainha*) commence the game; and the praise singer determines when the game ends while practitioners "co-choreograph open-ended and playful interactions."[20] This sequence also suggests players' responsibilities to the whole dynamic:

> Capoeira players sense and synchronize their call-and-response interactions through auditory perception (hearing). In capoeira angola, all movements, gestures, and intentions are (or should be) rhythmically coordinated in relation to a player's response to both external/shared rhythms (e.g. percussive music, chanted songs, and the opponent's kinesthetic cadence) and internal/personalized rhythms (e.g. breathing, heartbeat, perceived sounds, and melodic memory).... Moreover, since performers are not encouraged to communicate verbally, this rhythmic synchronization provides an additional sensorial channel between the pair at the center and ensures a constant connection between them and the musicians controlling the entire event (circle of capoeira) from the periphery.[21]

Rosa's discussion here illustrates multiple levels of calls and responses operating synergistically.[22] Rhythm is felt kinesthetically, including the physiology of one's own internal rhythms as players' co-choreography is synchronized with the musicians on the periphery. More experienced practitioners can play with being in and out of sync with the musicians as a challenge to their opponent. Rosa looks to the "*ginga* aesthetic"—a foundational movement in capoeira of side-to-side swagger that "juggles" the body's weight while maintaining a flow—as an overarching approach that teaches deeper embodied knowledges and is informed by Africanist aesthetics. In her assessment, rodas illustrate the fundamental dynamism, innovation, and openness of Africanist aesthetics, despite discourses of them through the lens of tradition, which is often seen as static, singular, and homogenous.[23] Overall, call and response entails a set of participatory exchanges that are at once sonic and kinesthetic, and that draw individuals into practices of collective responsibility or a part to play in the whole.

Call and response also includes a spiritual dynamic. In his analysis of call and response in ring shouts among enslaved African Americans, folklorist Roger D. Abrahams remarks that everyone in the circle was expected to participate in "keeping up the spirit," which was part of the utility of call-and-response chants that accompanied their shuffled, rhythmic, counterclockwise movement around the circle. "Keeping up the spirit" is a kind of double duty, demanding one attend to one's own spirit and thus simultaneously keeping the spirit or energy of the whole elevated. All three practices tell a story of call and response as an approach that deepens an individual's relationship to the collective through the body. Alim writes of this as "complete[ing] the cipher (the process of constantly making things whole),"[24] which is where the extraphenomenal begins to take shape.

The Extraphenomenal in Diasporic Circles

Circles infuse the immediate physical space with new meaning. In doing so, they become worldmaking practices in their capacity to create and enclose small worlds unto themselves. In moments of performance, circles can become an *other* place, beyond what is evident to the physical eye. Capoeira is a great example. In capoeira, two martial artists play in the center to the buzzing twang of the berimbau and a chorus of singers.[25] Though today capoeira is a symbol of Brazilian national culture, at its birth it was an urban practice among enslaved Bantu-speaking peoples (of present-day Angola) who were taken in large numbers to Brazil's major cities of São Salvador and Rio de Janeiro.[26] Their worldviews were informed by martial arts and rites of passage that organized ancestral forces to attend to their new conditions.[27] In *Ring of Liberation*, J. Lowell Lewis describes rodas as rings that set aside "special or 'sacred' space," an aspect of all games where the rules of play distinguish the world inside a circle from that outside.[28] The ways people interact with one another, address each other, and deal with challenges are fundamentally determined by the world within the roda.

> In the songs of capoeira, reference is frequently made to fellow players as *camará* (...'comrade'...) or ...*mano* (... 'brother'). These terms refer not just to one's own close companions in the sport, but ideally should extend

outward to include all capoeira players. . . . The fact that players usually express regret over [incidents between rivals], however, and see them as departures from the correct standard, reinforces the view that comradeship is seen as an overarching principle, a kind of communitas, even when honored by the breach.[29]

The roda dictates modes of sociality within it, and thus entering into a circle is entering into a distinct space with its own set of rules. By extension, feelings of comradeship and kinship reinforce cultural codes that inform how practitioners move through the world outside of the roda. That capoeira is a practice historically tied to the Afro-Brazilian religion of candomblé reminds us that the roda blurs demarcations between secular and sacred as well.

Though it receives less scholarly attention than the technique, capoeira has a sacred dimension that deepens this sense of a roda's worldmaking capacities. In both his book *Fighting for Honor: The History of African Martial Art Traditions in the Atlantic World* and his article "Combat and the Crossing of the *Kalunga*," historian Thomas Desch-Obi examines capoeira's sacred capacities in relation to its inherited elements of Kongolese martial art and ritual cultures, and he refers to the *yowa* cross to make his point (see Fig. 1.2).[30] In fact, bomba, capoeira, and ring shouts have all been linked to this cosmogram, depicted as a cross superimposed on a circle. The *yowa* cross represents a philosophy wherein the physical world exists simultaneously to an ancestral/spiritual realm across the horizontal *kalunga* line, which is often represented as an ocean, river, or dense forestation meant to demarcate the borders between the world of the living and the realm of the ancestors.[31] Desch-Obi describes the *kalunga* as referring to elements of the natural and supernatural worlds under an entire cosmological system "that understood bodies of water to be bridges between lands of the living and the dead."[32]

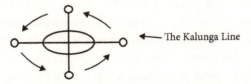

Figure 1.2 *Yowa* cross. The Kalunga line marks the threshold between worlds, often symbolized by water or deep forestation.

The cross itself can also be thought in relation to the cardinal directions, with each small circle at the ends of the cross representing the path of the sun rising in the east and moving counterclockwise around the inner circle to set in the west. The path of the sun corresponds to the path of the human soul from physical birth at sunrise to physical death at sunset, which begins rebirth as an ancestor below the horizontal *kalunga* line. In *Flash of the Spirit: African and Afro-American Art and Philosophy*, Robert Farris Thompson cites the following in explanation: "Bakongo believe and hold it true that man's life has no end, that it constitutes a cycle. The sun, in its rising and setting, is a sign of this cycle, and death is merely a transition in the process of change."[33] In this formulation, the ancestral world mirrors our own, and is inverted relative to our perspective.

This inverted world of the ancestors becomes an especially important detail. Desch-Obi argues that capoeira angola[34] is a variation of the *ngolo* combat system of Central Africa, wherein practitioners mainly balance on their hands or heads so that "they ritually mirrored the ancestors, as the other world across the *kalunga* was believed to be an inverted one."[35] Crossing into the ritual circle and being upside down meant "mediat[ing] power between the spiritual world of the ancestors and the world of the living."[36] Desch-Obi ultimately argues that there is a profound spiritual conception of the world underlying the physical plane of capoeira. His argument contextualizes dance scholar Barbara Browning's observations about the relationship between capoeira rodas and candomblé rodas: "Many capoeiristas feel a profound link to the orixá principles, and particularly to the idea of ancestor spirits."[37]

Ring shouts are another example of circle rituals wherein spiritual communion is a dimension of the practice. In African American history, the ring shout is a shuffled dance in a counterclockwise direction with singing, humming, and moaning accompaniment geared toward spiritual worship and Christian conversion. Ring shouts were first witnessed among enslaved Africans in the seventeenth century, eventually becoming a common practice among African Americans into the twentieth century. Historian Sterling Stuckey discusses ring shouts as "counterclockwise dance ceremony" tied to the *yowa* cross, and derived from Kongolese traditions that performed rituals of continuity between a physical life and spiritual existence after death.[38] In other words, the counterclockwise shuffle enacts the *yowa* cross. Historian Michael Gomez notes that among enslaved West and West Central Africans who lived in concentrated numbers throughout the South, "Ring ceremonies were very much used to invoke the presence of both ancestors and deities and served as media by which human beings entered into a shared experience with them."[39] While the necessity of shouts lessened over time,[40] as a danced practice it nonetheless maintained a choreographic stipulation that one's feet must never cross in order to distinguish it as sacred rather than secular dance. Stuckey and Gomez go on to argue that, in addition to facilitating acts of communion with ancestors and God, ring shouts were instrumental in bridging various African ethnic identifications into an African American identity.

In *Blackpentacostal Breath: The Aesthetics of Possibility*, religion and Black studies scholar Ashon Crawley draws particular attention to the movement of Afro-Arabic rings and Blackpentacostal shouts, describing them as both choreosonic and centrifugitive social worlds.[41] He defines centrifugitivity as "coterminous centripetal and centrifugal force," or the drawing toward and simultaneously away from a center, evident in shouts by the "individual twists and turns of individual flesh" that happen within "circumambulatory counterclockwise movements as a social form."[42] The counterclockwise movement enacts a centrifugitive logic of *decentered* social organization:

> Each shouter intentions their own motives and movements in concert with and as relation between the social form created at the moment of danced encounter. Perhaps this is an Enlightenment grounded in social relation between, where what the dancers escape into is the social world against the conditions of being shored up against sensory deprivation, where they enter into the social space in order to perform otherwise organization. These persons moved their flesh with intentionality of the social form they were in the process of creating in mind; they had to think the social to make the social.[43]

The "perhaps" embeds the language of possibility in his analysis, a philosophical consideration of the shout as a ritual whose enactment manifests otherwise forms of life and living. Crawley defines the "otherwise" as the infinite alternatives that already exist as possibilities alongside what *is*.[44] The "Enlightenment" of the ring occurs in the doing of it and the creative "thinking" of it at the same time, rather than thinking as some act separate from the dancing body. Think body-mind-spirit as whole rather than mind-body split. If sensory deprivation is an expression of the hierarchical world one must be prepared to re-enter, then the circle becomes a space of redress, which Crawley articulates as ways of releasing the flesh from its confines and its armor. Hence, centrifugitivity. His analysis demonstrates that diasporic circle rituals are, in the least, deeply layered social forms that enact otherwise modes of being that allow the flesh to escape the confines of daily life or steal away (discussed further later). Shouts are "aesthetic modes of existence as preparation for battle" in a "violent, violative world."[45]

That ring shouts are distinctly sacred practices does not alone account for their spiritual components. I contend that it is precisely the ever-present possibility of a circle's extraphenomenal capacities that captures why ring shouts become popular conversion practices.[46] All of the circles discussed in this chapter activate some form of the extraphenomenal too, even as primarily (though not exclusively) secular practices.

Writings about both capoeira and bomba discuss their spirituality to a much lesser degree, though they all note strong feelings of liberation and freedom that capture the spiritual or extraphenomenal in a different way. For example, in Lowell's discussion of capoeira, a sense of liberation within communal experiences develops in the form of both "freedom of motion" that tests the body's physical limitations (the flesh becoming), and an "ideological communitas" that "springs from, and is reinforced by, 'spontaneous' experiences of harmony and kinship with others in the course of play."[47] In bomba practices, the relationship between dancer and drummer helps to foster what Halbert Barton calls a "palpable excitement," a thrill so tangible it is a potent force.[48] Historian Lydia Milagros González adds that "the dancer mounts his dance until his entire body is shaking, very much in the way dancers tremble when possessed by a spirit in ritual ceremonies. Nobody interrupts the dancer; his or her time is respected and each person is allowed a space for freedom."[49] Alex LaSalle, bomba percussionist and founder of the Afro-Puerto Rican bomba troupe Alma Moyo, also acknowledges "an almost trance-like state converting him or her into a conductor of the spirit and energy."[50] LaSalle adds that the Ki-Kongo definition for the word "bomba" means "the action of spiritually cooling down a community or a member of a community,"[51] arguing that bomba's rhythms do just that. At times that cooling down was in remembrance of the struggles one's ancestors survived through the traditions they left; at others it is to create balance between oneself and the ancestors.[52]

Journalist, Hip Hop scholar, and bomba singer Raquel Z. Rivera expands on the spiritual/ ancestral dimension of bomba in her work "New York Afro-Puerto Rican and Afro-Dominican Roots Music: Liberation Mythologies and Overlapping Diasporas." In it she makes a case for what she terms "liberation mythologies," stories that we tell through song and dance that may or may not be "true," that specifically center "spirituality/ religiosity," and that are explicitly tied to social justice struggles for liberation, particularly with regards to class and race.[53] Rivera links this term to Robin Kelley's notion of "freedom dreams," bringing in multiple forms of mythmaking as creative expressions purposed to both "describe the world *and* to change it." Similar to LaSalle, Rivera locates this mythmaking in the rhythms of African ancestors and traditions, and in songs about freedom, marronage, and Africa—sung collectively and in call-and-response manner.[54] Ultimately Rivera argues that the stories that get told through song and dance should be thought of as both acts of medicine for the spirit *and* practices of liberation.

All of the preceding points demonstrate that circles practices channel extraphenomenal possibilities. Dance scholar Benita Brown refers to it as the Òrìṣà Paradigm, which she uses to describe African and African American cultural modalities manifesting in kinesthetic practices that prompt a dancer to open up to a spiritual realm: "That is the goal, and it is purposeful."[55] She continues, "Dance is a communicative phenomenon that creates a spiritual connection and permeates the well-being of society as a whole."[56] Overall, these practices share the invocation of a force or energy of some kind, whether that be spiritual, liberatory, or ancestral.

I have taken a somewhat lengthy departure from the subject of breaking to draw particular attention to how the extraphenomenal, spiritual, liberatory, community-building, and healing dimensions of circles are central to the embodied experience *when we center their Africanist aesthetics*. Breaking has these qualities too. Typically, breaking is represented as a dance-sport, getting more attention for its acrobatics or power moves than anything else. If, though, we recognize the cypher in relation to spirit and not just competition or spectacle, the comparison to diasporic circle rituals lends insight into cyphering experiences that oftentimes do not get named. Practitioners engage a multiplicity of discourses to explain their experiences in a way that nondancers understand, choosing accessible comparisons to describe them without settling on any singular language. Nonetheless, what persists is that the extraphenomenal is welcomed and *anticipated*, just as with other diasporic circles. This last point bears repeating because, while the liberatory, ancestral, and sacred are never guaranteed, they always remain a welcome possibility. How that force is conceptualized in cyphers gets at the heart of people's experiences in breaking culture, and their connection to its Africanist aesthetics.

Highs, Church, and Shifts in Time

While most of the breakers I interviewed spoke of some version of an extraphenomenal capacity to cyphering, oftentimes they had trouble finding the most fitting words. It makes sense then that some of the most poignant descriptions of this force within cyphering practices come from those who have been breaking the longest, perhaps because years have provided additional perspective. Others approach the topic more reticently, offering only peeks into their experiences, at least to me. Here I look to interviews with former b-boy Silky Jones, the late Boston-based b-boy Float of Incredible Breakers, and breakers Poe One, Triple7, Miss Little, Aby, Pia, and Jaekwon. Most were US-based, while the latter two are out of Austria. This group represents a sampling of the types of experiences voiced by breakers, and in terms that signal the extraphenomenal in their cyphering experiences. I organize this discussion around three main descriptions of the extraphenomenal: highs, church, and shifts in relation to time.

One of the most common descriptions of a cypher's extraphenomenality is to compare it to a high. Though he no longer breaks, Silky Jones tells a vivid story (in second person) of his high; a memory of a cypher at a New York club in the early 1980s (more than twenty-five years prior at the time of his telling):

> You know how it is when you've got a whole bunch of people that'd be like, "Yo! Get 'em Silk!" You know normally you might be like, you might be a little bit [cool] . . . it's all that nervous energy and all that shit's coming out and you got all the people behind you getting you geeked up. And the next thing you know you did some incredible shit that if you tried you can never repeat. And this is the best shit you're dancing—when you're doing your shit and you don't know what you're doing! And all you're hearing is "*Ooohhhhh!!!! Oooohhh!*" . . . Then the song'll be over and the scene'll fade and shit. And like, the circle'll be over and you walk with your peoples and they're giving each other pounds. And they be like, "That's nice Silk!" And you'll be like, "Yeah" [*nods in agreement*]. And you can't even look at 'em. Just be sweatin', all geeked up. Your boy gives you a pound. You can't even look people directly in the eyes, but you got the runner's high. Like the pupils are like this big! . . . Yeah man, it was like very—like a high. That was the high. Like, the rest of the night, you start to downshift. You'd be calming down but that was, that was the get high. . . . Every week at a particular place,

you're guaranteed to get high. That was my get high. . . . And sometimes, that's what you lived for. I work all week. Thursday, Friday, and Saturday, it's fucking on! And anybody could get it. *Any*body. . . . There's nothing like the feeling when—we're talking culturally—everybody you knew, everybody you bumped into had that, that beast that was right at the tip of they tongue or right behind their eye waiting to come out.[57]

This vivid tale of Silky's moment in the sun was an entire scene of activity. His story captured the sheer tactile pleasure of dancing with your friends to the music that literally moved him in his formative years. His personal high was clearly shared by an equally elevated crowd, and by his crew who pumped him up for the challenge.

While telling his cypher story, Silk performed the high he described to the camera, as the emotional flow of his story played out in his expressive eyes. He began the story with relaxed shoulders and a calm expression on his face, embodying a cool pose adopted at the beginning of a battle. As he turned to his dancing, the re-memory broke that cool demeanor, mimicking the point of the story where his friends hyped him up. The pace of his narrative jumped along with the urgency of the moments he recounted, paralleling how quickly he went from nervous to "geeked up" to the high that followed and lingered even after he left the cyphers and later the club. In his excitement, he cursed, repeated himself, and stumbled over his words in a rush to express the thrill of an unprecedented and unrepeatable moment of skill followed by enthusiastic validation by his peoples. And because our interview took place in a crowded and darkened nightclub following a battle earlier that day—my camera had the only bright light—the club itself served as the perfect backdrop for his re-enactment. The music—so loud that our conversation was more shouted than spoken—further lent to our lively exchange, as I felt free to play along in his memory, laughing and cheering.

Though Silky compared his "get high" to a runner's high, his description resonates with a drug-like euphoria too, another frequent comparative. Aby compared breaking with drugs in a different way, having experienced both: "With drugs I would get high, a couple hours later I'd go right back to my pain and misery, you know? But breaking, *rocking* was always there. All we had to do is get somebody with a record player, throw in a [record], you got, you know, we got the escape. And then we was on top of the world."[58] While both offer an immediacy and a sense of escaping to another reality (a prominent theme in comparisons to a high), the high from dancing was healthier, longer lasting, more readily available, and cost-effective. Silky ended his story by emphasizing that everyone shared in the cultural understanding of the cypher because they had their own beasts to release, and for both him and Aby, it was a meaningful form of release.

Float's comments brought out a similar sentimemt. At the time of our interview in 2007, Float was only beginning to return to the breaking scene in Boston, welcomed back as a respected figure. His emphasis, though, was on the conditions that contextualized his feelings about cyphering:

> It was definitely a way of letting out your aggressions or of like venting out what you were feeling in other areas of your life. 'Cause we, as poor people living in poor neighborhoods, we didn't really have the finances to go out and have fun. Some people did; some people didn't. I didn't, personally. So that was the way of having fun, just getting out, venting out. Seeing all the nastiness. And sometimes get raw battles and, you know, and compete. And sometimes for me, I wasn't so much into the hardcore competing like a lot of the guys were. If you jumped in the circle with me, and you jumped at me I'm gonna come back at you. You know? But if you didn't and you wanted to just dance with me, we dance together and we just go back and forth, and it's all good. But for me it was just, like, a way to get out. And just, I loved it. It was just fun. As I got into it and then passionately, I looked forward to just, "Finally, where's the jam? What we're doing? Where're we going?" You know? "Call the brothers. Let's go hang out. Let's go." It was my way of just escaping. I used to, in a sense, for me it was like an escape. You know, it was an escape way from getting away from all the nonsense. . . . It's like, some people did drugs to escape life. This was a positive of way of escaping, but into something that is good and positive 'cause it was a dance . . . Where we were pent-up energy just being in the neighborhood doing nothing, guys would normally end up killing each other or getting into bad things. This was a way of, you know, evolving into something more positive, you know? Getting into something that was actually, down the line, was beneficial . . . It was like guys that don't have much are able to build on something . . . and make something that was *great*. Not just regular. It was something that was great, that was a great feeling that is hard to capture anywhere else.[59]

Like Silky and Aby, Float contextualized the need for breaking and cyphering as a response to the conditions of everyday life. An inability to participate in expensive leisure activities is not an uncommon story and reiterates why cyphers were important. Also like Aby, Float proposed breaking as a positive form of escapism, with drugs as its negative equivalent. Breaking offered a kind of collective release, as "*we* were pent-up energy," like they were powder kegs ready to blow. While this imagery attests to the importance of the release, in his initial description of what the escape felt like, he opted for more simple terms like "love," "great," and "not regular," which are as far as words would go for Float, at first.

When he began to reflect on being "in the zone," Float captured aspects of cyphering's escapist extraphenomenality, clarifying that "the zone is the mood, the spirit, the spirit you're in at the moment. You're feeling the music. You have energy. You feel alive. And just, your body's gonna take you over. Then all of sudden, you're just, you're somewhere else. You forget everybody around you. You're just, you're out there. You're out for lunch! You're gone." Time and place change in ritual. "Out there," perhaps similar to Aby's "top of the world," is some other place or plane of existence that his body took him to, tapping into cyphering's version of ritual time and space. (See the discussion of dimensionality in chapter 4.) Perhaps, too, that is why Aby draws a link between the couple of hours of a drug high and the heights of cyphering. All of their discussions move beyond a high to something not quite named.

Silk, Aby, and Float also emphasized "escape" and "release," which echoes ideas of bacchanalian celebrations as social safety valves that releases tensions and discontentment, deemed necessary to maintain a given social order.[60] I would argue, in contrast, that their stories tap into a "steal away" logic. Stealing away historically refers to defiant acts of self-possession wherein enslaved Black people left the plantation without permission, trespassed across properties, and assembled clandestinely for various activities, from praise meetings to dances to meeting family or lovers.[61] As they ventured deep into "densely wooded areas . . . hidden from their oppressors,"[62] they also gathered to pray for freedom—prayers that manifested in dance, song, and ritual. Saidiya Hartman, scholar of African American literature and cultural history, writes that stealing away was also "an abrogation of terms of subjection" made possible by "investing in the body as a site of sensual activity, sociality, and possibility, and, last, redressing the pained body."[63] "Investing in the body" intervenes politically by propagating a transformative corporeality, one that was necessarily social, sensual, pleasurable, and healing.[64] Hartman goes on to state that "rather than the dance providing an occasion for forgetting or escaping the 'reality' of slavery, the pleasure such opportunities afforded were bittersweet, fleeting, and tempered by the perpetuity of bondage."[65] Hartman notes that stealing away offered limited and incomplete redress, yet its logic prioritizes the act of gathering together and laboring for one's own spirit and community on their terms and in ways that critiqued the very grounds for their subjection.

These stories expressed the necessity of breaking and cyphering as acts that counter the conditions of everyday life in urban America, whether those conditions be about wage labor or the absence of resources and outlets for youth. In the face of that, they invested in their bodies and cultivated a different way of being in the world. Their stories are extraphenomenal, not simply because a high signifies an altered state of mind, but because their stories are about otherwise possibilities for life. This sentiment is more pronounced in comparisons to church.

Poe One, for example, talked about a communal sense of euphoria in more overtly religious terms, bringing in a comparison to church, fellowship, and performance:

> You can even say that being in a church and praying is a cypher. . . . You know how in church sometimes, you just, everyone's singing a certain joyous song and you just . . . feel so happy inside? Or so united, so in sync. And you feel very powerful. There's a word for it. It's . . . in tune. Like, in tune. When that moment comes in a cypher, it's like that. You can even look across the cypher—like, say like, I'm looking at you now, right? That could be your side of the cypher [*he points to me*]; this is my side [*gestures to himself*]. There's a whole circle and everybody's channeling, we're channeling this energy. And we don't even know each other, right? Let's say we don't know each other, and you just walked to the cypher and you want to dance too. And I'm looking toward the floor of the person who's dancing and I'm feeling this beat. And a certain beat comes on, a new one, and I just raise my hand like, "Whoa!" like, "This. *This* is my jam!" But then it's your jam too! And I see you raise your hand too! We'll look at each other and we just nod our heads like . . . and our eyes just give this certain connection. And the next thing you know, we know each other now. We know each other. That moment of connection. We just met each other there. And it's like that song united us; that energy united us. Then all of a sudden you throw down and I throw down. Then it's like afterward we're talking and the next thing you know we go eat. It's a connection with everybody, it's that connection. It's like . . . it's, it's . . . it's real. It's that one moment of being real. No mask on. You're finally out there. Those are the people that know how to cypher and

let that energy of the cypher take you in. 'Cause there is a negative part and a positive part, you know like in anything.[66]

He began his comments with multiple, related but inexact terms to describe his experience: "happy inside," "united," "in tune," "in sync," "powerful." The connection that Poe described wavers between a state of being and a shift in perception, awakening him to new relationships. Music played a major role in his recounting, where the beat captured the shared harmonic vibration of breaking together. In his description, cyphering was also an act of worship, a reverent practice honoring something bigger than himself. On the dance floor, that reverence was actualized in breaking together ("throwing down") and the aftereffects. Poe One's description captured a spiritual component to cyphering that is often overlooked in analyses of street dance cultures. It is not spiritual simply because he compared it to church. Instead, cyphering conjures spiritual elements through the immaterial aspects of dancing: connections through music, in the eyes, being in sync. There is no guarantee it will happen, but the moment is ripe with anticipation and possibility.

That Poe ended with it being "real" may appear trite given past oversaturation of the Hip Hop's phrase "keeping it real," but his characterization of cyphering as "real" is quite fitting. The term signifies doubly. First, it is an expression of acting without facade or pretense ("no mask on"). Cyphering enabled a kind of self-exposure, not in the sense of lacking protection but in the chance to take off his daily armor or mask, at least for "that one moment." In the second sense, real refers to the genuine existence of a connection to the participants in the circle, something grounded in reality. They are connected through the culture; they are "united" in the act of dancing. Ultimately, the comparison to church is productive both because it is a broadly accessible example that accurately captures a genuine feeling, and because it establishes a degree of reverence for cyphering and the connections that continue to build beyond the momentary euphoria. It is real.

Poe was not alone in using religious discourse. B-boy and MC Triple7 described a cypher's energy in terms of a Christ or anti-Christ energy: "To me Hip Hop, if you want to get deep with it man, it's nothin' but an energy. And in reality to me, it's more to me like the energy of a Christ. I'm not—I don't want to get all religious, but to me, Hip Hop is the Christ. So, if the Christ is—the Christ is something that uplift[s] your spirit; Hip Hop uplifts your spirit. It could also suppress your spirit. So that means it's anti-Christ when it's doing that."[67] For Triple7, Hip Hop was not solely a product to consume, but a practice meant to uplift. He echoed MC KRS-One's discussion of the Christ in his piece "The Milk and the Meat," wherein he states that the "basic idea of the *Christ* is not exclusively Christian, nor is *Christ* the family name or last name of Jesus. *Christ* is who Jesus became."[68] In naming Hip Hop "the energy of a Christ" (not *the* Christ), Triple7 brought attention to its meaning as an anointed title for a messiah or liberator, extending that title to Hip Hop.

Carrying on with the biblical comparisons, Poe One described an almost opposite kind of cypher, one rooted in personal battles and collective demons:

> I think stress, like arguing with people, trying to make ends meet, bills, maturity, injuries, work, a regular job working 9 to 5 . . . you know, life! That kind of holds me back. But also drives me. Because when I do get the opportunity to go to a club and form that circle, that's when I let all that held me back out. I let it out. Sometimes it comes to memory. Sometimes the abuse of my father comes into my picture. Sometimes when there's a circle and everybody's afraid to go out, that's a demon right there to me. For me that's, that's a negative energy trying to break a chance for positive people channeling together, trying to hold them back. And for me that's like, it's time to fight. Let's do it, let's do it now. Let's fight it. . . . And it gets me, at the same time like a warrior, like *bah*! . . . When I do, I feel I conquer something. . . . When there's a positive energy and not a negative energy, that means we booted it out! It's like the negative energy went away and went into the other little corner over there and everybody now is channeling that most happiest moment. And that's like, that's being free.[69]

Poe One described a righteous act, one that fostered self-possession and connection to others through acts of channeling together. It was not simply that the negative energy had a form (a demon); each individual is engaged in their own version of struggling against that negative force. They are collectively in a spiritual battle. "Booting it out" is part of the drama rather than an impossible endeavor. This is an important aspect of Poe One's definition of freedom. He later stated that freedom is "no damn worries of nothing in your life whatsoever," which for him included "not worrying about where you gonna get your next meal from. Not your bills or not how you gonna get home, not when you gonna get your gas money. Not worrying about you gotta wake up in the morning early. It's just you, the floor, and the music. It's *now*!"[70] Poe depicted cyphering as a means of directly confronting the mundane stresses of laboring under capitalism, and banishes them in the now. This, too, is an investment in the body, one that prioritizes the immediate present over returning to a world of precarity under capitalism's scarcity model.

Similarly, Miss Little—who had already learned some breaking moves by the mid-1980s at the age of six or seven in the Bay Area of California—roots her feelings about cyphers in a spiritual certainty of dance's necessity and power, though from a non- or not entirely Christian angle:

> Once you go and dance, you think about how strong you really is and you just try to override that. And if you do, man, that's what'll keep you going. It's that you know that you can dance and feel good about whatever is hurting you in the inside. And keep it going. And dance is—I know I gotta keep dancing, because it's my protection. If I stop dancing, things start goin' bad for me. Because somebody's gotta go out there and brew up the spirits. Somebody's gotta go out there and clean the air with the movement. 'Cause that's who we are as Black people. We are movement people.[71]

Miss Little's discussion was influenced by having trained in various techniques since she was little, a background shaped by her mother's insistence that she was going to learn "*all* the dances," including "African dance" and capoeira.[72] The idea that dance can brew up spirits and cleanse the air is likely evident in some of these forms as well, which she learned alongside street dances and was reified in her belief systems. It is a sentiment that registered for her at the level of identity, in our shared blackness, and that manifested in breaking as well. Note too that dancing is simultaneously about the body and the spirit; attending to one is to attend to the other. Less about God or demons than a relationship to multiple and likely too ancestral spirits, Miss Little's comments add to the many voices that speak to the spiritual work of cyphering.

Finally, the spiritual in breaking has also been articulated as a kind of shift in time. Aby, who started breaking in 1974, interacted with a multiplicity of spirits, though his discussion moved in unexpected ways. With earnest admission, he talked to me about cyphering that very day, minutes prior to our 2007 interview:

> When you're rocking or you're breaking, now as you call it, you become free, man. And you're flying.... When I'm in the cypher and I'm breaking. Well, let's suppose I'm not breaking and I'm in the cypher. Ask Corey [Icey Ice, who introduced us], man. I go in a zone, and I place myself in that cypher. And I remember, and instead of picturing all these different faces, I picture all my people. All my people. Like damn, I see Jimmy Lee. I see Jimmy Dee. I see L-Mac, I see Baz, you know. I see us when we was young, doing that. You know? And that's what I see. And sometimes man, I get choked up . . . And with the music! Maaann. I got music that—you know, I sometimes, I put music on man and . . . it brings you back. 'Cause you go through so much pain. And to figure out that you made it and you livin' to see some seventh generation doing this?! And, you know, it brings you back. It brings you back. You know when a man cries, it cleans the soul? So that's what's going on right now. It's real man.[73]

It is worth amplifying that Aby described an experience as an active participant in the cypher, an experience that was *not* tied to breaking in the center. Within that experience he was still moved. Every time he said, "It brings you back," tears welled in his eyes and he would give me a little smile. Despite words like "remember" and "memories," and his reference to "picturing" all of his people, what he recounted of his experiences that day in the cypher felt less like a recall of the past than the past meeting him in the moment as the music took him back. The heavily seventies soul, funk, and rock breaks that were played that day paved the way for the conflation of time and place in the cypher. He described his experience as a simultaneity of the past and present. Fort Lauderdale in 2007 became the Bronx in the 1970s. Seeing his friends, those who have passed on or have left his life in some way, bridged past and present, bringing him back to an originary cyphering experience as an adult who survived in a way that his boys did not or could not—losses from death, disease, addiction, and prison. The extraphenomenality of cyphers is ultimately not exclusive to dancing bodies on the floor because there are more spirits present than meets the eye (see Fig. 1.3).

Cyphering allowed Aby to cross states of existence (dead and alive) and the social death of incarceration. The cross section of oppressive sociological and political forces that perpetuate addiction, criminalize Black and Brown youth, and extract people from communities were not things that he could escape, but cyphering continued to offer healing from those old wounds. His

Figure 1.3 Open circle, Evolution 3, Fort Lauderdale, FL (17 Mar 2007). This is one of the open circles during the weekend of my interview with Aby.

tears added weight to his words, and veracity to his story. He closed with the following comments that seem to reveal the stakes of telling it to me: "So don't ever underestimate us, depreciate us because who we are, how we dress. You know what I'm saying? Like us. I'm talking about *us, mami*. And these people gotta know, you know, we're human beings. We just doing what is given to us, you know. This was given to us. This is, you know, this is a gift from God. So look at it that way." He closed his cypher story with this pointed declaration of "our" humanity. He patted my hand gently when he emphasized "*us, mami*," which I took to mean African Americans and Puerto Ricans. That all of this is part of his cyphering experience, the *becoming freedom* of participating in the ritual, stays with me because this is not just about his individual freedom, but one shared with others in spirit, with others who are struggling, and with me.

In a 2012 interview, b-girl Pia offered a more hesitant yet overlapping description of a merging of time. She recounted cyphering with her crew at a practice session and its unexpected results:

PIA: Last year we had a practice in Salzburg. In Austria. And then we danced together and I was very . . . I've thought a lot of this day. . . . When I danced there, I only had my past in my mind (because it happened a lot), of the group, and my last relationship. Yeah. And . . . I got so into it that I started to, *not really* cry, but I was like [*gestures with her index fingers tears trailing down her cheeks*] a little bit. And I danced and danced and it was . . . it was like . . . meditation or healing myself in another way. So that was very interesting for me because I was like, "Oh my god. What is this? What am I doing here?"

IKJ: Were you in a circle?

PIA: Huh?

IKJ: Was it in a circle, in a cypher?

PIA: Yeah, it was in a practice room that we had. Everybody danced in the middle, so the others stood around.

IKJ: What do you think helped to make that happen? Was it the music or the people, the lighting or the space? What do you think helped to make that happen?

PIA: I think it was the mixture of all. 'Cause the people, they, we . . . It was before we start the new big—or the old—but the new version to the big show. And we had a big aim, and we had this dream. But we knew that it would be over after that, after that big show. So it was the energy of the people. We were all very . . . melancholic?

IKJ: It was like your last time together or something?

PIA: No, it was— It wasn't the last time together because we, we had the practices for the show for I think three months or something. But it was the last practice that was like this, like with this special feeling. And yeah. It was very interesting for me, that feeling. Yeah . . . I was very free also in dancing. It was also the music. We put on some also melancholic music, but . . . also very powerful.[74]

My own fascination at the time with how these things happened—the roles that music,[75] space, lighting, ruminations about the past might have played. In retrospect, my follow-up questions muddle the point, but I was also trying to jog her memories of the sensorial experience. That she thought about that night "a lot," that she felt "free," that she surprised herself, that her own questions ("What is this? What am I doing here?") were left unanswered, hints at how the experience continued to convey its embedded and embodied lessons inexactly, over time. That is, we both understood that the cypher opened up something unexpected. Its parts may have played a role but they were not items in a recipe. The question of *how* it happened remains unclear, yet its impact was abundantly evident. The "not really crying" but crying seemed to happen almost against her will, marking a material trace of the "meditation or healing" or whatever it was for her.

In my interview with Pia, there was also a more pronounced gap between what she was able to communicate in English and what I understood. With that said, it was clear that this cyphering experience stood out as a unique one for her. Pia spoke candidly about it, but in a hushed tone. In fact, as she gauged my reaction to her story, I felt like the one on the spot. I initially assumed that her apprehension was because of the camera. I was there to interview b-boy Jaekwon, whom I had met several years prior on a trip to Germany and kept in loose contact with to ensure an interview when next we met. Pia accompanied him but had not planned on taking part in the interview. Although she agreed to participate when I asked, Pia was largely quiet most of the time. Nevertheless, she was paying close attention. Less than five minutes before she recounted her experience, Jaekwon and I had this brief exchange that might have impacted her decision to participate:

IKJ: You said that sometimes you think of other things or other people [when you dance]. Can you give me examples?

JAE: Yeah, sometimes it's, sometimes it helps me to, to cope with other experiences that I've made. Maybe that I'm thinking about persons that I was close to and am not anymore. Or maybe even that I, that it helps me to recognize more where I'm at, at the moment, and to enjoy myself. Yeah. . . . Maybe that sounds a little bit funny, but sometimes it feels like you go through different time zones. Sometimes it is what could be in the future. Sometimes it just helps you go back to the moment again. Yeah. . . . That's how it feels.

IKJ: I've heard similar things from other people, so it's not strange. But everyone describes it in different ways, in unique ways.[76]

I remember the looks of relief on Jaekwon's face and piqued curiosity on Pia's. Jaekwon's description of a shift in relation to time resonates with transport, traveling back and forth "through different time zones" (versus a linear experience of time). It only occurred to me after reviewing the interview transcripts that perhaps I had unwittingly made it okay for Pia to share her story.

So, if these experiences happen with some regularity, then why the concern that it sounds absurd? It made me wonder if breakers spoke to each other about these things. I would argue that verbal language might not adequately express the full scope of their experiences to begin with, especially across language barriers. In a subculture that crosses so many different nationalities, sometimes the "right words" do not exist; yet their conversations through dance can be expressive in ways that are nonverbal. As well, the lack of specific language captures an incredible range of experiences.

While not all breakers would characterize cyphering through religious language, highs, euphoric stealing away, shifts in time, or ancestral and spiritual connections, the dark matter of cyphers captures a through line across practitioners' chosen language. Somewhere in the realm of experiential knowledge, amplified in the act of cyphering among a group of people who share a danced cultural language, unexpected possibilities manifest. A diasporic lens matters profoundly to our ability to recognize, appreciate, and learn from cyphering experiences of liberation, community healing, spirit, and fellowship because that is built into the technology of the circle. The *yowa* cosmogram, in its representation of the circle as a space to engage with spirits and ancestors, captures an understanding that is then danced or enacted in circle practices.

Diaspora, Race, and Power

> I simply want to say that in the histories of the migration, forced or free, of these societies . . . whose cultural traces are everywhere intermingled with one another, there is always the stamp of historical violence and rupture.
> —Stuart Hall, "Negotiating Caribbean Identities"[77]

The invisibilization of Africanist aesthetics is indicative of that stamp of violence.[78] It exemplifies the profound degree of ignorance about African diasporic histories and people. The general permissiveness granted to the public to consume Black dance with no "sustained contact with the corporeal fact of Black people in the world," as dance scholar Thomas DeFrantz describes, extends that ignorance and is a function of power.[79]

Case in point: in a December 2006 discussion thread on a popular Hip Hop dance website, locker Ill Kosby stated emphatically that Hip Hop dances in all forms are "rooted" in Africanist practices. Responses in support and against this claim raged on for several weeks, spilling over to another website.[80] Folks contributed their opinions, links to other sources, and archival photographs to support their claims. It came down to two arguments: (1) Hip Hop dance is rooted in Africa; (2) Hip Hop dance is American, and Africa has little to do with what people in the Bronx were doing in the 1970s. Faulty binaries, overly literal interpretations, and righteous indignation constituted many of the responses. On both sides of the debate, people struggled to either articulate or understand how Africanist "resonances and presences, trends and phenomena" can manifest in everyday acts of contemporary cultural production outside of one-to-one, unidirectional transmissions.[81]

For example, even in cases when one might concede a connection, diaspora detractors often argued that recognizing African influences in breaking's history was somehow ahistorical, or an illogical approach to history. Most frequently, this stance equated chronological and geographic proximity with cultural influence, meaning that the most worthwhile influences to acknowledge happened directly within a particular environment over a significant period of time. The more direct the relationship to breaking, the more legitimate the claim to an influence. Detractors demanded "proof." They wanted to know who took African dance classes, when did they took them, and where these classes were made available in the 1970s. Without pictures and documentation (which largely do not exist) to explain the actions of young people in the Bronx, for this group any arguments favoring African diasporic influences were deemed meritless.

While these naysayers might accept, for example, that tap dance influenced breaking—many early breakers talk about their admiration for the Nicholas Brothers or Sammy Davis Jr. seen in movies and on TV—those opposed to diaspora did not see any Africanist elements in tap either. And those that did only acknowledged African influences alongside Irish ones too, as if multiple and overlapping cultural influences nullified any impact of Africanist aesthetics. The reverse logic was evident as well: that all of humanity "comes from Africa," as if Africa were a country and DNA stood in for culture. This particular argument concluded that everything is African "on some level," just not in a discernible way.

Such a debate matters precisely because it sparked such heated exchanges, suggesting that there was more at stake than simple claims to roots or national culture. And demands that each piece of evidence be able to stand alone as definitive proof ultimately stymied the exchange. The staunch positions on both sides of the debate—emphatic about breaking's African retentions on one hand, and deeply invested in the denial of any influence whatsoever on the other—led to forms of oversimplification that left some to conclude that this is a Black dance for Black people, a postulation that saw breaking's ethnic and racial diversity as a testament to blackness *not* mattering. Missing from the debate was an assessment of the workings of power running through their exchanges. While antiblackness abounds in some responses, when read generously, it seems that everyone struggled to name an analytical framework that "made sense," that could explain or account for the kinds of connections noted in the original posts, and that could penetrate the cognitive dissonance that prevented some from even entertaining the consideration.

In a 2007 interview with b-boy Viazeen about this very topic, he pointed out that such oversimplifications made claims to Africa seem empty, or that they obfuscated more than they revealed. Viazeen argued that appeals to Africa often replaced the work of studying the movement, and thus fully respecting the dance:

> We haven't really understood or studied the movement enough. So we always go, "It's origins is from Africa." Yes and no. There's some things that, you look . . . you can't say that's from Africa. It came from exploring what only their body can do. Falling out of something, trying to do something and it not working, or just, you know, pushing your limits. Using your imagination. I learned to roll around the floor because I rolled around the floor. . . . So, you know, a lot of that stuff doesn't *come from*, doesn't have *an origin* that we automatically go, "Yeah. This came from the East Coast. This came from the West Coast. This came from Africa." There's some things that we can't put a finger on that. . . . We have to look at it, you understand. Even the stuff that comes from Africa or anywhere can be broken down, so it becomes influential to how things are created.[82]

The implication is true at times: appeals to African origins could stand in for *not* knowing how to articulate why that connection matters to breaking experiences, beyond crediting Black people, (which is still important). While Viazeen contextualizes those claims in terms of regional classifications of moves and style (East and West Coasts)—and in contrast to my own argument that Africanist influences are epistemological—his emphasis on moving away from claims to origin reminds us that identifying such influences alone does not exhaust what we need to know and understand about the dance.

However, even if, for example, one argues that "rolling around the floor" is an aspect of Africanist aesthetic practices—and Gottschild reminds us that "Africanist dance idioms . . . reaffirm contact with the earth"—recognizing this tie to Africanist aesthetics (and the constellation of aesthetic elements it activates) should springboard to a deeper discussion, not signal the end of one.[83] My approach to looking at Africanist aesthetics is both an effort to start from specific qualities of the dance and its culture, and to allow that specificity to unearth new layers of understanding.

I draw attention to evidence of Africanist cosmologies within capoeira, bomba, ring shouts, and cyphering because, without a diasporic lens, we miss something *vital*. Acknowledging the parallels between cyphering and other circle practices in the African diaspora does not mean arguing for unidirectional or uninterrupted lines of influence from Africa (or the diaspora) to the Americas (or New York). Instead, it is the active reworking of inherited diasporic cultural aesthetic imperatives. To be clear, diaspora is a heterogeneous formation that "necessarily involves a process of linking or connecting across gaps—a practice we might term *articulation*," as literary scholar Brent Hayes Edwards proposes.[84] Diasporas can also "overlap" (as historian Earl Lewis theorized), or be "mutually interlocking" (as ethnic studies scholar Juan Flores once described).[85] Thus they touch, interconnect, mutually influence and link people in a range of ways and across various differences, nurturing a sense of something shared.

One could easily make the case that breaking, for example, encourages a degree of philosophical literacy with East Asian cultures as well. Many breakers were influenced by or trained in various Chinese, Japanese, and Korean martial arts.[86] Breaking's history recognizes the influence of kung fu movies in the seventies and eighties on Hip Hop,[87] but ideas of apprenticeship, training, and the diversity of styles (e.g., drunken, monkey) within breaking are at least in part adopted from these influences too. Even the idolization of Bruce Lee is in part because his philosophy of martial arts lent itself to breaking. In *Tao of Jeet Kun Do*, Lee writes:

> The martial arts are based upon understanding, hard work and a total comprehension of skills. Power training and the use of force are easy, but total comprehension of all of the skills of the martial arts is very difficult to achieve. . . . To put the heart of the martial arts in your own heart and have it be a part of you means total comprehension and the use of a free style. When you have that you will know that there are no limits.[88]

A philosophy that recognizes the symbiotic relationship between technique and freedom in movement overlaps with breaking culture. In fact, during an interview with Krazy Kujo, he remarked that breaking *is* a form of *jeet kun do*, though breakers may not recognize it as such.[89] Though the language of "diaspora" is not invoked in this example, there is still an understanding of overlapping cultural influences within breaking. It is also clear that these types of connection demand further exploration.

In the face of violence and oppression, cyphering is part of a tradition of African diasporic creative expressive practices of survival and liberation.[90] Nonetheless, a fear of African influences resurfaces in the histories of capoeira, ring shouts, bomba, and breaking. And while I argue that cyphering in particular is influenced by African diasporic aesthetic imperatives, the fact that these influences remain underacknowledged, underrecognized, and repressed tells me there is still a lot of work to do.[91]

Research on capoeira and ring shouts, for example, discuss their being interpreted as dangerous African practices, and efforts to end them were fueled by racism. Desch-Obi notes that up until the 1930s, before politicians began to engage capoeira as "national" culture, capoeira had been criminalized and repressed by the state since the second half of the eighteenth century in an effort to "exterminate" the martial art as a dangerous and "unsightly" remnant of Central African culture.[92] Though capoeira is now an accepted dimension of Afro-Brazilian culture, Desch-Obi argues that the growth of origin stories that do *not* acknowledge Africa or capoeira's Central African elements surfaced after its "co-optation by populist politics,"[93] reframing what was once deemed a fact into a debate.

While ring shouts are today acknowledged as sacred, animated forms of worship, they were once looked down upon as savage vestiges of Africa and deemed disrespectful and insufficiently devout, at least to Euro-American sensibilities. In an era of racial uplift, danced religiosity was deemed a problem holding African Americans back, preventing our being accepted as intelligent and rational human beings. African American community leaders like Bishop Daniel Alexander Payne sought to purge ring shouts from Black Christian worship in order to combat stereotypes of blackness and primitivity.[94]

In the case of bomba, anthropologist Isar Godreau's "Folkloric 'Others': *Blanqueamiento* and the Celebration of Blackness as an Exception in Puerto Rico" explores the celebratory banner of Afro–Puerto Rican folk culture and a discourse that situates Africanness as an essence to be retrieved from the past for national projects that help safeguard Puerto Rican culture from threats of US imperialism.[95] Simultaneously, these traditions are located in specific places like Loíza and San Antón, which are depicted as sites "where black people live" that consequently constructs the rest of Puerto Rico as "not black."[96] In this case, blackness is acknowledged, contained in specific locations or traditions, and ultimately disavowed, shoring up ideologies of *blanqueamiento*, or the whitening of Latino peoples. Godreau furthers that such ideological projects are meaningful only when they are "informed by an anxiety" over the contemporary presence of Black subjects.

Each genre confronts Black subjecthood as a crisis to the meaning constructed around the practice. Breaking is no different. Put simply, blackness is often treated as antithetical to multicultural dreams of a global Hip Hop, perhaps because of the ease of co-opting multiculturalism for apolitical, deradicalized, and profitable ends. To recognize the dark matter of cyphers, then, demands that one also reckon with internalized antiblackness and anxieties about being perceived as appropriative or exploitative.[97] Gottschild avows simply that "we desperately need to cut through the convoluted web of racism that denies acknowledgement of the Africanist part of the whole."[98]

Conclusion

At their best, cyphering experiences are deeply spiritual, freeing, and community-affirming. Cyphering offers an embodied understanding of Africanist cultural inheritances, and it facilitates acts of collaboration and community among participants across racial and ethnic differences.[99] But a truly multiethnic and multiracial global breaking culture necessitates addressing antiblackness, and disabusing ourselves of the belief that dance transcends difference. With that said, the potency of cyphering experiences tells us that palpable feelings of connection, or joy, or release do exist and have changed lives.

I believe that those feelings are an underacknowledged driving force behind global Hip Hop. A diasporic lens helps us recognize that force, and I have argued as much in this chapter. At the same time, those aesthetics must be contextualized by New York City in the 1970s and early 1980s, which is to say the conditions under which these aesthetics came together as breaking cyphers, which I discuss in the next chapter.

Superheroes Among Us

B-Boy All Stars Block Party in the Bronx, New York, 13 August 2006
It is supposed to be just a forty-five-minute interview with Kid Glyde, president of the Dynamic Rockers, following a KR3Ts (Keep Rising to the Top)[1] rehearsal. Before I can leave, Kid Glyde approaches me as if he has forgotten to tell me something important, smiles briefly, then gestures to the woman beside him and says softly, "Oh, um this is Peaches. She's a popper." Within minutes, Peaches Rodriguez—a tall, boisterous blond—looks down at me, smiles, and announces, "There's a block party in the Bronx right now. Wanna go?" She shows me the crumpled, printed-out email announcement of a block party hosted by the B-Boy All Stars, which has already started. If we're lucky we can catch the last hour or so. Peaches graciously offers me a ride as Glyde heads out first, and off we go.

On the drive we chat: I tell her about my project, she tells me about the early eighties Hip Hop scene and her audition for the movie Beat Street. I spend most of the drive listening to her description of the day's events, and jokes about life. Peaches is an expert storyteller and an actual stand-up comedian, which eventually contextualizes her abrupt delivery, good-natured and somewhat candid sense of humor, and infectious laugh. We arrive at Watson Gleason Park on Rosedale Avenue sooner than I expect and luck out with parking Peaches' black SUV. We follow the music to find the party, and as we walk I note the train tracks overhead (my first indication of how to get home).

B-Boy All Stars is a community event organization headed by Veronica Star, a "b-boy events organizer" who also hosts. The block party is well underway. Vendors sell hot dogs, meal plates, and various sweets. The streets are a blur of laughing and running children, skinned knees from hard play, ice-cream stains on oversized T-shirts, with at least a couple of hundred people hanging out and enjoying the summer weather. As I take it all in, Peaches brings an old friend over to meet me. His dance name is Cartoon, a popper like Peaches, with a friendship dating back to the early 1980s. He too auditioned for Beat Street, but his part ended up on the cutting room floor, which he tells me at least twice.

The onslaught of sensory information overwhelms me, so I walk to get my bearings and explore. I wander to the edges of the block party just shy of the music's outermost reaches. I return in less than ten minutes to see a cypher already formed. I join the stream of people doing the same, and with camera in hand I make my way to the center just before Cartoon steps in (see Fig. 2.1). With a focused intensity, he struts into the circle as if he were stepping into the song itself. Each part of his body corresponds to a different aspect of the music: his legs move to the left, his torso faces the right, and his hand turns the brim of his baseball cap to the left, creating the illusion of a segmented body moving in different directions at once. Cartoon begins to send waves through his arms and then through his torso; but when the iconic DJ Grand Wizzard Theodore scratches, each additional layer of sonic disruption prompts Cartoon to follow suit, breaking his flow mid-wave, turning his body in a new direction as if to start again. He matches the cut and flow of the music to circle around himself, waving and twitching, his arms outstretch and ripple, and the rest of his body follows. He seems satisfied when he completes his run, and steps to the side, arms extended as if presenting the cypher as a beautiful buffet for the next dancer. Applause and head nods in approval follow. A young girl sitting on her father's shoulders taps out beats on his head. A b-boy anxiously jumps in as if he's been waiting for hours.

After one dancer finishes, a few b-boys do some toprock and brief footwork. A couple of older men do unfamiliar footwork that reminds me of an especially rhythmic game of hopscotch. One little boy performs a somewhat coordinated combo of the Funky Chicken and a Michael Jackson leg jerk with the finger snap. It doesn't seem to matter what people do because it all fits. And after each turn, everyone applauds the effort. At one point, three adolescent boys looking for my camera's attention get in the circle together while a dancer patiently waits for them to finish. Seeing this, a preteen girl snatches one of them by the collar. He looks at her surprised, his big eyes asking, "Why!?" But she can't be bothered with an explanation and impatiently motions for him to get out of the way, pointing to where he should stand to wait his turn.

Though most cyphers expand and contract as people enter or leave, this one moves like an organism breathing in and out. It swells and undulates, shifting a little to the left, then a little bit forward. We are never quite centered on the flattened and duct-taped cardboard boxes. Though we only move a foot or two in any direction, it feels like we are adrift and unencumbered in the wide-open space. I see heads bobbing, hands clapping, necks craning to see, kids bouncing around, people shaking hands, giving hugs, shouting greetings across the circle.

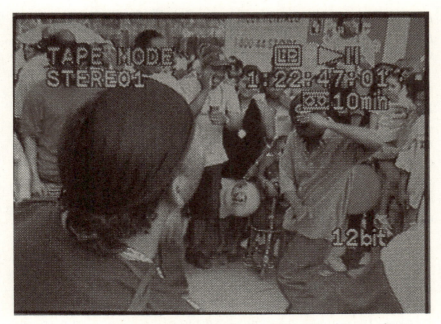

Figure 2.1 Cartoon entering the cypher. From ethnographic footage of B-Boy All Stars Block Party, South Bronx, New York, 13 August 2006

As one b-boy finishes, his friend excitedly pats his arm and points a finger at Peaches as she readies herself to enter the circle. When Peaches steps in, she amplifies the anticipation, first by stillness. Then she slowly begins to pulsate and twitch until the moment her entire body spasms and the crowd explodes. Peaches juxtaposes mechanical staccatos and wave-like fluidity. Her strong arms robotically guide her body in one direction, as her head moves in the other. Then she sends a wave through her entire body. I can see it move down her frame and then up through it again. Each time her muscles contract, she turns to face a new person in the crowd, leans forward, and holds their gazes with unfaltering intensity. In the end, she holds her hands up, palms facing the crowd, and fingers spread wide so that when she pulses her body, I half expect electricity to actually shoot out of her fingertips. Each shockwave makes her shoulder-length hair tremble. The applause is loud and joyous. High fives, pats on the back, and accolades follow.

"Shout out to Peaches! Pioneer popper, locker. What up Peaches? Representing for the ladies!" Cartoon gives her a hug and a kiss on the cheek. A little girl rushes toward Peaches, who picks her up, hugs her tightly, then deposits her

back on the ground careful to keep her out of the way of the little boy who is finally able to take his turn. After watching them dance, my introductions to Cartoon and Peaches seem complete.

Veronica Star interrupts the music's flow with a commentary that propels the activity forward in a different way. "Throw your hands up if you're from Brooklyn?!" Instead of the customary hoots and hollers this question typically elicits, people here boo. Expecting this, she tries again: "Is Queens in the House? Queens? . . . Queens was never in the house." I see Kid Glyde, who hails from Queens, smirk at the diss and respond by jumping in the cypher. With a relaxed approach, Glyde combines swift footwork and quick hip swivels (reminiscent of a salsero) while weaving his feet in and around each other and wearing down the cardboard underfoot.

Star continues her call and response: "What about Manhattan? Anybody from Manhattan in here?" A few people cheer halfheartedly. Then finally she asks, "What about the BRONX!! Throw 'em up!" Hands shoot up and the vocal response is huge. This time the DJ chimes in: "Yo, if you go to any other borough and they sayin' that they started Hip Hop, they lyin'. It started right up here in the Boogie Down Bronx. Bronx River y'all!" In this moment even I feel it: the fleshy embrace of a community.

2

Battling in the Bronx

Social Choreography and Outlaw Culture

A 2006 block party in the South Bronx was my first experience of a cypher that seemed to breathe; it had a pulse and was alive in a way that was unique in my field experience. It was also an act of self-declaration: the South Bronx as the birthplace of Hip Hop. As Hip Hop studies (rightfully) complicate South Bronx origin stories, bringing attention to the cultural practices and places that influenced Hip Hop beyond a Bronx origin story[1], when it comes to breaking there remains a culturally situated relationship between the practice and the place. The South Bronx is embedded in breaking, and knowing that matters to how we understand cyphering. This chapter uses a Hip Hop lens to focus on the living that happened in the South Bronx, and its aesthetic influence on cyphers.

Breaking cyphers carry the traces of how life and living in the South Bronx in the 1970s and early 1980s shaped the sensibilities of its early practitioners, particularly in a battling context. While in other chapters my argument hinges on what Africanist aesthetics are doing, this chapter balances focus on the imprint of the South Bronx on battling sensibilities alongside the Africanist aesthetic resources used to express those sensibilities. In the 1970s and early 1980s, the time period framing the interviews featured in this chapter, the ethnoracially segregated social lives of South Bronx youth began to blur as they convened around shared music and shifting standards of cool. The majority of this youth hailed from the African diaspora. I am not arguing, though, that the Africanist aesthetic resources that they drew upon were the most salient points of identification among them; instead, it was living in the South Bronx together.

The South Bronx lives in breaking, not simply in its origin story but in the everyday ways the dance was lived in the margins of the state. In *Foundation: B-Boys, B-Girls and Hip-Hop Culture in New York*, Hip Hop scholar Joseph Schloss states that "as New York City was abandoned by the federal government and working-class neighborhoods were abandoned by

New York City, youth in those neighborhoods were, in turn, abandoned by traditional institutions.... As a forgotten minority of a forgotten minority of a forgotten minority, their culture was almost totally ignored."[2] For Schloss this amplifies "a profound lack of documentation" in the archives of this era.[3] Despite the limited archive, it is obvious that their cultural world in the South Bronx, as a forgotten minority three times over, had bearing on how they moved through the world, and that mobility in turn shaped breaking. Their maneuverings through the city under the rubric of dance illuminates a culturally meaningful sensibility, despite the state's neglect. Part of what this chapter attempts to do, then, is orient itself to the perspective of those who lived the contradictions and hypocrisies of state violence, who came of age in such a place, and who expressed the sensibilities and values of life in an embodied aesthetic practice that they had a direct hand in cultivating.

In this chapter I pivot to cyphers occupied by those who were "there" and whose stories about Hip Hop in New York City get at the relationship between South Bronx living and a battling sensibility. These cyphers are occupied by breakers, poppers, and other street dancers,[4] roughly between 1976 and 1984 and namely in the Bronx. I draw on oral histories from breakers Aby, Baby Love, Kwikstep, and Trac2, and popper Cartoon; and supported by insights from popper Mr. Wiggles via documentary footage. Though popping may appear to depart from the book's focus, poppers and breakers in New York City shared overlapping social spaces and friend groups; as well, by definition Hip Hop culture is multigenre. Each person tells coming-of-age stories, stories that also illustrate how their corporealities influenced their maneuverings in their transition to adulthood. Through two key terms, "social choreography" and "outlaw culture," this chapter explores the inherently political ways that practitioners activated counter choreographies of moving through the world just as breaking and Hip Hop were beginning to cohere into distinct forms.

Social Choreography: Intersecting Dance and Politics

The South Bronx is a site of life and living on its own terms and in its own dance. Social choreography, as a concept, lends itself to thinking about that life and living in the shadows of the state. I describe social choreography as the ways that the people of a given society are trained to move (both physically and spatially) and to contort and comport their bodies in keeping with and in (sometimes counter) production to a given social order. In this chapter, I argue that the day-to-day living of Bronx street dancers reinforced social choreographic lessons that were then instilled into their own burgeoning social dance practices.

Though invoked by various scholars across disciplines, Andrew Hewitt's *Social Choreography: Ideology as Performance in Dance and Everyday Movement* offers the most sustained discussion of this concept. Hewitt posits that, in the relationship between art and society, "dance has served as the aesthetic medium that most consistently sought to understand art as something immanently political; that is, as something that derives its political significance from its own status as praxis."[5] Hewitt argues that our everyday embodied experiences of moving through the world as sociopolitical subjects of bourgeois society (Hewitt's focus) is in "aesthetic continuum" with dance, a medium wherein a "utopian social order" or "fantasies" of social order get rehearsed and performed for audiences.[6] Social choreography thus "functions as a space in which social *possibilities* are both rehearsed and performed."[7] Though focused on questions of modernity, modern dance, and the ordering of bourgeois society, Hewitt's discussion lends itself to conceptualizing a relationship between how we are socialized to move through our worlds and how one physically moves in a social dance practice. "Dance" for Hewitt may not have included practices like breaking, but social choreography helps us understand how breaking can rehearse a relationship to society on proletarian terms.

Hewitt's Eurocentrism and his investment in modernity and bourgeois societal demands might account for why he eschews the impact of sociopolitical identities in his analysis. Whiteness is allowed to remain unmarked. Thus I also draw on Aimee Meredith Cox's work *Shapeshifters: Black Girls and the Choreography of Citizenship*,[8] which shifts focus from modern dance to the social choreographies of young Black women in a Detroit homeless shelter, centering how race, class, and gender necessarily shape "the socially constructed meaning *shackled* to [their] bodies."[9] To be independent of "socially determined representations of their self-worth," Cox argues that these young Black women's choreography or movement through the city and the shelter integrates "improvisation, borrowing, and sampling to disassemble and reconstruct current social realities."[10] For Cox, "choreography" captures a politically informed cultural production that allows young Black women to "read social inequalities" and deploy tools like improvisation to "demand legitimacy on Black women's bodies."[11] Terms like "sampling," which are particularly meaningful in Hip Hop spaces (discussed further later), highlight a convergence of social strategies and Hip Hop aesthetics. Like Hewitt, Cox recognizes how social choreography attends to the ways that people are made to move through normative society; yet Cox's point is that social choreography can act as a method for subversive moves in places like Detroit or the South Bronx.

I am also drawn to dance scholar Anurima Banerji's activation of "choreography" for a political analysis through dance. Banerji shifts focus from social order to the state in *Dancing Odissi: Paratopic Performances of Gender and State*. She writes:

> The state and dance are intimately connected—they are not entirely separate institutions in terms of their workings; indeed, what choreography does to the individual body, the state does to the social corpus. . . . My contention is that both choreography and the state are centrally concerned with the body and its orchestrations, and imposing prescriptions and proscriptions for its exemplary movements in space. While dance organizes the body in an aesthetic milieu, the state scripts and arranges corporeal relations in the social. . . . Thus, choreography shares a metonymic and metaphoric relationship with the state.[12]

If Hewitt and Cox help us understand battling as, not just aestheticized combat, but performative acts of social possibility for embattled social actors in marginalized contexts, then Banerji reads that not just as a consequence of social order but in intimate relationship to state functions. Banerji draws an explicit connection between dance's aesthetic "prescriptions and proscriptions" and the state's need to control bodies, both of which operate in social terms. How people can and are told they should move through the world is profoundly political. I foreground the forgotten minority who cypher a distinct relationship to the state.

Choreography here should also be thought of as improvisational, which Cleis Abeni writes of in "Improvisation as Choreography in Black Vernacular Dance." In it, the choreographic is infused with culturally specific values:

> Delineating improvisation as choreography in black vernacular dancing reveals the intrinsic value of oral communication and sensing in the

dancing. By oral communication, I mean the passing on of values, aesthetics, and actual movement traditions through experiential knowledge and ritual work.... Sensing also signifies a heightened, in-the-moment, understanding of one's relationship to forces in the environment around the body (like gravity and the weighted pull of the ground) and the acknowledgement of psychosomatic forces that embrace the unknowable, mystical forces perceivable by faith.... [I]n African-American vernacular dancing in its original sociocultural contexts ... there is no division between improvisation and composition. In black vernacular dancing, improvisation means the creative structuring, or the choreographing, of human movement in the moment of ritual performance.[13]

The structure of the ritual, alongside Africanist sensibilities that communicate values and demand heightened sensing, inform the nature of the choreographic within improvisational Black vernacular forms. In the context of rituals, the structural parameters of battle cyphers are thus informed by several factors, including its aesthetic and cultural imperatives, individual repertoires, and the "aural-kinesthetic environment" for play.[14] Improvisation is more than an extemporaneous or unrehearsed approach to technique. As dance scholar Naomi Bragin emphasizes in her dissertation on West Coast street dance forms: "*For street dance practitioners, improvisation is both practice and disposition, an attitude enveloped within everyday life processes and elaborated through movement study and practice.*"[15] In my use, the choreographic in social choreography is the creative, improvisational (which is to say compositional) structuring of movement and gesture that are attuned to particular cultural parameters, whether embedded in street dance culture, in rituals like cyphers, or in the necessary everyday modes of moving through the city.

Taken together, Hewitt, Cox, Banerji, Abeni, and Bragin demonstrate how social choreography captures the correlation between battle principles and everyday life. If breaking cyphers choreograph a particular kind of social relationship to the state, then theirs is a social-corporeal choreography of a kind of outlaw positionality relative to the state. Cyphers are the ritualized training ground for tactical maneuvering and improvising through societal structures, and perhaps too rehearsal sites for new social possibilities. Just as the state moves people, street dancers innovated strategies that allowed them to move themselves in outlaw ways.

Outlaw Culture in South Bronx Living

"Outlaw" captures how practitioners have identified themselves from the outset for their antiauthority, counterconventional, sometimes criminalized, combative, and confrontational styles.[16] For a time, the word circulated primarily to identify motorcycle clubs or gangs, both groups from which breakers adopted aspects of their style (e.g., denim vests with frayed edges where the sleeves had been cut).[17] Yet outlaw also spoke to Hip Hop's cultural elements. In an interview between Jeff Chang and aerosol artist Lady Pink, for example, she states that graffiti is "an outlaw art. When we train other graffiti writers, we're not training fine artists to exhibit in museums. We're training criminals. We're training kids how to take life in their own hands and go out there and hopelessly paint on some wall or some train that will do nothing for you except get you fame with other vandals and criminals."[18] Playing on mainstream assumptions that graffiti is only ever vandalism, Lady Pink immediately launches into those values that it teaches and how it empowers youth in a way that is easily discernible from normative professional aspirations under capitalist terms. In another example, San Bernardino, California, made national headlines in 1984 when the city council proposed, though ultimately dropped, an ordinance that would cite and fine breakers $100 for the first offense of cyphering in public and obstructing commerce, and $500 for future violations.[19] Which is to say that even cyphering could be seen as an outlaw act.

Breaking draws on "outlaw" in multiple ways, but I draw on what legal scholar Monica Evans and Hip Hop scholar Imani Perry write about as "outlaw culture"—a culture cultivated at the outskirts of mainstream values and social expectations because of racialized and classed subordination. In her analysis of Black women's empowering outlaw practices, Evans writes, "Outlaw culture refers to the process by which African-Americans shift within and away from identities in response to mainstream legal systems and dominant culture. It describes a conscious and subconscious series of cultural practices constituting life at the margins. Marginality is thus a strategy for carving out spaces in which to maneuver and resist."[20] It is not just or simply that "outlaws" are such because of how they are seen by the mainstream—as dangerous and deviant—but that the meaningful existences they have "carved out" in the margins entails cultural practices that are in opposition to the mainstream.

Perry elaborates on this concept in relationship to Hip Hop culture, specifying that outlaw culture "articulat[es] a kind of power within the hood, an overwhelmingly powerless context, and an exploitation of the power created by fear of the hood experienced by outsiders."[21] Her explicit attention to a knowing manipulation of stereotypes (i.e., claiming power in marginality), speaks to why she names one of her chapters "Glorious Outlaw." By extension, outlaw culture speaks to a repertoire for living within particular environments that are attuned to its values and codes.

In the early 1970s, an outlaw sensibility in breaking was contextualized by a nationwide economic crisis—manifesting in increased gas prices, stagflation, stagnant unemployment, and the neglect of urban communities contradictorily in the face of urban renewal programs. This prompted and exacerbated the downward spiral of inner cities across the country. The South Bronx became "a symbol of America's woes," dubbed as such in a 1977 article in the *New York Times* (and other articles as well).[22] Historian Evelyn Gonzalez's *The Bronx* details the political and economic incentives for its unofficial abandonment by the state, private owners, and some residents.[23] Multiple contributing factors to the South Bronx's deterioration include but are not limited to urban renewal programs, unreliable city services like garbage collection, the closure of multiple firehouses, the deterioration of facilities like Lincoln Hospital, and the twelve-year Cross Bronx Expressway project, all of which left direct community activism as the only means for change.[24] An economic and political matrix of destruction was made even more intricate by questionable federal and city policies, insurance industry changes, greed, and a general political disregard, producing the literal reality that the Bronx was burning.[25]

The infamy of the Bronx's burned-out buildings was itself a representation of that confluence of forces. Gonzalez goes on to write about the literal burning buildings from the perspective of landlords, illustrating how the South Bronx was a place to exploit:

> Some landlords used their derelict buildings as tax shelters or transferred their properties back and forth to increase valuation for sale to the city or to acquire second mortgage loans. Others cut down on maintenance, deferred paying taxes, rented to undesirable tenants or "problem families," aggressively collected whatever rents they could get, and "ran for the hills." . . . Some, however, went a step further and burned the structures. When low-premium fire insurance became available in the 1970s, many

investors bought Bronx apartment buildings with the express intent of burning them.[26]

As Gonzalez makes clear, the borough's infrastructural and economic deterioration was cumulative, typifying systemic violence. Abandoned buildings were representations of congealed political neglect, topped off by profit-making schemes wherein the flagrant disregard for people's lives and well-being paid off for absentee landlords. That abandoned buildings decorated the landscape further solidified the South Bronx's reputation as the national symbol of urban blight. Though no one was ever convicted of arson, newly homeless families were placed in relocation buildings or "welfare hotels," which somehow became the solution.[27] These conditions broke up communities and social networks, putting the burden of survival on the residents themselves.

The lives behind these kinds of sociological facts tell the story of burned-out buildings differently. In his documentary *Everything Remains Raw*, director, locker, and embodied dance historian Moncell "ill Kozby" Durden features a 2007 interview with popper Mr. Wiggles of the Electric Boogaloos and Rock Steady Crew.[28] As Durden and Mr. Wiggles sat in a Boston diner looking at a series of photographs of the Bronx in the 1970s, Wiggles began to identify the ones taken near his former home in Longwood, then launched into a description of life behind the black-and-white photos:

> The landlords were burning down the buildings to collect on the insurance. The mafia was buying the buildings on purpose, burning them down with people in them, giving them very little notice. And then they would put them in a relo building. A relocation building is like—they had a relo on my block in Longwood. They had relos in different parts of the Bronx, where when your building got burnt out, they already had a building to put you in. *Now don't that look systematic to you?* So, relocations were common. And you know, people used to make fun of the relo people. So, they'd call them— you know, they'd snap on them, "*Relo! Relo!*," 'cause you lived in a relocation building. You know, didn't make no sense to me because . . . instead of prevention they had the building already, because they *knew* they was going to burn them buildings down and they had to put people in those [relo] buildings. That's how it was man. It was like a war zone.[29]

While the topic seems to fall in line with persistent narration of the South Bronx's deterioration in the 1970s, Mr. Wiggles's comments more so addressed the systemic violence of dispossession from the perspective of one who lived it. He emphasized a war with the state that saw it better fit to protect property rights—or rather the right to exploit housing policies for profit—over protecting people. A tone of frustration and disbelief resonated throughout his discussion, especially as he talked about the irrationality of relos as a fix. When he stated, "They had the building already," the word "already" aurally conveys two meanings: (1) that relo buildings were already in place or preemptively established in response to *anticipated* fires; and (2) that they were *all ready* or pre-equipped and thus invested in or resourced in a manner that not-yet-homeless families could have benefited from, without the trauma of the fire. If the burned-out building came to represent the Bronx of that era to the media, then from within the South Bronx relos could be seen as emblematic of life under this kind of state oppression.

It is no wonder that young practitioners would conceive of themselves as outlaws. Wiggles went on to describe how moving through the world, in part by way of the burned-out buildings, contextualized Hip Hop for him:

> You could find anything in these buildings, bodies. You smell the bodies being dumped into the building. Everything was sold out of those lots and buildings, and abandoned buildings. It wasn't crack back then. It was dustheads and heroin addicts. It was just like that movie [*City of God*]. I saw the movie and I saw the little kids in the movie. You saw the little kids that were always caught up in the middle? That's, that—reminded me of me. Me and all my friends. That's how we rolled. *That* young I was already in the street in the Bronx, running around just like that, witnessing crazy shit; witnessing rumbles happening in Echo Park. Watching people walk in and crawl out. It was crazy. It was hectic. It was *really* scary man. Hip Hop was scary during that time. And we didn't call nothing Hip Hop. We didn't look at anything as culture. It was just something to do to keep our minds off of the bullshit that we had to deal with on a regular basis. And those parts of the Bronx, to me, in my opinion are the reason why Hip Hop was so important—it was that one gift that God was able to give us to help us get past all that bs.[30]

If Hip Hop's outlaw status represents forms of existence outside of normative, bourgeois notions of lawful citizenship, then it does so not simply as a matter of rebellion for its own sake but as a condition of everyday life. He rightly emphasized their young age, referencing the Brazilian film *City of God*

(2002), a coming-of-age story set in Rio's favelas in the 1960s.[31] While wealth, white privilege, and political clout can turn the types of violence accompanying drug addiction and overdoses, murder, and peer-to-peer assaults into "private" affairs, when experienced in 'hoods from the South Bronx to Rio, these things were a dimension of public life. Wiggles offered a deeply visceral account, attending to sight, smells, and most importantly the emotional and psychological distress of it all. Thus, Hip Hop was not simply a means of distraction; it offered a way through.

The social choreographic elements of Wiggles's story attests to why Hip Hop was a gift that kept him and his crew protected. He repeatedly referenced two modes of activity: their running around from place to place, and their witnessing "crazy shit" not typically associated with childhood. Wiggles used "witnessing" multiple times in reference to rumbles, addicts, and dead bodies. To be witnesses is not just to *see* something, but to know it and attest to that reality to others. His multiple, terse statements about this violence—as crazy, hectic, and really scary—are a hauntingly matter-of-fact invocation of the trauma of such experiences. His social choreography also entailed a sense of his 'hood's boundaries, codes, and customs even in the midst of their capacity to move through it with seeming unbounded access. They learned to stay mobile, to witness but not linger, and to travel in groups, which Hip Hop interwove into its developing culture.

The outlaw nature of Hip Hop is not a euphemism for illegality, violence, nor simply a cool pose aesthetic. Instead, it is a term that captures entire dimensions of social life that are informed but not limited by the state's war against those who inhabit society's margins. They moved through their neighborhood in a demonstration of a choreographic practice informed by outlaw culture. By extension, Hip Hop and battle cyphers became the medium through which outlaw stances were organized and rehearsed.

"True" Breaking and Battling Principles

To draw out the relationship between battle cyphers and the sensibilities that informed early Bronx breakers' social choreography, Trac2 is a great person with which to start. Trac2 of Star Child la Rock Crew, started breaking in the Bronx in the mid-1970s. I met him for the first time in the summer of 2006 at the Rock Steady Crew Anniversary in New York City. He was generous with his time, and spoke with me for over an hour under the street lamps at dusk as the battle was letting out. His daughter and nephew stood nearby, seemingly familiar with these sessions but nonetheless impatient. Trac2 told stories of epic street battles and local club scenes, illustrated with exact addresses, songs, and fashion choices. Multiple battle stories started to bleed into each other, and played in my head like a movie...

When he was young, battling meant combat not competition. Though battles often took place in abandoned buildings, this one was on concrete. No cardboard. They were in Spy's neighborhood. Trac2 and his crew walked there, and as they moved between territories, their community followed. Trac2's sister told him that a pregnant woman in a cab saw them walking and got out to join them. They arrived seventy-five people deep. The battle cypher was riddled with broken glass and other debris that they swept away with their feet.

Rocking, as it was called, was more rudimentary then. Still, Spy, dubbed "the man with a thousand moves," likely began with a basic toprock: rhythmic steps forward one foot at a time, arms open just enough to bare his torso, presenting himself to the opposing crew, challenging them.[32] *Perhaps he would've added a short hop from one foot to the next, or James Brown-inspired shuffles, or a twisting dive, maybe following it with front sweeps or cc's (front-facing, side-to-side, crouched twists with kick-outs), or low-to-the-ground spins in a tight circle some call a top spin. Each move had a name and was fired on opponents like a bullet, complementary to the herky-jerky and staccato style of seventies breaking.*[33] *Trac2 ordered his crew out one by one to battle, and when they returned each took a knee while awaiting his orders. He still carries a scar on his left hand from a broken Coke bottle that cut him while he danced. He says he kept dancing, only getting it checked out once the battle finished.*

There were no handshakes afterward. They didn't even talk across crews until the next day. Losing meant forfeiting some money or maybe even their sneakers. Trac2 doesn't name what he lost that day, but he and Spy would battle again, and eventually battle on the same side.[34]

While the preceding story aggregates several Trac2 stories in our actual interview, what struck me were the pictures he painted of Hip Hop–inspired ways of moving through and across territories in the South Bronx. He illustrated his own social choreography through stories that captured essential battling qualities. How they danced in the literal streets, amassing followers along the way, premised a sensibility that foregrounds a dynamic and shifting collective of people, from crew to community (sometimes one and the same). Whatever part one plays, walking-following-dancing-kneeling, everyone had a stake in their triumph. As well, embedded in its warrior aesthetics are implicit valuations of training and an approach to discipline, down to following the orders of the one in charge or literally dancing on broken glass. How they moved reflected both a Hip Hop belonging and a deeply situated, neighborhood-specific belonging, both of which informed the other and reinforced a sense of place and deep loyalty.

As he told these stories, Trac2 also began to name particularly important qualities that he repeatedly referred to as what he felt "a true b-boy" would do. In our conversation, that phrase came to signify the knowledge and understanding necessary for any breaker to competently enter a battle cypher. While he did not list or number them, by the end of the interview I noted ten such qualities. To begin, "true" breakers battle, and they do it for "ghetto celebrity status" (i.e., the respect of their community and their peers rather than solely for money or commercial fame). A true breaker knows "the four elements of breaking" or the fundamental techniques of one's practice.[35] Breakers are illusionists, and they "know the difference between a new move and a variation" of an already established move. True breakers are "gypsies" who travel to battle other people.[36] They know their opponents and their own repertoires. They are strategic in battles, improve as the battle continues, and know that battles are won by "last man standing" and not by crowd response.[37] For the sake of analysis and time, I have condensed his list into four overarching battling principles: survivalism, strategizing, nomadism, and illusionism. While my summary of Trac2's list into four principles *does not explicitly exist*, they are useful stand-ins for embodied sensibilities learned from battling and the underlying social choreographic principles enacted within battles.

Perhaps because "true b-boy" is also clearly a term of high regard, using "b-boy" as a stand-in for everyone who breaks "erases women from the discourse upfront," as Hip Hop and gender studies scholar Jessica Pabón-Colón puts it.[38] That is the case despite that the qualities he names are applicable to all breakers. At the same time, Trac2's word choice may not be just habit. I propose that his word choice also signals that battling and breaking were meaningfully gendered for him. Breaking was a vital experience in his formative years, taking him through adolescence to adulthood. The "true b-boy" qualities he names are thus also wrapped up in his own coming of age as a Puerto Rican cis man and teen father in the South Bronx. This is especially important considering that he was active during an era when "retirement age" was seventeen years old.[39] Ultimately, these values are intimately tied to the particularities of everyday life. Moreover, these four principles still matter to breaking today.

Survivalism reminds us that in battles, the goal is to be the last person standing, not just the crowd pleaser. In practice, Trac2 specifies that a loser will begin to repeat moves, give up, or be seduced into applauding for their opponent. The literal concept of survival values perseverance through struggle, which is to say that in order to survive one must contend with the possibility that one might not make it, or was never expected to in the first place. And while this might imply or outright signal victimization, Imani Perry clarifies: "Hip hop resists victimhood, preferring ... the concept of the survivor. Survivors do not define themselves by their victimization, instead fighting against it and examining the social practices that lead to such violence."[40] Wiggles's eye on systemic state violence resonates here in his emphasis on the conditions leading to Hip Hop's hectic early years. Anishinaabe scholar and writer Gerald Vizenor's concept of "survivance," which he describes as the stewardship of Indigenous innovations and forms of knowledge as a means to survive, also influences my understanding of survivalism. Carrying generations of cultural knowledge, *ancestral* knowledge, through tradition amplifies the responsibilities of those who carry it. It also signals the possibilities of an ongoing accumulation of such practices, which are essential to surviving present-day struggles. Where Vizenor notes that "survivance stories are renunciations of dominance, tragedy, and victimry,"[41] in contrast I would argue that Hip Hop exalts triumph and the art of getting over.

If survivalism attends to a repertoire for survival, then strategizing captures the capacity to put that repertoire into action. Strategizing is about intervening in the social world through imaginative means, which also entails changing one's conditions into something personally advantageous. In a battle, strategizing necessitates understanding oneself and an opponent enough to launch a counterattack. Trac2 adds that dancers need to know their skills and quickly assess an opponent's capabilities—for example, poor musicality, good balance, sloppy footwork. It calls forth creativity, discernment, and a focused study of opponents. In his own stories Trac2 was the strategist, sending out breakers when the conditions of the moment called for a particular talent, energy, or skill set, echoing the role of a general in battle. In that depiction, Trac2 is reading the cypher and constantly assessing how best to respond.

Nomadism is about street-level social interactions in marginalized communities through networks established by way of ritual competition and a readiness to show and prove. Nomadism reminds us that street dance is social, and demands interaction with others beyond one's own circle to prove and elevate one's skills. In his story, nomadism builds a network of both street dancers and those who share in their sensibilities. This principle includes traveling to compete, which builds reputations for "ghetto celebrity status" and self-ranking. This concept is not bound to a particular ghetto, evident in that he contrasts it with "a neighborhood dancer," someone only known around their 'hood. In a contrast to normative versions of fame tied to wealth and recognition by mainstream white audiences, "ghetto celebrity" status celebrates and respects their own, in the context of an outlaw culture. Nomadism thus alludes to a shared understanding of people living in the margins of society, across 'hoods.

Finally, illusionism captures the magic of street dance, making spectators wonder what they saw and how it was done. Yet a "true" breaker should know the secret or put in the work to learn and master it. Illusionism speaks to understanding the layers of cultural knowledge embedded in the dance, and the implicit challenge to execute that understanding well. Being able to dissect a move's nuances reflects both cultural knowledge and a sociocultural sensibility. Aesthetically, one need only look to b-boy Spy, a contemporary of Trac2's known as the "man with a thousand moves." Trac2 clarifies that the nickname is not because every move Spy did was brand new, but that they were variations on established moves, thereby conveying a seemingly endless repertoire. This example represents a lesson Trac2 still carried. Illusionism speaks to an insider knowledge encoded in practices that confound expectations of physical possibilities. In other words, illusionism captures a capacity for insider knowledge to dance into existence new forms of bodily comportment and moving through the world that seem impossible.

On their own, these principles give us some insight into the sensibilities that shape battling. Survivalism recognizes a context of power but does not capitulate to it, instead drawing on inherited knowledge. Strategizing anticipates obstacles that one must improvise through, thereby valuing training, preparation, and the creative use of all available resources. Nomadism speaks to perpetual preparedness to battle while expanding one's social competitive network on community terms. And illusionism showcases expertise as the impossible actualized, performatively bringing a new reality into existence. Each of these principles is multifaceted and tell us what is at stake and what knowledge and values matter. Together though, they indicate distinct qualities of life and living in the South Bronx in the seventies and eighties, and perhaps other places and historical moments like it. While they do not cohere into an exact framework for understanding breaking or battling, these embodied principles bridge an outlaw social choreography in the South Bronx with a burgeoning Hip Hop culture.

Bronx Tales of an Outlaw Social Choreography

Early breakers animate these four principles through stories about their everyday lives in the South Bronx. Considering breaking's history is most often transmitted orally, stories from breakers who started in the culture's first decade should be understood as part of that tradition. Their memories and accounts have likely been or will be offered to younger breakers over and over again. While they do not represent the earliest documented practitioners of breaking,[42] within my research pool many of them are OGs. People like Aby and Trac2 started breaking in the mid-1970s; and others like Cartoon, Baby Love, and Kwikstep got introduced to it and started learning in the late seventies to the early eighties. The following discussions draw attention to a particular subsection of street dancers whose stories of Hip Hop are deeply intertwined with living in the South Bronx.

Surviving and Strategizing: The Clubhouse

Strategizing and survivalism were pronounced themes in those stories about marginal spaces. For example, for The Bronx Boys / The Bronx Girls Rocking Crew (TBB/TBG), the burned-out and abandoned buildings that decorated the South Bronx were "clubhouses." In a 2007 interview with Aby, president of TBB/TBG, he had this to say:

> We saw an abandoned building around our area. Nobody living, burned down. We'd go in there: everybody gets a floor. We used to go take—we used to steal the extension cords from our houses or we used to go into Woolworth's (at that time there was a store called Woolworth's) and steal power cords. And we'll connect them to the light outside, bring it all into the building. All the way, every floor, and everybody'll have lights, electrical lights. We'll get crates, milk crates, and wood, and mattresses—old mattresses burned out or trashed out—we'd go and put it and we'll furnish our apartments. So everybody had a floor. An abandoned building mind you; this is a building that's been abandoned. So it's like, it's *our* building.

That'd be our second home. Whoever wanted to run away, you run away, you run in there. You stay there. We had shelter. In the winter we cold, but we had shelter. When it's raining, we go in the house, we go in our apartment. That was ours. Nobody could take it away from us but the state, police; and they really never did 'cause they was afraid to even go up in there. The only ones that we would bump into there, they were the drug addicts. That's it you know. We'd go up our flights, see one by me with a vein, you know, shooting up. And [we'd say] "Yo, what's up?" [and] keep on going. Keep it moving. We never was scared 'cause we had a group! We had a big group.... You had crews of thirty guys, twenty girls. It was a big family. That was our family.[43]

Their outlaw social choreography meant rolling in crews of large numbers because by doing so they could rely on their own self-made families to back them up. They also learned to move in relation to others and in relation to the proverbial Other, those who have also been marginalized, criminalized, and forgotten. They were crew even when the crew was not physically there, enacting a sensibility wherein they carried the collective with them to sites that others feared.[44] Aby's initial emphasis is on a certain kind of independence and the freedom to cultivate his own family and his own home without parental rules. He and his crew took advantage of what was available to them: stolen and found objects, other people's trash, abandoned property. The overwhelming tone of his story is not about victimhood but of subsistence—everybody had a floor, lights, makeshift furniture, beds, shelter in poor weather, and a place to go when they ran away from home. There is a triumphant tone to it, getting over by way of the very resources symbolic of blight.

Crucial too is their *right to claim* abandoned property, to seize it from its uselessness and recreate it as a resource. His repetition of "an abandoned building" makes the case that they were not trespassing. While some might argue that they stole from their homes, from Woolworth, and the power company, that was beside the point. The building's abandonment was the problem. His emphasis was not on trespassing or the laws that would criminalize them for it. Instead, he stressed a retrieval of sorts. Rather than a necropolitical approach that found profit in arson—which in turn resulted in a proliferation of buildings that literally held the dead bodies of other forgotten people—surviving and strategizing emphasize use over waste, a sensibility wherein abandoned buildings are repossessed for their social interests.

The crew is an especially important organizing entity here. From one perspective, crews fortify a group identity and nurture fellowship, echoing an Africanist aesthetic quality that constantly reasserts the collective.[45] At the same time, it is in that collective that other kinds of violence took place. Aby goes on to explain how day-to-day interpersonal relationships were organized around breaking, and how that played out specifically for the girls in the crew:

> We ain't have the money. . . . Half of our moms was on welfare. Single mothers, six to seven kids. You know what I'm saying? Like that so, my sister—every time, I had my sister. So, [to] my own sister [I'd say] "Yo! Sis, don't go out there." We'd chase them out and beat them down. "We don't want you out here!" It was like that. We was real protective. No fathers, so we would, we would be the fathers. You know, and after a while my sister started, you know, doing the dance, so then they got into it, and we would leave them 'cause we could trust the guys because they [his sisters] was running with the crew.

While no one was really "safe" and they protected themselves by moving through the world as a group, within the collective they still reproduced violence specifically around gender. Given the conditions of the South Bronx neighborhoods they traversed, Aby's concerns were not unfounded, and the urgency for protective maneuvers was logical (see Fig. 2.2). But by stepping into a guardianship role, he interpreted those parental responsibilities through a patriarchal lens. For Aby, "protecting" his sisters was his job, and physical force was one of those means available to him to do it. That he did not trust his peers around his sisters until they learned the dance too implies that learning to break was a way to shift how crew members related to each other across genders. (More on this in chapter 3.)

Yet for those girls, learning to break and being in a crew meant being subordinated to b-boys as a prerequisite of participation. In his own words, being in the crew happened first on b-boys' terms. Aby continued:

> Ponytail Rosie, Chica and Chickie, Sugar. These girls were like our backbone. You know they kept us together. We used to date a lot of them. If not, they was considered sisters. And up to today a lot of them are still together. Twenty-six, twenty-seven years, still together to this day. . . . So that was, you know they was kind of like our sister/mother type. Or our loved ones.

Figure 2.2 "Bathgate Avenue and East 173rd Street (2 girls by chain-link fence)."
Source: National Museum of American History, Mel Rosenthal Photoprints. Photos in Rosenthal's series on the South Bronx were taken between 1975 and 1983.

Or family. We was a family. . . . The girls, I have a lot of respect for the girls out there at that time because they took a lot of shit. They was kicked to the back, you know. After we done our stuff, because we was breaking and we're doing all our shit, so we'd have them go out there get the beer. Stuff like that. Sometimes it's abusive, you know, *mentally*. You know it does inflict a lot of inner wounds, but altogether it's a strong bond. They was pleased to do whatever, 'cause we would do for them as they would do for us. But they would do more.[46]

Insofar as the clubhouse was both congealed political and economic neglect *and* the home base or refuge for an outlaw sociality, ultimately a survival sensibility amplified the art of getting over but still left room for abuse. This meant that the crew—a family crafted through this "gift from God"—perpetuated the same gendered discourses and dynamics of larger society, burdening b-girls with yet another layer of violence. Surviving was not freeing in itself, and it inflicted wounds along the way. Yet the sisters' initiation into the developing world of breaking and cyphering (before either term even came into regular use) was a strategy that expanded their social possibilities. That is to say, breaking offered new resources for everyone's ongoing improvisational-compositional maneuverings through the South Bronx, though differently along gender lines.

Illusionism and Nomadism in Training

While strategizing and survivalism are directly about battling in the context of a larger sociopolitical war, illusionism and nomadism speak to how those forms are put into the body through training, or embodied in practice. Illusionism gets at some of the magic of street dance and the deeper terrain of an initiate's knowledge, while nomadism attends to the social networks that enable that learning. For Cartoon, a Bronx popper who saw it for the first time in the late 1970s, popping's illusions seduced him, and he sought out ways to participate and learn.[47] In so doing, he mapped a new relationship to the city. For Baby Love, the first widely known and commercially recognized b-girl (Young City Girls and Collective7, formerly of Rock Steady Crew), her relationship to breaking started with her crew, friends who lived nearby. The conversation between Baby Love's experiences and Cartoon's offer insight on how training happened in and out of the context of a crew and distinctly in terms of gender.

To begin though, it is important to consider the distinct illusions in popping as a genre. Dance scholar Naomi Bragin points to differences in creative intention, noting, "The popper's groove is less invested in constructing a spectacular end to the performance than in building a groove in time-space," a groove she describes as more "cyclical" relative to breaking's linear structure (footwork, floor work, power moves, freeze).[48] Bragin describes popping, and the other forms sometimes erroneously couched under that name, as "innovative aesthetics of movement isolation, contraction and release."[49] At times the illusion is of an external force moving the dancer like an invisible puppeteer. Other times the illusion comes back to a "stop-and-go" effect of cycling between contracting and relaxing the muscles. The illusion is amplified by hitting the beat. In popping, isolations (or the ability to articulate different parts of the body) are central, demanding two types of control: muscle contraction *and* its relaxation between pops. Bragin refers to this as "not-seen/not-known until *kinesthetically* engaged through prolonged practice, a practice that necessarily entails improvisation."[50]

Formerly Mr. Chill, Funk Maker, and Super Sugar Crisp, Cartoon (the name he eventually settled on that he said described his style) is a little-known but dedicated popper who grew up in the Bronx. In our 2006 interview he stated that he never got to travel to the West Coast (where the various illusionary styles he practiced originated). His story showcased how he traversed the South Bronx between fourteen and fifteen years old expressly to learn as much as he could. When we met, he repeatedly referred to his being cast in the 1984 Hip Hop movie *Beat Street* as a testament to his skills, though his part ended up on the cutting room floor. He kept the proof on him: a paystub for $542, rather than the $25 paid to extras. Though Cartoon was without a crew, popping had shaped his life since he was a teen. He described being awestruck by it, and spoke with such passion that he regularly stuttered, forcing out every pertinent detail before his mouth could catch up. The beginning of his story was rich in the cadence of his enthusiasm about the people and places that prompted his love of popping:

> So, I seen Pauly G and Loose Boots and I was like, wow! I seen these two people floatin' all over the floor on 42nd [Street]. . . . And I was like wow! *People can float all over the floor, and defy gravity with their body!* Now *that!*—I find that to be very intriguing. So I had a couple of friends with

me—it was Thanksgiving in 1979—and they laughed and said, "You never gonna learn how to do that." So I took it home with me and I practice it. And I practice and I practice and I practice, you know? And then finally, I got the backslide. And I got the frontslide. So then I went to Kips Bay Boys Club and then, I met Wiggles. I met Wiggles. And Wiggles, he was the first person I ever seen who was doing waves like water through his body.... Wiggles, he prolly been about fifteen maybe at the time, maybe.... And-and then there's another guy called Electric Boogie Fat, and Electric Boogie Fat, he was part of the Shack crew. And he was able to do arm waves that were really like water. So I was really—you know that he was doing these illusions, and I was like, wow, you know? So I went and-and I took that home with me and I worked on that. So at the time I was going to Gompers [High School], and I met a guy named Al. And Al was down with the Electric Company. I was learning from Al. And Al was like, showing me how to do the arm wave, and how to do the tick, and how to do the backslide, and do the sideslide... I would dance, and I would practice, and then, at that particular time there were a lot of contests going on. There was th-th-the "Lets Boogie" contest over at Skatin' Palace. And I went to that contest, and I competed in that contest. I didn't win that contest. But I [got] a lot of experience.... [Eventually] I would battle people, and I never lost.[51]

This is how Cartoon began a near forty-five-minute narration of his life, largely unprompted and with few interruptions. To be honest, I sat with his story for years before I really began to appreciate the nuances of its details. One detail is that the trajectory of his journey began with the power of the dance's illusions. That Pauly G and Loose Boots floated and defied gravity changed his sense of a body's capacities. In response Cartoon sought out teachers of that initiated knowledge to learn new ways for his body to move through the world. The illusions in this case are tied directly to the isolations he learned. Cartoon describes his growing repertoire move by move, which is to say body part by body part: arm wave, tick, backslide, and more. Others have noted a similar approach when they were learned popping.[52] Isolations, which depend on the repetition of a move in order to build muscle memory and gain control, were his entryway into learning popping's secrets.

Isolations demonstrate how Africanist aesthetics become more meaningful when understood in concert with other key aesthetic elements. Dance scholar Brenda Dixon Gottschild addresses isolations in relation to a "get-down stance" that allows for polycentric movement. She writes that to practice "isolating and playing the body parts one against the other so that chest, rib cage, back, belly, pelvis, and buttocks have the option of working independently or separately" is to "carry on a tradition of polycentric, polyrhythmic body fluency."[53] In her discussion of six characteristics of African American dance, dance historian Jacqui Malone draws attention to the element of "control" in movement both in body and demeanor, or the maintenance of an "aesthetic of cool," which values elegance or a presentation of effortlessness that lends itself to the illusion. She contends that to be inside the tradition, one must adhere to its specific "technologies of stylization."[54]

Learning isolations, which is to say enacting an ensemble of Africanist aesthetics, translates directives about stance, control, and demeanor into a specific technology of a style. To achieve it requires building "extreme self-control of isolated muscle groups" that can either affect the "visual illusion of jumpiness, tension or at times chaotic lack of control" while diverting attention away from the mechanics of the body. Bragin offers, as example, how a shrug of the shoulders (which looks like moving one's bones) in popping is actually an effect of an "intense muscular contraction," with contraction *and* relaxation as dual forces.[55] The illusion is a consequence of "improvis[ing] within a set of limitations imposed on the body's freedom to move," the implications of which reach beyond the cypher.[56]

Popping's illusions also prompted Cartoon to be nomadic, mapping a new set of relations to other practitioners who taught him. Though his story begins on 42nd Street in Manhattan, in his own words he makes his way to the Kips Bay Boys Club (once located in Midtown Manhattan but moved to the Southeast Bronx in 1969).[57] From the Boys and Girls Club, he goes Gompers High School near East 145th Street, which only factors into the story as a site for dance and little else. (He would eventually drop out to pursue his art.) The last spot named in his story is the now defunct Skating Palace, once on the corner of Rosedale and Soundview Avenues, where he first battled. That mapping suggests that his mobility allowed him to maneuver in ways that did not depend on having a crew. By remapping the Bronx into sites for dance training, Cartoon created a network of inconsistent but substantive social ties.

Cartoon's map of the South Bronx reflected the social choreography of a developing street dancer, enabled by his degree of mobility as a young man. He learned to control his body in order to hold those illusions, and in so doing he also etched out new social possibilities that, even if they did not pan out, gave him a way to step into a sense of self. He told me early in our interview that after seeing a cypher, he knew he had to learn either breaking or popping because "I didn't have no identity, so I needed an identity. So, I needed to learn how I can be able to be a part of that." He learned. Cartoon could always enter a cypher, as he did in the opening story "Superheroes Among Us," and imbibe the cheers and admiration that came from showing and proving.

For young women practitioners, social networks could be tenuous in a different way, producing a different kind of map. Cartoon's training can be contrasted with Baby Love, who can provide some context for the experiences of women practitioners of her generation. In our 2007 interview Baby Love remarked,

> My mother did not like me hanging out at the park [Rock Steady Park]. So a lot of the time I went there—you know 'cause I was young. I was fourteen [or] fifteen. So a lot of the time, I would sneak out. I would say I was going to a friend's house and then I would find my way in the park. And then when my mom would realize that I *wasn't* at my friend's house, she would come out looking for me. And it was great because all the guys would be like, "Yo! Yo Baby Love, your mother is coming!" And we had ways to get out of the park so that I could sneak out and then my mom wouldn't find me, but she always knew. . . . The park was like three or four blocks away from where I grew up, where I lived. So by the time she walked home she would be, "I know where you were. I know you were in the park."[58]

Sneaking out of the park with the help of her crew demonstrated a different kind of illusion that teenagers are stereotypically known to practice. Baby Love's mobility was specifically shaped by the social and cultural pressure to remain close to home, a common expectation of daughters and typically a means of protecting her reputation (e.g., accusations of promiscuity) and her person. Negotiating those terms while hanging with groups of boys meant her map of the city, at least initially, was geographically narrow. It included the immediate blocks surrounding her home and Rock Steady Park (at 98th and Amsterdam Avenue). This suggests that, in contrast to Cartoon, she was more reliant on a crew to learn at all. Yet only parts of her repertoire were nurtured.

Baby Love was among only a handful of practicing b-girls in New York at the time. Even within her own crew, the Young City Girls, not all of the female members were dancers. The only other dancer in the crew, Lady Rock, "didn't do a lot of footwork, but she did headspins."[59] Baby Love is much more known for her footwork, and even has a move named after her, but she did not get sustained instruction on how to do more power moves. In contrast, she was given a lot of room to develop footwork. I inquired:

IKJ: Give me some background as to why you think there was not as much support around you developing in areas other than footwork.
BL: I'd like to say probably because of my size, you know, not being strong enough to hold my body. Maybe that's not true. And I think I will never know. You know, I think we'll never know that it was because, "Oh let her just do the footwork and that's good enough. We don't have to teach her anything else." I don't know if their perception was that I didn't want to learn more. You know, I guess I will never know. Those are questions that I don't have answers to. You know, I can speculate. I will always speculate. But I won't let it take away what I have today with the women that I'm involved with, with Collective 7, and what that represents to me. And what women in Hip Hop represents to me. Because I am a woman in Hip Hop.[60]

In *Black Noise*, Tricia Rose captures some of Baby Love's unspoken concern about the barriers to participation for b-girls, namely that sexist attitudes among b-boys meant that they "heavily discouraged [girls] from performing break moves because they were perceived by some male peers as 'unsafe' and 'unfeminine.'"[61] Yet, for Baby Love there was no "answer." Was it perceptions about her size and strength? Was it their disinterest in teaching her power moves, or perceptions about her lack of interest? At the same time, she made it clear in our interview that "the Rock Steady Crew made it comfortable for me."[62] Her crew took care of her both in teaching her certain aspects of the dance and in helping her avoid punishment for hanging out with them in the first place. That, though, did not mitigate the possibility of having been tokenized to some degree.

Whatever the obstacles, being in a crew nonetheless gave Baby Love a sustained network that Cartoon seemingly lacked because he was not in one. It also suggests that without a crew, Baby Love might not have had access to teachers in the ways Cartoon could more openly pursue. With that said, while Cartoon's nomadism did not depend on a crew, it also may have left him without consistent connection. As principles about embodiment, illusionism and nomadism reveal how a dancer's corporeality impacts processes of learning and the cultivation of support networks. Gender clearly played a part in distinguishing Baby Love's and Cartoon's experiences. At the same time, these principles also amplified the social work of participation, or the on-the-ground social labor an initiate had to put in to truly embody these forms.

Cartoon did not achieve the level of celebrity—ghetto or mainstream—to which he aspired, and Baby Love would go onto international recognition. Both nonetheless placed themselves within a larger Hip Hop legacy. Baby Love named hers in relation to women in Hip Hop: "I am a woman in Hip Hop. That is who I am. And maybe I've been out of the scene for so long, but it never left my heart." Cartoon outright named the genealogy of his own identity. He finished our interview by stating, "It was the most beautifulest time of my life." Then he looked directly into the camera and gave "a very special thanks," "props," and "love," to Poppin' Taco, Jazzy Jay, Mr. Wiggles, Popmaster Fabel, DJ Afrika Bambaataa, Poppin' Pete, Boogaloo Sam, Skeeter Rabbit, and DJ Shakes for "passing on the information" and giving him what he "necessarily needed." In thanking Skeeter Rabbit, who died well before our interview, icons of popping whom he had never met like Sam, Pete, and Taco, local and well-known poppers he met or learned from like Wiggles and Fabel, and two DJs, Shakes and Bambaataa (a man anchored to the history of Hip Hop), Cartoon's list is more than an expression of gratitude. It is a narration of a lineage that now included him.

Nomadism: Two Sides of the Street

Nomadism, as a battling principle, foregrounds engaging with others, or the proverbial Other, as a matter of moving through the world. It is part of the social life of breaking culture. At the time, as breakers started to catch people's attention because of how they moved through New York City, they practiced and showcased a sensibility about the nature of that movement within the urban terrain of the US in the 1970s and early 1980s.
With a perspective on moving through the city, dance and public policy scholar Randy Martin saw the mobility exhibited in breaking as a practice of risk and mutuality, alongside other subcultures and contextualized by the 1970s debt economy. In analyses of risk, dance, and finance, Martin explores what he calls a "social kinesthetic" evident in postmodern choreographer Trisha Brown scaling buildings, the Zephyr crew skateboarding in empty swimming pools Southern California, and breaking on New York City

streets. Social kinesthetic refers to the way "that we move together, that we're oriented towards movement that we could say is a way of reclaiming and reinvesting in a different principle, a lateral, distributed, but also difficult-to-concretize principle of people moving together but not as one."[63] In each practice one "would need to move off-center, fly low, gather its forces laterally," and as such "risk is reward."[64] With regards to breaking, Martin singles out the "iterative process of rehearsal, of taking turns doing movement *for* one another, [which] amounts to a continuous shuttling between viewer and actor so as to render the spectacular internal to performance."[65] In other words, a cypher.

Martin notices and hinges his argument on two unnamed Africanist aesthetics: blurring the lines between audience and performer, and the multifocal approach demanded by the circle. In "The Case for an African American Aesthetic," American studies scholar Gena Caponi notes that, even if you were not the one at the center, "the circle helped to keep everybody involved, active, and interdependent."[66] That everyone plays a part and cannot be easily separated out as audience is formative of call-and-response exchanges. And the loose audience/performer divide that results creates a very different dynamic than the linear unidirectionality of the proscenium stage, according to Gottschild. She writes:

> There is always the possibility that the person who is an onlooker may be drawn into the action and become a performer. In addition, since there is no proscenium stage separating audience from performers, spectators may choose where to focus their attention, and performers may choose where to locate themselves while performing. Frequently there is more than one "performance" going on simultaneously. No one person is capable of knowing/seeing all that is going on at any particular moment in time. But this is not to be mistaken for chaos (a cultural bias emanating from those who see linear structure as superior to other possible alternatives). Instead, this is a democracy of structure that is characteristic of Africanist-based performance modes. . . . When linearity is disrupted and the performer-audience divide is blurred, the force of the unforeseen gains ascendance.[67]

Blurring the performer-audience divide is not simply that anyone might take part, but that they are invited to, or even seduced. The invitation, though, comes with conditions, including that one enter in the right way, attendant to the cypher's etiquette and its cultural responsibilities and including active participation. Since there are multiple, simultaneous, mutually influencing, dialogical exchanges happening, taking in everything is impossible and all you can do is participate with others, improvisationally. Perhaps where Martin sees a social kinesthetic that values risk and mutuality, from inside the cypher one can recognize and experience the force of an ensemble of Africanist aesthetics working in concert to reassert the collective (which supports dancers precisely at those moments of risk) and open channels to the unforeseen.

In Kwikstep's story, the concept of a blurred relationship between practitioner and audience is evident in his relationship to the streets he traversed. He spoke to me in a 2007 interview about his nomadic journeys as a b-boy to different schools and boroughs during his adolescence in search of other breakers:

> I was in the streets and I knew that there were two sides to the streets. . . . There's a saying in Spanish: *Mira pa frente, no mire pal lado; tú es un santo, pero tú no eres babalao*. Meaning look forward, don't look to the side; you might be a saint but you're not God. That means mind your fucking business, and don't think you too bad for anything because you will get tested. I knew that at a young age. Where I was going, I kept focused [on] where I was going. I didn't look at anybody. I went to go break. That's it. And after a while they'd be like, "Yo, I seen shorty on this block all of the time. What's he doing man?" I mean, they saw me at the jams and block parties, in the schoolyard. Like, "Yo, money's nice." 'Cause thugs, they love dancers. [Dancers] got skills that [thugs] don't got. Plus, girls come around you. So, you know, they have a different reason why they hang around you. But part of it is admiration, so there's a little bit of respect there.[68]

As a principle, nomadism speaks to the need to travel; as an embodied experience, Kwikstep emphasized *how* he traveled. His primary lesson was simple: mind his business and stay on his path. He understood this in a proverbial kind of way, a folk wisdom he rattled off so quickly that my beginning Spanish skills could barely keep up. In Yoruba-based spiritual practices in the Americas and in West Africa, the *babalao* is a spiritual leader who offers healing or divination services as a kind of high priest; a different kind of MC, a master of spiritual ceremonies.[69] If the rules of the streets are that no matter how godly, no one is above street life, then anyone he encountered along the way was just part of what he needed to expect in a nomadic practice. As a consequence, Kwik had to walk with an unwavering focus, watching out for what he could not predict nor control. The unforeseen, which is not necessarily coded as good or bad, is instead foregrounded as inevitable and thus to be respected. The blurring of audience and performer brings a logic of "gather[ing] its forces laterally" to everyday social encounters.

Kwik's ability to navigate "both sides of the street" was likely wrapped up in his admiration for the older cousins and brothers, "gangsters" and "thugs" he grew up around and who introduced him to these social dance aesthetics:

> You know, when you're a child and you look at heroes, they're on TV, but then you look at your block and they're right in front of you! They look heroic, you know: the way they dress, the way they primp their hair, the way everybody says hello to them, everybody gives them a pound. You start to emulate them, you know, and you want the same kind of attention. So when you're in the neighborhood, you know, you start to do things that call attention. And as soon I saw it [breaking] I knew I wanted to do it. And I remember one of the first things that I saw. It's a basic move and I think it's been in a lot of cultures. Some people call it a coffee grinder. And it's part of a front sweep in breaking. But I saw one of my alleged cousins doing it ('cause he wasn't really my cousin, but I was part of his foster family).... I saw him in the poolroom. I looked in and I remember the paneling very clear: beige, old seventies paneling, bar, pool table. And he just like, he moved his body in a way that caught my attention. And then my mom pulled me, and you know I ignored her and looked some more. And she was like tugging on my shoulder like it was a shirt, but she was pinching my shoulder. But I was mesmerized by what he was doing, which is coffee grinder, and I wanted to do that. I wanted to go and say, "How did you do that?" and she just grabbed me by my hand and she pulled me down the block. "You're not going to go hang out with him. You're not going to go over there with that thug!"

Despite his foster mother's best efforts, like Cartoon, Kwik was awestruck. It was less about the move itself, noting how common it was, and more about the style of its delivery and who embodied it. Part of the appeal in this case is not that it was an illusion that seemed impossible but that it just looked so damn cool. Pulled in by the aesthetic, the movement amplified his admiration for local figures. Under the gaze of the streets, Kwikstep learned to sample both sides.

Sampling is a Hip Hop aesthetic practice that borrows excerpts from previous songs and uses them in the production of new music. Rose writes of sampling as a demonstration of key Hip Hop aesthetics, namely layering, rupture, and flow. She reads sampling as an act of invocation and paying homage through "intertextual references" embedded in the music.[70] In *Making Beats: The Art of Sample-Based Hip-Hop*, Schloss states explicitly that "African-derived aesthetics, social norms, standards, and sensibilities are deeply embedded in the form [sampling], even when it is being performed by individuals who are not themselves of African descent."[71] Specifically, repetition and "looping" the break "creat[e] a cycle out of linearly conceived melody." Both Rose and Schloss draw on literary scholar James Snead's exploration of repetition in Black culture to contextualize the looped break, which Snead argues "builds 'accident' into its *coverage*, almost as if to control . . . unpredictability."[72] All of these aesthetic features are evident in sampling as a music practice.

Beyond rap, sampling is conceptually useful here in relation to identity. As stated earlier, for example, Cox's use of sampling highlights how young Black women "captured in the white and adult gaze . . . respond with their own self-possessed, and often politically-informed, choreography."[73] Their choreography was "a process of meaning making" by "borrowing" and "sampling" from the very people under whose gaze and power they were subject. Hip Hop theater scholar and artist Nicole Hodges-Persley argues that sampling "can be a subversive methodological and theoretical tool of identity construction, negotiation and representation . . . [that allows] the opportunity to manipulate the boundaries and limitations of existing categories of difference and essentialist notions of being."[74] In Hodges-Persley's research, sampling registers how performative codes in Hip Hop (specifically in Hip Hop theater) sanction "sampling" blackness via language, self-adornment, and embodied gestures. In Kwik's case, he too borrowed and sampled from figures in his environment, and out of an *identification with* those cool, older thugs and gangsters he expressed that appreciation through self-adornment and embodied gestures. His identification signaled both respect *and* an awareness of who he was in negotiation with on his nomadic journeys. Sampling is not simple mimicry but part of a practice of dynamic and ongoing production. In this case, it was in service to *becoming* a b-boy.

Moreover, if being a b-boy was a passport of sorts to cross territories that thugs and gangsters controlled, it was not the dance alone that enabled that mobility but a mutual interest in attracting girls. Kwikstep elaborates: "They [thugs] had the girls, and you know they always had the jokes, and they looked tough, and I wanted to be like them. I remember them carrying their radios, listening to music, and just having a good time. And it was soulful, and I wanted to be a part of that." Where b-girls of this era likely needed to move furtively (e.g., Baby Love on the lookout for her mom, Aby making his sisters stay inside), b-boys seemed to have been able to move in more open exchange with thugs and gangsters across territories. Kwikstep comported and contorted his body in ways that were respected in the streets, and that allowed him to negotiate different power dynamics by way of his new identity as a b-boy.

Similar to Cartoon, breaking gave Kwik an identity, a mode of expression for a shy kid trying to find ways to come into his own sense of self: "Because I didn't know how to speak—didn't know how to let out my emotions. When it came to dancing, I could speak as loud as I wanted to." Within the larger social landscape, a b-boy identity at the time cultivated a unique aura, one that sampled from "both sides of the street," and balanced looking outward with caution while compelling others to look at the illusions they projected.

Conclusion

And think about the terminology. "Yo I'm going to a *battle*." I mean, you're already in a war and then you're going to a battle. You didn't call it a skirmish.[75]
—Kwikstep, personal interview, 26 May 2007

Early generations of breakers and New York–based poppers who grew up in the South Bronx contributed to the creation of a culture that basked in its own invention, celebrated its own practitioners, and valued the sensibilities that perpetuated their worlds. Rather than private ownership, consumerism, and individual mainstream fame, they spoke of squatter's rights, do-it-yourself artistry, cooperation, and ghetto celebrity statuses. At the same time, differences in gendered experiences illustrate how breakers used the dance to negotiate internal struggles too. Battles were not solely contests or bitter rivalries but training grounds for an outlaw sensibility, reinforcing battling principles while activating a set of culturally meaningful repertoires, critiquing mainstream values, and teaching these lessons in how to carry those messages into any given context. Such lessons continue to transfer to new generations of practitioners.

Breakers' social choreography in the 1970s and early 1980s informed battling then and now. They moved beyond survival to cultivate an ever-expansive lateral network of Others. This contextualizes battling's possibilities, especially since a forgotten minority three times over is not supposed to be powerful. Even as other regional histories and influences rightly get greater attention, the social choreography of early practitioners in the South Bronx still matters.

While street dance techniques get passed on globally, underlying street sensibilities are only sometimes explicitly articulated, but always relevant. Even if only evident in traces, breaking allows one to embody the repertoire of cultural outlawry, challenging structural relations of power through *and in* this embodied practice. Chapter 3 extends the possibilities of battling, outlawry, and a warrior aesthetic to cyphers dominated by b-girls.

Crossing the Line

Train Station in Braunschweig, Germany, 22 October 2006
It's 3:30 a.m. and I am tired. It is the night of Battle of the Year, and I'm walking alone on the cobbled streets of Braunschweig, Germany. The battles are over and even the after-parties are fading, but I hear that the train station is the place to be, so I go. As its glass, automated double doors slide open, a very bohemian scene greets me: a hall packed full of breakers dancing, sleeping, lounging. Some are in sleeping bags on the floor or atop unattended countertops, or curled up in darkened corners; others are grouped with friends laughing and talking; and others still are dancing in small cyphers, first to a live DJ and later to a live drummer. Nearby are a couple of cops, who I expect to disrupt any revelry in favor of "order," but to my surprise they just watch unfazed by it all.

I venture a bit further into the spacious main hall of the station, and finally approach a nearby cypher in time to catch the tail end of a battle between Ardit, an Albanian b-boy from TNT Cru, against b-boy Kiprana from Soul Runnings Crew out of Mexico City. I met Ardit two weeks prior at the UK B-Boy Championships, and a familiar face makes me stick to this particular cypher. I watch him and his opponent go back and forth, and am intrigued by how their exchange bridges language gaps through dance. From the outset, Ardit speaks the language of power moves and contortions. Each turn in the circle is his opportunity to display those skills, using his hands like most people use their feet. He spins on one hand with his body extended vertically above him (a move called a 1990), hops from one hand to the other while working the space of the circle, then pulls a leg over one shoulder while balancing on a hand. Ardit's style is dynamic and skillful, drawing the support of friends and strangers.

As the true language of their exchange is breaking itself, when Ardit demands, "Power! Do power!" in his clipped English, everyone understands the terms by which he insists that the battle proceed. His opponent Kiprana has demands of his own. He skips into the circle right on beat and begins making cutting and stabbing motions toward Ardit's head, gestures of an impending massacre. Kiprana quickly shifts to the floor, incorporating traditional footwork in a distinct combination that culminates in several crouched cartwheels wherein his head touches the ground when he is inverted. He choreographs a rich testament to the creativity of the dance. Kiprana moves his arms in the air like an off-balance scale, mocking Ardit's arm stylings. "Power move?" he questions out loud, and then waves away Ardit in refusal and begins dancing again without going to the floor at all, denying Ardit's and the some of the crowd's demands to see more power while performatively accusing Ardit of being unable to dance. I see these ideas play out in battles regularly, but in this case the terms of their confrontation quickly change.

Several white and (guessing from their side conversations) German breakers, and one b-girl in particular, start obnoxiously bellowing, "¡Ándale, ándale! ¡Arriba, arriba!" every time Kiprana enters the circle. I remember the phrase from the Warner Brothers cartoon character Speedy Gonzales, a Mexican mouse who is perpetually running away.[1] Kiprana—who is decked out in green, white, and red flag colors with "Mexico" airbrushed across the back of his personalized T-shirt—lets their taunts pass . . . at first. Eventually, though, he gets more openly tense as they get louder. The hecklers seem oblivious to the offense of invoking an openly racist stereotype (or maybe just don't care), pleased with its effects as others in the cypher join in the laughter. The young b-girl intends to piss him off, to distract him during a battle, and she succeeds. Eventually, Kiprana reaches his limit. In the middle of a run, he just stops dancing altogether, walks directly to her, and thrusts his middle finger in her face. The gesture both signals a loss (of cool and the battle), and invites a new battle. The crowd's mood shifts decidedly against Kiprana because he seems to be taking out his frustrations on an "innocent" b-girl bystander rather than the b-boy opposing him in the cypher—though from where I stand a gestural "fuck you" is a more than reasonable response.

The crowd eggs on the confrontation with dramatic "Oooh's!" There is a palpable change in Kiprana's energy and his body language suggests uncertainty: he stands half in and half out of the cypher, as if debating whether to walk away. In contrast, she's just getting started. She immediately rises, unfazed, removes her jacket, enters the cypher, and boldly begins to break, starting with a little toprock before going to the floor. Some are impressed as they bounce their hands in the air in approval, suggesting that the majority of this circle is on her side. Kiprana does not respond to her challenge.

How people read his refusal to battle is unclear. It was once not unusual for some b-boys to avoid battling b-girls, sometimes assuming a too-easy win, other times thinking it's a no-win situation. Yet the cultural codes around gender are *changing with each generation; and though misogyny persists, challenges to it increase. The codes around race in this moment though seem almost nonexistent since, to most of the onlookers, Kiprana went too far. Only a small few of us felt that those who taunted him were the ones who crossed a line.*

A young Black man goes to Kiprana and pats him on the back for support. A b-girl who's been watching on the sidelines takes Kiprana's place in the battle. As the players change hands and the original tensions dissipate, the situation ends unresolved. I watch as Kiprana eventually leaves the cypher altogether, and can feel the familiar pain of accumulated, microaggressive cuts. And with that, I figure it's time for me to leave.

3

Badass B-Girls Dancing the Dissonance of a Breaking Sociality

> Battles give women an opportunity to show a side of them that's not necessarily socially acceptable. You go to a battle and the idea is to be aggressive, really offensive, like you're attacking somebody. That's not something you can do in your normal day life; you're expected to be polite and ladylike. Breaking is an opportunity to talk shit, be angry, and be a badass, and it's cool. You suck if you can't do that.
>
> —Chyna, *We Be*Girlz*[1]

> Because I'm dancing now for twelve years, for a long time [my mom] she didn't understand what I was doing. But she was like, "Well, one day, she will settle down and have kids." And, um, yeah—it didn't happen up till now! So she's like *waiting*, you know? Especially when I started doing more breakdance, she's like, [*shrugs*] "Yeah, spinning on a dirty ground. What the . . . ? What are you doing?" You know? So I don't even bother to explain it that much. As long as I'm happy, I hope she can be happy too.
>
> —Black Pearl, personal interview, 21 October 2006

After years of watching b-girls in cyphers, "badass" was a fitting (if not obvious) term for their energy. It is in fact, as b-girl Chyna points out, what breaking demands, and as a result perhaps why an ever-increasing number of b-girls take advantage of the "opportunity" to spin on a dirty ground, often literally. Insofar as cisgender women are raised or even coerced into socially acceptable versions of femininity, breaking offers a means of embodying alternative femininities to be badass in a cypher. Yet they have to first choose to push against social expectations writ large and in the context of their home life. Since Hip Hop often challenges normative expectations of the socially acceptable *as a matter of practice*, b-girls' embodiment of a warrior imperative does a certain kind of work both in and out of the culture.

In scenes dominated by b-boys, b-girls experience the discord in breaking's gender politics (the culture's expectations of how b-girls should dress, dance, and embody gender), and learn to dance the dissonance between the pressures coming from outside and competing expectations from within. In doing so they continually muddy or dirty up a conflation of biological sex, gender, and gender expression in performance. At the same time, though being badass might simply code as empowering or progressive, those positive connotations belie how the interplay of gender, race, and nation continually shifts the meaning of badass and muddles the political stakes in any given moment, which was unmistakable on my trip to Germany.

When I first began research in the mid-2000s, there weregrowing numbers of b-girls in the scene, and increasing efforts to nurture women practitioners through mentorship, classes, and b-girl-centered events. B-girls were, nonetheless, often reticent both about new women in the scene whose intentions for being there were unclear (was I dabbling, dating, or down?) and of researchers likely to ask predictable questions about gender (guilty). Over the years, as my relationships to specific b-girls deepened, candid conversations remained cautious in tone, and, when on the record, b-girls often still purposefully undernarrativized the details around sexism and misogyny in the scene to outsiders.[2] My focus then, like theirs, is on practice and the possibilities of their creative interventions in cyphers.

I also directly engage with recent studies of b-girls in China, Australia, Canada, and Norway, in contrast to chapter 2's focus on the South Bronx as a local place. Across the literature and in my own interviews, b-girls disrupt assumptions about what femininity is supposed to be, whether they intend to or not. In *We B*Girlz*—a collection of commentary by and photographs of b-girls from around the world edited by Nika Kramer and famed Hip Hop photographer Martha Cooper—Aruna, founder of the Hip Hop Huis in Rotterdam Holland states, "Girls who are breaking are very aware of their choices. Because if you're a girl, you really have to make a choice to start breaking. You have to give up more socially than a guy to be able to break."[3] Paying those social costs can be high because choosing to break is more than learning the dance. For example, in an article on b-girls in China, authors Mathew Ming-tak Chew and Sophie Pui Sim Mo write, "The embodied experiences of breaking compel Chinese b-girls, sometimes even against their will, to defy major patriarchal and cultural inequalities including thin-body ideals, the moral burden of fertility, Chinese indecent exposure discourses, and the norm of submissive Oriental women."[4] While only one example, across the literature being a b-girl threatens social standing, induces sexist discourses about health, and undermines major cultural tenets. Thus, making the choice to break has stakes in all of these areas too.

My use of "badass" comes directly from Chyna's comments. The word captures something palpable while pushing against other more obvious references (e.g., tomboy) that read b-girls as performing masculinity,[5] language that never felt sufficient. (Moreover, the b-girls I interviewed never articulated themselves in terms of masculinity.)[6] In 2014, I defined badass femininity by way of performances that "eschew notions of appropriateness, respectability, and passivity demanded of ladylike behavior in favor of confrontational, aggressive, and even outright offensive, crass, or explicit expressions of a woman's strength."[7] It mostly captured how cisgender women opted into alternative performances of strong femininity rendered permissible within particular cultural milieux (like breaking or the blues).

In "From Blues Women to B-Girls: Performing Badass Femininity," I looked at blues women and b-girls as two points in a lineage of badass femininity in Black performance cultures. I oriented badass femininity expressly to theories that were responsive to the historical violence of enslavement and the colonizing project of a gender binary. For example, I engaged what Black feminist literary critic Hortense Spillers calls the "ungendering" of enslavement, referencing the ways that blackness tests the limits of gender precisely because enslaved Black people were held outside of its social and legal meanings.[8] Cyphers bridge global breaking to this Black lineage of badass femininity through Africanist aesthetics. Whether practitioners recognize that is another matter.

This chapter, thus, pivots to explore cyphers occupied by b-girls from around the world with badass femininity as our point of entry. Across this global research and in my own, b-girls open themselves up to the shit-talking, in-your-face, aggressive, hard, badass approaches that the practice demands—and if not that exactly, then certainly an "alpha energy."[9] As a result, b-girls play in the gray areas between femininity and masculinity, and consequently trouble binary gender through practice.[10] They do so in the embrace of a ritual circle that values improvisation, experimentation, originality, and a willingness to get dirty (see Fig. 3.1).

Figure 3.1 B-girl at footwork challenge, B-boy Summit B.O.S.S. (Battle of the Sexes) Jam 2006, Los Angeles, CA, 31 August 2006. Note the sweat and dirt on her back.

The Dissonance of Breaking's Gender Politics

Though Hip Hop is comfortable with masculinity, it has an ambivalent relationship to femininity, and a gender binary further obfuscates what femininity can mean in Hip Hop. For example, following a screening of Popmaster Fabel's 2010 documentary *Rock Dance History: The Untold Story of Up-Rockin'* at a South Bronx community center, during the question-and-answer period a woman in the audience made a plea for the greater inclusivity of "feminine energy" at Hip Hop jams to mitigate the violence of interpersonal beefs. On the all-male panel of rockers, one vigorously shook his head back and forth before the "No!" could even be uttered. He stated that "feminizing" Hip Hop meant sanitizing it, pacifying it, making it "nice" or "pretty," and thus stripping it of its spirit. Read generously, the woman in the audience offered up "feminine energy" as a kind of balance to a hyper-masculine environment, but when her words are funneled through a gender binary, femininity is deemed to lack a capacity to carry rocking's quintessential battling spirit altogether.

In discourse, Hip Hop's most authenticating terms for breakers are "b-boy" and "b-girl," which seems to reify gender bifurcation at the culture's linguistic foundations.[11] In this binary, "b-boy" is already dominant and gets positioned as the representative cultural figure (e.g., Trac2's "true b-boy"). As a result, b-girls can all too easily be read as simply performing some version of masculinity, justifying assumptions that combat dances like rocking and breaking are decidedly *not* feminine. Though framed in that way, when breaking, b-girls upend these assumptions whenever they hit the floor.

A number of scholars have teased out the intricate gender politics of Hip Hop culture within particular genres (e.g., rap, graffiti),[12] and explored women practitioners' embodied experiences.[13] In such scholarship, which covers multiple fields, Hip Hop both acts as a site that can reproduce Western gender norms (social expectations based on the reassertion of a masculine/feminine binary) *and* offers paths to disrupt those norms through engaging in a Hip Hop *practice*. That is to say that physicalized practice is key because it opens spaces wherein women practitioners can embody and play with energies and approaches that are already disruptive to the binary. So, even when the social environment reifies the binary, practice troubles it. Thus, by focusing on ways of being that are put into the body, practitioners forge new possibilities in gender expression for themselves and others that are ripe for deeper exploration.

It is equally important to recognize how expectations of how b-girls should embody the dance can further delimit the room to play and experiment. Dance scholar and b-girl Mary Fogarty warns:

> Many bboys and bgirls spend time policing how women *should* act in the scene. Males aren't held to the same test or told to perform a particular type of masculinity on a regular basis in their development as dancers. . . . Not only are females trying to figure out how to do the dance but are often told what sort of femininity they should adhere to in their performance. I think instead people need to be who they are whether this presents as a rugged, battle mentality or an experimental expression of a monster personality or a cute and flirty performance. We are so much more than our gender and have so much more to say about the world through our dance than a performance of our gender.[14]

Though b-boys likely get messages about appropriate performances of masculinity from inside and outside of the culture too (e.g., a "dominant Hip Hop masculinity"),[15] there is still a lot of room for audiences to register b-boys' expressions as sometimes rugged, humorous, flirty, or experimental without questioning how they performed their gender. In contrast, Fogarty argues that b-girls get told regularly how they *should* perform femininity, often at the expense of their own self-actualized original styles. In that vein, badass femininity can easily become a controlling narrative that simply repackages compulsory masculinity. Hence my reconsideration of this term.

Reconsidering Badass Femininity

Despite badass femininity's possibilities, its critical intersections along lines of sexuality, race, and nation highlight its limitations. Though it treads theoretical ground established by queer life—for example, Marlon Bailey's work on butch femmes in the ballroom scene and their "collapse of the masculine/feminine binary of gender presentation and performance"[16]—it would be a misrepresentation to suggest an uncritical political alignment between the two since, as previously stated, badass femininity can get used to police rather than expand gender expression. As well, some cisgender and heterosexual b-girls might purposefully distance themselves from queer people to mitigate assumptions that they too are queer (precisely because they disrupt conventional notions of femininity), and thereby reassert dominant structures of power through gender.

National and racial differences also inflect how badass femininity can be meaningful. Writing on b-girls in China, Chew and Mo acknowledge that expectations for b-girls to be badass imposes an *American* strategy that is so far outside of traditional notions of femininity in China that it seems unviable in their dancing. They suggest that one informant "has probably internalised the traditional image of women so thoroughly that [she] cannot dance in an aggressive way even if [she] intends to."[17] Instead, they propose that Chinese b-girls often use their bodies in a badass way through tattoos and more visible musculature to resist.[18] In this chapter's opening story, "Crossing the Line," we see again how overdetermining gender limits the analysis, this time with regards to race and how whiteness was operative in producing that moment in the first place. Insofar as sexuality, nationality, and race structure our relationships to each other, badass femininity does not transcend those dynamics just because it has an empowering aura.

In mainstream use, the term "badass" seems to most attend to a tough femininity that breaches the binary in some ways, and reifies it in others.[19] For example, sociologist Mimi Schippers uses the term to describe a group of high school girls who "embodied a sexualized, heterosexual femininity and were also physically tough and aggressive."[20] Schippers's definition is specifically tied to what she calls "pariah" or "subordinate" femininities, because "they are deemed, not so much inferior, as *contaminating* to the relationship between masculinity and femininity."[21] Her formulation correlates to Hollywood portrayals of badass-ness in action films with women anti/heroes who tend to embody the same qualities as male action heroes (e.g., hard hitting, hard drinking, often emotionally stunted) while remaining "sexy" (typically white, thin, pretty).[22] In the visual terrain of pop cultural representations, badass-ness both "contaminates" the binary and gets corrected by ensuring her sexual desirability, locking her into a white heteromasculine gaze. And perhaps that is all people think about when they come across the term. Nonetheless, badass in my use moves along a different trajectory, one paved by Africanist aesthetics.

While badass femininity is a point of entry, my focus overall is on what becomes possible in a practice of Africanist aesthetics. In this chapter I focus on ritual derision, the prioritization of originality, and the ensemble of Africanist aesthetics that they activate. Through them, focus shifts from badass-ness in general to enactments of aesthetics that yield badass performances in battles, especially in relationship to an African diasporic lineage of such practices.

Burns, the Profane, and Rituals of Derision

Battles are not only driven by technique but also by wit, savageness, and humor. Dancing these qualities can completely change the game. "Burns" or "burners" capture some of the more combative elements of the dance, and are a staple of battle culture. In his book *The Art of the Battle: Understanding Judged Bboy Battles* b-boy Alien Ness writes that burners are in-your-face attacks or expressions of disrespect (a diss) against an opponent that makes fun of them.[23] Dance scholar and b-boy Serouj "Midus" Aprahamian argues that among first-generation breakers, "burning was a kinesthetic concept dictated by originality, musicality, wit, and competition. A dancer might put a more unique twist on a popular step, act out a humiliating insult, or drop to the floor and come back up with their hand in an opponent's face."[24] Burns typically attempt to humiliate, exploit a flaw, or establish dominance over someone.[25] While moves themselves can be burns depending on timing and quality,[26] gestural burners are very common in battles. They signify by way of an accumulation of pantomimed actions that tell a story or paint a picture, and often act out forms of attack using an array of weaponry (from machetes and switchblades to various types of guns).[27]

In the same way that explaining a joke can evacuate the humor, describing burns does not do them justice and makes them sound harsher than they appear in practice. Nonetheless, gestural disses are important combative weapons in a breaker's arsenal.[28] Many of breaking's traditional burners, like pulling out a gun and shooting an opponent, were adopted from the rock dance.[29] Breaking employs a similar pantomimed narrative approach that rocking is known for, but rather than taking up a whole song and battling in parallel lines, breakers' stories stand out as attention-grabbing counterattacks within a predominately breaking-driven technique. In their most common iterations, burns allow b-girls to play in the profane (through crass and explicitly sexual expressions) and aestheticized violence (shootings, decapitations, stabbings, breaking backs, etc.).[30]

Two examples of memorable burns stand out for me. In a battle between b-girls Vendetta and A-Plus at the King of the Hill Exhibition in 2011, posted online, Vendetta acted out digging a grave, dragging A-Plus into it, racking a shotgun, shooting the body, and kicking dirt over it. Finally, while staring directly at A-Plus, Vendetta did a little dance *on her grave*. Then she started breaking.[31] All of this took less than ten seconds, and every time I think about it still makes me chuckle. In an example of "sistas who rock outlaw style" offered by rocker Papo Luv—featured in Fabel's *Rock Dance History*[32]—he recalls a woman rocker he saw over thirty years prior. He describes the burn as he performs it, pantomiming grabbing her opponent with one outstretched hand, rolling him into a ball with both hands, then inserting him vaginally, which he describes "as a douche" (but to me seemed more reminiscent of a tampon), pulling him out, and flinging him across the room.[33] Papo Luv recites this story as he bounces and drops to the floor, reenacting the unnamed outlaw sista's exquisite burn. In response to his own story, he proclaims the subsequent dilemma: *"How the fuck can you burn that?!"*

In his 2020 article, "'There Were Females That Danced Too': Uncovering the Role of Women in Breaking History," Aprahamian speaks with members of the very first generation of breakers of primarily African American practitioners who stopped breaking well before media attention. He argues that their repeated stories about girls instigating battles by "throw[ing] her hand in your face" implies that b-girls specifically helped to establish battling culture in breaking. Aprahamian comments further:

> Contrary to the assumption that such competitions emanated from male aggression, firsthand testimony from practitioners indicates that young women were heavily involved in this burning stage of breaking as well. In fact, many accounts suggest that it was often specifically the girls who would challenge the guys on the dance floor.
> " . . . The hand is old. That's from the '60s. Giving somebody the hand. A girl would drop down with both of her hands in her lap, and then come up and throw her hand in your face. You were done. You had to leave the circle." (Disco Daddy)[34]

When I was growing up, I always attributed the hand in the face gesture to Black girl culture, and probably, foolishly, thought my generation invented it. The narrative shift that this perspective requires, then, is that we understand breaking, battling, and burning as having been heavily influenced by women from the beginning.

Burning is an integral part of the culture that speaks to a freedom in practice, at least from broader social strictures that may discourage playing in the profane. But if we only think about burns in terms of Hip Hop's outlaw aesthetics, the discussion could stay here. Through Africanist aesthetics we can consider other dimensions to this practice. For example, the Africanist aesthetic of blurring the divide between the sacred and secular leaves room for us to consider the profane here as an expression or extension of the sacred or spirit in cyphering (see chapter 1). Consider African American studies scholar L. H. Stallings's term "funky erotixxx," which identifies an already present Black Atlantic genre of cultural production that narrativizes a "sacredly profane sexuality [that] ritualizes and makes sacred what is libidinous and blasphemous in Western humanism so as to unseat and criticize the inherent imperialistic aims within its social mores and sexual morality."[35] Stallings instead argues for a history of funky erotixxx in Black sexual cultures as an opposing sensibility that disrupts Western humanism and "subvert[s] hierarchies of gender and sexuality" because it "has a lineage that exceeds its destructive imperialist mandates within Western patriarchy, *and that is sacred.*"[36] What if burns extend the sacred profane into ritual practice of battle cyphers? B-girl practitioners must, in some way, reject Western humanist tenets of civility and respectability to roll around on dirty floors, redefining notions of decorum and appropriateness through breaking and in the ritual cypher.

Ritualized mockery is another key element. It is a common practice throughout the African diaspora, and gives precedence not simply to the literal insult but to the cleverly stylized manner of its delivery, including making use of the profane. There are limited references to *dances* of derision in the African diaspora, with the primary example being the cakewalk, a pre-emancipation nineteenth-century practice wherein Black dancers mocked formal white dances in a stylized manner that was later adopted to the minstrel stage.[37] Battling in breaking, though, is more aptly comparable to verbal rituals of derision, where much of the scholarship seems to rest.[38] Familiar examples in African American life include playing the dozens, "snapping," or simply "ya mama" jokes. Such games are highly stylized traditions of ritual verbal combat.

Scholars have written about verbal rituals of derision throughout the African diaspora, including Cuba, Brazil, Colombia, Ecuador, Guyana, Puerto Rico, the US, Jamaica, Trinidad and Tobago, Suriname, Nevis, and the Bantu-Kongo region.[39] In his comparative analysis of Black snapping practices in Columbia, Ecuador, and the US, Spanish linguist Armin Schwegler writes,

> The language appropriated for such ritual events is rough, insulting, aggressive, crude, disrespectful, and, at times, downright foul, and is meant to produce comic effects in the participating audience. Not surprisingly, persons unfamiliar with this ritual tradition may find its language deeply offensive. To the practitioners too the words are rough, but these are never to be taken literally.[40]

Like breaking, these games prioritize originality or a distinct style, and its characteristics include well-timed, somewhat personalized, creative, and exaggerated insults that are performed in cooperation with an audience who referees the exchange. Insults are meant to be "boorish" expressions of wit and cunning that also entertain—largely through humor, originality, and clever wordplay, the dexterity of which is a testament to one's skill and style. One should not lose their cool lest they lose the battle, and no one is to touch. Verbal games are "profoundly competitive," rest on rhythmic cadences or structures, and express skills through a range of linguistic signifyin' practices that convey multiple meanings at once (e.g., hyperbole, puns, double entendres), "with accompanying body language of its own."[41]

Folklorist Roger D. Abrahams adds that such rituals are "training grounds" for the "man-of-words," his catchall term for various cultural figures in the English-speaking Caribbean who are especially dexterous in their verbal oratory abilities (to charm, con, entertain, seduce, etc.). Though Abrahams largely neglects women practitioners—which, to Aprahamian, reduces "complex articulations of creativity and joy" into fantasies of masculinized "resistance to urban destitution and deprivation"[42]—even Abrahams concedes women were always part of such rituals as both practitioners and community members. Skilled orators in these practices are "capable of turning any conversation into a show" for the surrounding community, a circle of culture that offers both a platform for them and holds the ritual overall.[43] He notes that "such contests were a community-accepted manner of establishing and maintaining a public (or *street*) reputation."[44] (It is no wonder that ritual insult games are among the cultural progenitors of rapping.) If we extend these qualities to breaking, then battle cyphers train breakers for a related though distinct set of skills.

When b-girls adopt these practices, their aggressiveness, strength, and play in the profane comes to represent how b-girls disrupt assumptions about what femininity means. In my first exploration of badass femininity, I drew connections to African American blues women of the 1920s and 1930s as "physically and psychologically strong, sexually free, and authorities over themselves and others."[45] They sang of their own pleasure, violence both received and given, and occupied spaces deemed primarily for men. Blues women are also among the "riotous" women that Saidiya Hartman writes about in *Wayward Lives, Beautiful Experiments: Intimate Histories of Social Upheaval*. Hartman explores Black women whose existences were always already criminal and criminalizable because they walked "the errant path," which Hartman describes as paths tread by Black women who refused the "state surveillance and police power [that] acted to shape and regulate intimate life."[46] Hartman depicts errantry as a kind of counterlogic to society's choreographic attempts to control everyday Black women's bodies and mobility.[47] Their errantry expressed a freedom they were never meant to possess; hence their power and society's fears.[48] By situating b-girls in this lineage, it extends Hip Hop's outlawry beyond the culture's own historical framework, with a particular focus on women.

I also look to African martial arts historian T. J. Desch-Obi to better contextualize my approach to warrior women. In his forthcoming historical analysis of *grima*, a machete fighting technique in Colombia that traces back to the era of enslavement and built upon African martial traditions,[49] he argues that Western scholars have tended to misread African diasporic women martial artists as "pretending to be" or "posing as" men when in fact that perspective was more indicative of Western researcher's imposed worldview that disarticulated aestheticized and actual violence (as in combat and sport) from Western "common sense" notions of appropriate femininity.[50] Desch-Obi furthers that in certain Central African contexts, masculine and feminine were principles in an overarching cosmology rather than biological imperatives. (The feminine principle included qualities like "tactical morality," "just violence," and a ferociously "protective motherhood.") For example, while the potency of *grima* was read through a masculine principle, one needed to also inhabit the moral character of the practice (the feminine principle) to not shed blood unless absolutely necessary. The technique itself enacted this balance because it used the sides of a machete, which stings like a whip, rather than the sharp edge so as not to cut.[51] Under such a cosmology the feminine is part of everything, including violence, and is not determined by *who* is fighting. While I cannot simply apply Desch-Obi's argument to breaking, I do propose that, as in *grima*, breaking gives primacy to its internal values and codes *regardless of the body doing it*. Breaking is seen as relatively egalitarian with "no division of labour or difference between vocabularies."[52] For b-girls, who train in warrior aesthetics like burns while improvising with the profane, battling creates opportunities to move in ways that are already seen as a problem to Western patriarchy.

Despite b-girls' gender-troubling possibilities, street dances that explicitly aestheticize violence and play in the profane are still popularly seen as exclusively masculine, an unbalanced understanding of breaking as a practice. One particular burner allows us to pause on the kind of contradictory space b-girls occupy as practitioners who carry knowledges embedded in the battle cypher training ground, but who are still questioned about their participation in these cultures.

Battling Emiko: Throwing the Dick and Other Sexualized Burns

Not too long into my initial ethnography, gesturing and burns began to capture my interests. More than power moves or contortions, they added a touch of humor and personality. One in particular, though, "throwing the cock" or "throwing the dick," is especially popular.[53] In it one grasps an imaginary erect penis with both hands as if it were absurdly long, thick, and heavy, and then shoves it towards someone's face, butt, or in their general direction. When it was first brought to my attention by my homegirl Sadio, I assumed breakers were pantomiming a bazooka or a rocket launcher fired from the lower half of the body because it was so exaggerated. (The connection between a penis and such weaponry is obvious.) Throwing the cock can be an act of retribution for a diss, or a quickly incorporated general diss in the midst of a set. The tone of the gesture is a strange combination of obvious and still at times unexpected, as trash talk often is. And no one is exempt from it: it happens in battles between young and old breakers, between friends and against enemies. Depending on the circumstances, throwing the cock can even overtly signify an oppositional politics, a poignantly directed "Fuck you!" to police, for example.[54] Overall, though, the thing to recognize is that it is a ubiquitous staple in breaking's repertoire that practitioners learn even if they are not formally "taught" it or told what it means.

The spirit in which a burner is given is also shaped by who delivers it and to whom it is directed. Throwing the dick caught my attention for two specific reasons. One is that I noticed that the gesture was performed with much greater frequency by b-boys in battles against b-girls, making it seem less about the immediate battle than about her presence at all. Second is that during my research in the 2000s, a debate had ensued about whether or not it was "right" or "made sense" for b-girls to perform it, such that breaking's relative egalitarianism was, in this sole instance, sacrificed for a commonplace gesture implied to be for b-boys only. Ultimately, the politics around such moves opened up space for further inquiry.

Individual breakers respond differently to throwing the dick and other sexualized moves. While some breakers avoid them altogether, others do not care, and still some b-boys will intentionally not perform these moves specifically against b-girls though they might otherwise against a b-boy.[55] Multiple b-girls have told me of their own ways of engaging the move, especially after being told it does not "fit" them, but repeatedly still having to find ways to respond to it. B-girl and dance scholar Rachael Gunn attests to developing strategies for "depleting the potency" of the move, for example by biting off the dick.[56] The sheer redundancy then of being questioned if one performed the move,[57] and the repetition of the immediate retort that she "does not have one" amplifies the ridiculousness of the accusation, as if any *pantomimed* reference to a dick hinged on an actual penis. These incidents are indicative of the muddied playing field for b-girls.

In a 2006 interview with b-girl Emiko, a Japanese woman living in Philadelphia at the time (now a Los Angeles–based founder of Open House community dance collective), she considered the complicated politics surrounding this gesture:

> I think they [b-boys] definitely do something sexual. Not like . . . they don't come out right away, but yeah. . . . Even like little, tiny bit things, they will do something like, they come like, pushing their way [*thrusts her hips forward in a humping gesture*]. I don't know. But they definitely do it. 'Cause that's . . . that's how they see us, you know.[58]

Though Emiko confirmed my observation of the frequency of sexualized burns by b-boys when battling b-girls, she clearly did not want to linger there as indicated by her stilted response, partial sentences, and halfhearted inference, "that's how they see us."

She had much more to say, though, when she considered how things play out in practice. Emiko articulated throwing the dick in relation to a larger question about sexualized moves in her repertoire at all. She elaborated:

> I used to do that [throw the dick] because that's the only way, I thought. And I didn't really realize what that means, you know. Then after I've been in breaking scene for a while, I'm like, "Wow. This is not really cool thing to do." And one time I catch myself doing it, recently, because I was so hyped or so mad or whatever, that I couldn't think of a thing to do. But immediately I go, "Wow, what am I doing? I don't want to do this." I'd rather do something funny, something like, hmm, like not really sexual. Because b-boy has so many ways already to express. But a female to be sexual is not really, like, not funny way. You know what I mean? It doesn't fit into b-girl style. Like being sexual as women is "sexy" and like, sexy means . . . I don't know. You know like, it could be different kind of sexy but . . . compared to what they do, to what b-boys do to each other? I cannot really relate to that

as a female doing same kind of moves. I have boobies. And uh, what can I do? Throwing them? Juggle? [*Laughter.*]

I thought about it. Like, okay, what can I do? But people come up with that idea also. And they do the same thing. And it's not unique anymore.... And it's so limited too. First of all, I don't want to present myself like that anymore. And there's so many other ways to make fun of people. But regular b-boy who don't dance, don't know how to dance, they will come up like typical way. Whatever.[59]

Emiko learned the burner in the context of learning how to break, and it lived as a standard diss in her repertoire as it does for most breakers. Once she realized the literal reference, though, it no longer lived comfortably. The double bind was that she was expected to demonstrate, to show and prove that she knew and understood breaking's repertoire (which includes this gesture); but in doing so, her creativity was called into question.[60] She could not then imagine a diss that was sexual *and* read as funny or aggressive on her body; and logic told her that such a move would be more readily misread as sexiness.

She lingered on the question of what to do: "Sure the meaning [is] different . . . because we have different things in the body. So, a lot of people say, 'Oh, you do this but you don't have one,' and 'Be more creative,' [and] other stuff. But what can I do?"[61] She repeated, "What can I do?" a few times at this part of our interview, suggesting that "b-girl style" makes sexual (as in sexy) moves untenable. Throwing the cock became another discourse through which b-girls were told how they should dance and express gender, further delimiting the room to play and experiment. Emiko's consideration at the time to avoid such moves altogether was also a counterpoint to the "different kind of sexy" that was left uninvestigated. In the end, though, Emiko countered with the very critique lobbed at b-girls: that throwing the dick lacks creativity.

Intellectually, Emiko questioned the efficacy of sexualized moves, but weeks before our interview at B-Boy Summit in 2006 she *danced* a resolution. During a five-on-five crew battle, the only b-girls formally competing at this four-day event formed an ad hoc group for the sake of entering one of the battles. At one point during Emiko's run, a b-boy attempted to interrupt her set by feigning humping her from behind as he bent backward while balanced on one hand. But he was taken by surprise and burned when Emiko swiftly turned around, straddled his head, and humped his face, positioning him as being at her service. The audience's response was boisterous, and the applause and laughter echoed. Emiko quickly and seamlessly continued her set, unencumbered by his interruption as he sheepishly walked back to his crew. It was an unexpected, funny, and badass response that, most importantly, did not disrupt her flow.[62] She improvised her way around her seemingly limited options by deploying the very thing she could not reconcile in the context of our interview.[63] And at an improvisational moment in a practice of ritual derision, Emiko physically enacted another option. By embodying breaking imperatives and Africanist battling practices, she made a way through her own conundrum.

When Emiko employs profane gestures, they hit harder precisely because b-girls can play off the overuse of popular burns like throwing the dick. When read through Africanist aesthetics, the battle cypher training ground is precisely where one learns to deplete the potency of a fraught tradition. A culture that knows the varied possibilities of the battle—wherein, for example, neither experiment nor stock move can guarantee a win[64]—always maintains subversion as strategic resource.

Originality and *In Relation*

Originality is an Africanist aesthetics that also activates a distinct understanding of sociality in the circle. What I couch under originality heavily overlaps with what dance scholar Thomas DeFrantz refers to as "the African American expressive *imperative to innovate*." In "Hip-Hop Habitus v.2.0," DeFrantz describes this imperative as part of an "unprecedented alignment of desire, intention, and action" that prizes the work of individual innovation within a group dynamic.[65] To dance scholar Brenda Dixon Gottschild, a dancer's leap into improvisation and innovative movement happens when the collective circle operates as the safety net.[66] In her "Crossroads, Continuity, or Contradiction: The Afro-Euro-Caribbean Triangle," Gottschild focuses on Caribbean dance's Africanist aesthetic standards, placing originality under two headings: "improvisation" and "collective/communal trust."[67] B-girls can "let it all hang out" because communal trust and respect for tradition balance improvisation and "the force of the unforeseen."[68] For DeFrantz, the unforeseen in Black aesthetics is a through line between multiple capacities: the capacity to dance beyond what seems possible, the potentially unlimited capacity to innovate and express oneself, and the ways that such capacities defy the boundaries laid out for Black people. He writes, "Hip-hop dances surely arise from this tradition of dance that defies expectation, dances that confirm something beyond reach (freedom?) but present within the capacity of the physicality of doing."[69]

In addition, innovative or original movement can influence everyone else. Take into consideration, media and music scholars Rachael Gunn and John Scannell's 2016 exploration of b-girls' influences on the "Hip Hop habitus":

> No scene, no matter how conservative, is ever truly static, with the speed of change entirely dependent on the regulation of difference. For the b-girl to enact change in the breaking scene, she might employ such a repetition of difference as practice, where the stock b-boy moves are assembled in new ways with the end goal of producing triumphant moments of the singular. The critical difference is that instead of having such moves "corrected" or "trained" back into acceptability, the b-girl singularity might instead be further cultivated as unisex expression.[70]

Building on French philosopher Gilles Deleuze and psychoanalyst Félix Guattari's concept of the singular (as an expression of the "potential and capacity for change"),[71] Gunn and Scannell describe a dynamic wherein b-girls repeatedly practice a "difference" from stock breaking moves that shape the culture as a whole. While they name it as a particularly empowering possibility for b-girls, in practice it is what any breaker should do. I read their term "repetition of difference" as a variation of originality or innovation as aesthetic imperatives. Breaking's embrace of experimentation, improvisation, and original expression is not simply a cultural idiosyncrasy, nor a happenstance byproduct of a push for change, as Gunn and Scannell may inadvertently imply, but part of the overall project: to assert a sensibility that positions the individual within the circle collective, freeing them to experiment and play within the tradition.

The collective is key, and differences in experiences along gender lines do not supplant breakers' shared experiences. Fogarty states that "there is a careful thoughtfulness to [b-girls'] articulations of their experience as women, especially when asked to address gender explicitly.... At the same time, women are constantly asked about their gender simply because they break, and are resistant to setting themselves apart from bboys who share their experiences and journeys."[72] She names "resistance" outright, drawing attention to b-girls' careful framing that insists one listen deeply, and challenges researchers like me to understand beyond our own ideological premises. I experienced such a discursive pivot, one that delicately corrected as it modeled an approach, in a 2006 phone interview with b-girl Rokafella. After I asked if there were any support networks "available for b-girls," Rokafella responded, "I think we're creating them. I don't think they are there yet. It's not as if there are any real support networks for b-boys either."[73] It may seem a minor shift of little consequence, but her attendance to breakers' shared needs, even after a pointed question about b-girls, is an example of this subtle resistance that repeated itself in our interview and in my interviews with other b-girls.

With that said, differences in experiences along gender lines do create culturally internal frictions. Mastery of the dance or culture is one way to level the playing field. For example, in our interview, whenever Rokafella discussed the sexism she dealt with as an Afro–Puerto Rican woman in different kinds of dance spaces (streets, clubs, party circuit, theater and dance institutional spaces), she repeatedly returned to the significance of building up an expertise that comes from a deep knowledge of the dance and its culture: "I knew that I had to train, you know. And I was not trying to be treated like, you know, like a weaker gender, or a stupid person, or a groupie." And a few minutes later: "So to come in and see breakers try to, you know, present this to me again like, 'Look, there's a hierarchy and you're on the bottom.' [*Scoffs*] I wasn't having it. 'Cause I already had my rep." And then: "I knew that part of making them see that I was equal was learning the dance, and training, and learning the history, so, you know, I had to go and get into the lab once again and ... get what I needed."[74] Mastery of breaking is its own kind of armor, equipping her to battle sexism through practice. Developing mastery earns respect, can influence attitudes, and changes the dynamics of certain relationships.

I propose that breakers dance a competing formulation of relation that foregrounds practice, and that it is only sometimes verbalized precisely because it is danced. Such a formulation does not rely on a colonial gender binary as its organizing logic, and those careful articulations consequently counterbalance an overdetermined binary discourse. Moreover, b-girls are more likely to verbalize it because they repeatedly get asked about gender. Their subtle resistances, though, offer a way into thinking about what breaking enables in practice: "dances that confirm something beyond reach (freedom?) but present *within the capacity of the physicality of doing*."[75]

While playing in the profane can open space for alternative femininities, originality and individual innovation activate lessons in sociality experienced in the circle. By deprioritizing linear hierarchies, cyphering fosters a competing sociality that troubles the authority of a gender binary in breaking. I name this contrasting sensibility simply *in relation* because b-girls hint at it at precisely those moments when researchers attempt to position them in opposition to b-boys.

Originality further illuminates what *in relation* can mean. First, it calls for distinctiveness over sameness, which speaks to the embedded heterogeneity of breaking and the ideal that every breaker has their own flavor. Second, though battles and burns on the surface seem to be about domination, in practice they teach lessons on the collective enactment of the ritual. Everyone has a part to play and taking part comes with terms: one has responsibility to learn how to participate, give energy if they expect to receive, to carry on cultural imperatives and traditions (foundation), actively participate, and elevate (knowledge, skills). And it remains an invitation that is accepted across races, genders, nationalities, age groups, and sexualities. (I discuss this in terms of race and national difference in chapter 4.) Cyphers capture the dynamics of this coming together across differences while being brought into the folds of a shared culture. *In relation* is perhaps best understood as an already active "otherwise possibility," along the lines that Ashon Crawley has written about, one that reminds us that the normative world is not the only world.[76]

I chose *in relation* both because it is inexact—an idea rather than a self-contained theory—and to invoke a connection to poet and philosopher Édouard Glissant who has been taken up by some Hip Hop scholars because he offers language that captures aspects of Hip Hop sociality in a global context.[77] In *Poetics of Relation*, Glissant delves into a distinct formulation of relationality from a Caribbean perspective that moves away from one of origins or "roots," which likens relation to kinship or bloodline, in favor of "rhizomes" (another borrow from Deleuze and Guattari), which formulates cultural contact that produces an "immeasurable intermixing of cultures."[78] Glissant challenges what he calls "rooted relationality," which gets ideologically linked to European conquest and attempts to bring everyone the world over into its logics and control. Instead he privileges relational identities that focus on shared and expanding knowledge, since such relations are infinite. He writes,

> Relation is learning more and more to go beyond judgments into the unexpected dark of art's upsurgings. Its beauty springs from the stable and the

unstable, from the deviance of many particular poetics and the clairvoyance of a relational poetics. The more things it standardizes into a state of lethargy, the more rebellious consciousness it arouses.[79]

Glissant formulates a multiplicity irreducible to sameness as a "unity-diversity" wherein difference is a fundamental part of the whole rather than something to be eradicated or corrected.[80] As a consequence of the proliferation of connections through difference, cyphers foster horizontal relations across them by staging danced encounters with each other, in the same circle with those that would be Othered. Relationality, thus, manifests in poetics/aesthetics whose "upsurgings" resist standardization, and efforts to contain or control it consequently compel its rebelliousness.

Africanist aesthetics tap into Hip Hop's potential for internal cultural re/generation and expansion through the interplay of tradition and difference, an aesthetic expression of a "unity-diversity," and a complicity with otherness. While I began by exploring alternative femininities improvised in battles, through my focus on b-girls I have come to appreciate the possibilities (freedom?) in breaking's aesthetic sociality, a sociality that is operative even at the scale of the body.

Entering the Circle with Black Pearl

On a brisk night in October, Black Pearl, a b-girl from Amsterdam, brought her own unique brand of fire to a muggy dance club in Braunschweig Germany for a b-girl battle the night before International Battle of the Year in 2006. Watching Black Pearl felt like listening to James Brown. Her frenetic toprock embodied those classic drum breaks. The joyful chorus of a horn section was like her energy, it elevated the groove. She jumped into the sonic landscape and played there. Black Pearl reminded me of a James Brown song because she embodied a foundational sensibility, emblematic of the music pumping through the speakers. And even though I stood well above this battle, my view half obstructed by the railing of the balcony, I could feel her force and was drawn in by it. That is precisely what made her so badass.

Black Pearl wavered between a confrontational approach (common in breaking) and a dismissive attitude (less common for the in-your-face practice), and used her curves to accent her delivery. At moments, she would tauntingly shimmy her shoulders and breasts in her opponent's face to the rhythm or dance too close, daring the opposing b-girl with a sinister smirk; and then with a flick of the wrist and wave of the hand she would turn her back on the opposing crew, switch her hips and sashay away as if she couldn't be bothered (much like the countless times I have seen other Black women do the same). Black Pearl even top-rocked with her arms akimbo, a gesture expressive of Black and particularly Afro-Caribbean womanly impudence.[81] (Arms akimbo is also a Ki-Kongo stance associated with authority, "proclaim[ing] a person ready to accept the challenge of a situation.")[82] Black Pearl's style was already an expression of a certain kind of relational sensibility on a corporeal level, or rather a "corporeal orature" that I interpreted through multiple cultural and gendered approaches to confrontation and aggression.[83]

Despite the intensity of her approach and my general appreciation for her overall style, Black Pearl also stood out because of her physical body. Though slim and athletic—all evident despite her loose-fitting clothes—she was noticeably more curvaceous than the other b-girls competing. As well, she employed those curves distinctly, incorporating her breasts, for example, into her style. By using her curves in her battle arsenal, she ended up troubling commonplace assumptions about breaking bodies. I was not the only one who noticed. Later that evening in a conversation about Black Pearl with Rokafella, one of the battle's judges, she remarked that she would love to train Black Pearl but that she would have to "lose some of those curves." Rok explained how she was told the same thing when developing as a b-girl in the 1990s.[84] I draw attention to Black Pearl's body because there was something about her style that suggested to me that losing her curves might actually work against it.

Critiques about b-girls' bodies tend more so to speak of vulnerabilities and deficiencies, and sometimes express a contrived concern about health and safety. Criticisms about the capacities and vulnerabilities of women's bodies are central to how b-girls have historically been policed and discouraged from breaking.[85] For example, Gunn interviews New Zealand b-girl Sass, who states, "Some people say 'oh you know [girls'] bodies might not be made for it,' or you know, 'they don't have the strength,'" acknowledging how certain Hip Hop characteristics are deemed inaccessible to cisfemale bodies.[86] Chew and Mo highlight how Chinese b-girls are repeatedly told, "Do not get hurt by [breaking]! If a woman becomes infertile, she's in deep shit!"[87] As Latina feminist performance studies scholar Jessica Pabón-Colón puts it, "sexist discourse masquerading as commonsense knowledge about physical capacity" does a certain kind of discursive work that can discourage future b-girls.[88] "Losing those curves" is one example that can become a means to pressure conformity, not just to other b-girls but really to b-boys. It is a discourse that shapes how b-girls learn to break because it assumes a young cismale able-bodily ideal in the practice.[89]

In my interview with Black Pearl the afternoon following her battle, she both drew attention to the challenges her body presented when learning to break and breaking's affirmation of her body as it is:

> I was a dancer, becoming a dancer. And I met my current boyfriend, and ... he was a b-boy in the eighties. And because I was dancing he started going back into b-boying. But I didn't do anything with b-boying, so I was like, "What the heck are you doing?" you know. And yeah, I started to do things. But the first time that I went down to the floor, I didn't really have something like, "Whoa! I want to do b-girling!" because I was heavy as hell, you know? I couldn't do it. I was more into street dancing, Hip Hop dancing, doing tours for artists, and yeah. More like, image-building, concerts, and the like.... I decided that yeah, I would do something more for myself where I could express myself. I don't have to fulfill some kind of image, you know, of how you should be and how you should behave. Like size or hair or all those things. I just wanted to do me and express me. And that's when I started doing it more seriously.[90]

While the challenges of learning to break limited her initial enthusiasm about it, breaking nonetheless offered a path to self-expression that her commercial dance background foreclosed, a path that freed her from certain industry demands. While "image-building" type work meant conformity to music and dance industry standards of size, hair, and "all those things" that had bearing on her income, her remarks about the heaviness she felt while learning to break correlated to doing the dance, her literal capacity to bear her own body weight in a form that relies heavily on upper-body strength. What she found in breaking was a kind of freedom from industry confines, even as she encountered new ones. This is not a capital *F* freedom since it still operates within a set of expectations and regulations that look down on normative feminine qualities, but instead the freedom to play with gendered energies under the expectation that they innovate forms of expression all her own.

Further, breaking opened up understandings about who she was in the world. She reflected on the aforementioned battle, surprised by her own battle approach:

BP: So, it was really ... I was nervous as hell. It's like I couldn't—I didn't even realize I was doing it. So afterwards I was like, "Okay." And I didn't even want to look at the tape. That's something else I don't like when I'm dancing because it's so different from what I think I am, you know? In the sense that a lot of hostility comes free and [*chuckles*] attitude. And I'm like, "Oh my god!" ... But I know that, I'm a little bit confused about what happened yesterday to me so I have to let it sink in a bit more.
IKJ: What are you still thinking about?
BP: The aggressiveness. I look back and I was like really aggressive and I'm not really like, really aggressive, you know. So I was like, "Oh shit!"
IKJ: Actually, I really liked that part. I was like, "Yeah!"
BP: I like it too but I was like, *okaaay*. Yeah, I didn't know it was there, so that's good. That was the confusing part.
IKJ: So it just came out?
BP: Exactly ... I didn't know it was there.[91]

Both Black Pearl and Emiko were somewhat taken aback by how they performed in battles. In this case Black Pearl was "confused" by her overall aggressiveness and was more reflective about how far she deviated from her own sense of self. At the time of the interview, I thought it ironic that the qualities of Black Pearl's dancing that I was most drawn to were, for her, somewhat off-putting. Yet she was also clearly curious about what she *already* possessed, something already "there." Her originality was in part an improvisation through the unfamiliar territory of a self that was unpoliced and unrestrained by the expectations placed on her by commercial industries or society. Black Pearl would tell me at another point in the interview that one can see their "naked truth" in a cypher. In practice, though, that truth seemed to make her nervous and destabilized a certainty about who she "is."

In relation in the Black Pearl example is less about the connection to others literally in the circle than it is about the connection to the multiplicity of selves and the other within; that breaking cyphers bring all of those elements into conversation is key. In some ways, Black Pearl's discussion represents my interpretation of how these competing formulations of relation coexist: the binary may shape her learning, but it was not an all-encompassing force. Black Pearl's battle style, an amalgam of gestures of aggression from multiple repertoires and across various aspects of her identities,[92] was the embodiment of a sensibility that makes room for these multiple repertoires to coexist. Breaking offered her an otherwise way of relating to her own body and to the world through dance. Perhaps too this tells us something about the increasing number of b-girls worldwide who also find something liberating in the culture.

Multiplicity in Breaking Identities

In relation is far from easy. I cannot say that all b-girls (or breakers for that matter) value its possibilities, enact them, or care to. For example, when badass-ness is prescribed as a compulsory stance for b-girls or when it gets treated as a costume donned while hurling racist stereotypes, these are examples of a refusal of the Other. In contrast, *in relation* positions one relative to *another*. It does not fix difference in hierarchical relation but instead enacts a circle of varied and perpetually proliferating social identities brought into mutually supporting ritual practice. This sensibility competes with a Western hegemonic gender binary that constantly reasserts the logics of colonial hierarchies (along racial, national, and gender lines) and their violent othering that evacuates the ensemble of Africanist aesthetics of their radical sociality. As the vehicles for competing epistemological orientations to the world, Africanist aesthetics live by way of the particular people who practice them, their already existing cultural orientations, and the structures of power that contextualize how breaking gets learned and lived.[93] At the same time, cultural identities reassert themselves in and as breaking identities.

Black Pearl's pursuit of dance comes after her attempts to fulfill her immigrant parents' desires for her to have a stable professional life. Under her mother's direction she attended college to study tax consulting, but she was drawn more to dancing. It made no sense to them that a twenty-nine-year-old woman should be "spinning around on a dirty floor" rather than marry and settle down. She assumed their response was indicative of a larger pressure to "be somebody" respectable in society. At the same time and in defense of her dance life, she drew on the cultural inheritances and traditions of the African diaspora, remarking that dancing, storytelling, and "being a strong woman" were parts of "our culture," and thus worth exploring too. As one of the few Black b-girls from Holland, placing Hip Hop within that tradition presented an otherwise foreclosed path, away from her parent's expectations about conventional notions of professional, financial, and social success.

Similarly, b-girl Hanifa Queen's multiple sociocultural identities shaped her breaking identity because, as she would tell me, Hip Hop offered a different mode of femininity than that which was available in other popular Black music-dance genres in her era, like dancehall and R&B.[94] Formerly known as b-girl Bubbles, Hanifa Queen was the subject of a documentary short, *Redder Than Red*, bringing recognition to her as the first UK b-girl in the 1980s.[95] In a 2007 interview with her, she remarked that the filmmakers misunderstood and to some extent misrepresented her story precisely because they did not seem to appreciate why it was meaningful to explicitly name her as a "Jamaican-British daughter of Pan-Africanist immigrant parents." Their efforts to position her within a discourse on "women in Hip Hop" meant evacuating the specificity of her identity rather than its incorporation.[96] She says she insisted on the film's title, which on the surface gestured toward the red track suit she wore in her television debut, but it was also her nod to her Jamaican heritage by way of a Bob Marley lyric, subversively reasserting a more wholistic sense of self.

These examples give us a clear sense of how a breaking identity can inflect or be made sense of through national, racial, and ethnic identities. In reverse, breaking identities can also crosscut cultural identities. Returning to the previously discussed 2006 Summit battle with Emiko, the organizers included a "nations" battle, where breakers from the same countries formed ad hoc super crews and battled one another. Emiko told me about feeling pressured to join the Japanese crew but having felt ambivalent about being identified as a "Japanese b-girl" because, though she had trained in other dance techniques in Japan, Emiko's breaking identity was very much tied to experiences of moving to the US for college, making friends with other international students, and connecting to a broad and diverse network of people that brought her into the folds of American Hip Hop culture. She also felt more affinity for the American crew because, at that time, she was unfamiliar with the breaking scene in Japan. The disjuncture between Emiko's breaking identity and nationality evidences how breaking identities resist the confines of nation and gender as much as they can operate through them.

The preceding examples can perhaps be understood as the lived experiences of "rhizomatic identities." In *The Rhizomes of Blackness: A Critical Ethnography of Hip-Hop Language, Identity, and the Politics of Becoming*, linguistic anthropologist Awad Ibrahim draws on Deleuze and Guattari (rather than Glissant) to explore Hip Hop among Afro-Caribbean and African immigrant youth in Toronto. Ibrahim offers the following: "Rhizomatic identity is a line of flight that welcomes sociality with everything that it brings (the good and the ugly), but there are no guarantees about what its final product might look like, or what maze it has to go through to get there."[97] Key to his definition is a perpetual state of becoming that branches out in varied directions, resists linear hierarchy, and does so in a way that is inclusive of "the good and the ugly" it brings—the liberatory, the profane, the problematic are all part of the cypher.[98] Rhizomatic identities, in Ibrahim's formulation, is marked by uncertainty and the commingling with rather than the excision of its unsavory parts. These are preconditions for a welcoming sociality. B-girls' breaking identities and the paths that got them there are a material manifestation of rhizomatic identities.

If breaking challenges us to conceive of our relations to each other in expansive and rhizomatic ways, then *in relation* deprioritizes hierarchies and control in favor of horizontal relations made real in practice. When we focus on b-girls in battle cyphers, those aesthetics reveal connections that, even when expressed in binaristic terms, also operate in excess of them. I call that excess *in relation*. Emiko, Black Pearl, and Hanifa Queen have multiple cultural identities that inform how they experience breaking. Hip Hop did not amplify their existences as women over everything else, nor did it supplant the specificity of their identities. Instead, breaking was a meaningful way of living those particularities (see Fig. 3.2). In turn, practitioners recognized their relationality to each other (and themselves) under new terms. In other words, the "other" is always also them, and negotiating difference, internal or external, is part of the game.

Conclusion

> Hip-hop dances surely arise from this tradition of dance that defies expectation, dances that confirm something beyond reach (freedom?) but present within the capacity of the physicality of doing.
>
> —Thomas DeFrantz, "Hip-Hop Habitus v.2.0"[99]

In this chapter, a deeper study of b-girls' physical practice of Hip Hop's subversiveness and the freedom drive of Africanist aesthetics reveals the

Figure 3.2 Film launch flyer for *All the Ladies Say*, documentary directed by Rokafella, 2009. The documentary captures how seven women, practitioners across several Hip Hop dance genres, work collectively to promote the growth of women in Hip Hop.

contours of a new social arrangement made possible by dance. The force of the unforeseen in cyphering's participatory (yet conditional) openness makes room for a kind of freedom in physical practice, along the lines of DeFrantz's "(freedom?)." Parenthetically hushed and punctuated to leave the term unsettled-yet-in-reach, a kind of freedom is attainable through actual physical practice, at least in moments. By centering Africanist aesthetics, we move beyond superficial expressions of b-girls' badass-ness to a deeper understanding of how that badass-ness is attuned to the dissonance of a complex social environment shaped by both interlocking structures of power and its own internal cultural imperatives.

Chapter 4 continues in the vein of sociality and considers how differences in race and nationality get invoked, downplayed, and negotiated in discourse, in the cypher, and in a global breaking context.

Circles or Cyphers

Volkswagenhalle in Braunschweig, Germany, 19 October 2006
I have traveled to Europe, following a circuit of breaking events in search of cyphers. After England and Switzerland, I am now in Braunschweig, Germany, for International Battle of the Year (IBOTY), the culmination of over a dozen preliminary breaking competitions worldwide. IBOTY inspires two types of responses: some aspire to compete in it at least once; others see it is an Olympic-sized spectacle that treats breaking as a sport more than a dance. My initial feelings fall somewhere in between.

I get to Volkswagenhalle a few hours before the event and am immediately impressed by the 126,000-square-foot arena. A massive line grows, zigzagging from the front doors, across the entire length of the hall to within a few feet of the street. Vendors walk around selling pretzels, and a large jeep with Red Bull Energy Drink logos on it blasts familiar soul, funk, Hip Hop, and Latin freestyle music. In many ways this is what I imagine global Hip Hop to be, brand new yet familiar, and expansive. I walk through the throngs of people from all over the world who stand in line, and gravitate to the jeep's large speakers when I see a couple hundred people gathered, their backs to me, but clearly in a circle. The lack of crowd response isn't yet meaningful, but I am certain that at least something is going on, and I want to be a part of it. I make a beeline toward the circle and easily maneuver my way to a better view, but confusion and disappointment quickly replace anticipation and curiosity. No one is dancing.

The first person I see enter, a minute or so after I arrive, skips his way toward the middle with a sheepish grin on his face. Without transition or attention to the music he maneuvers into a one-handed handstand, and pumps his legs up and down to hop on it. He executes this move (called a hand-hop) well enough, but after several hops he eventually loses his balance and tumbles to the ground. So, he tries again . . . and then again in a monotonous display of twenty hand-hops before walking the several feet back to the circle's borders. Then again, circles are rarely so large as to warrant that many steps. It is over twenty feet across, and in the center are four four-feet by seven-feet thick cardboard pieces *(a stereotypically common breaking prop), taped together on the ground and immediately surrounded by several feet of cobbled sidewalk. I notice that the empty space is greater than the dance space the boards create. It is an intimidating circle to enter. And as he leaves, I feel his mix of embarrassment and accomplishment for even trying (see Fig. 4.1).*

Other breakers enter but the vibe stays the same. Each new dancer focuses on executing a single move, a head spin or a contortionist style freeze. Many fall, then attempt their move again, yet no one actually dances. The lull between dancers resumes. We clap respectfully and continue to wait and watch an empty circle. Those of us in the circle distance ourselves from the boards. And that's exactly the problem. It's clear that the circle preceded the dancing, a structure put in place for a show. We obediently play audience and wait for a performance that never happens.

It reminds me more of a hitter's circle in that the arrangement is for an audience who stands well out of the way and waits to be entertained. Hitters, groups of street dancers who perform in places where tourists gather, make that happen through a set of common practices. The key is to plan your show down to the

Figure 4.1 B-boy entering the (noncypher) circle, outside of International Battle of the Year, Braunschweig, Germany, 19 October 2006.

jokes the MC tells to get the crowd relaxed and the money flowing. Dancers do a few eight-counts of uncomplicated group choreography (maybe ten minutes), where each member of the group briefly performs a solo, usually demonstrating a particular talent: someone who specializes in flips, another in extreme balance positions, another with a nice body who dances shirtless. They're led by MCs, charming and charismatic individuals who gather the audience. Like a circus barker, they make a few jokes, tell the audience of the amazing feats they are about to witness, and make appeals to neighborhood pride to start the donations: "We got five dollars from Jersey! Hey! Ten dollars from Connecticut! They're making you look bad, New York!" The goal is to minimize physical labor while maximizing the entertainment in order to get through a day's work. The shows can be fun but are redundant, and they accomplish their goal every twenty minutes or so. After the money is collected, the old crowd is ushered out, and a new one is coaxed in.

In contrast, here we gather for no other reason than the false expectation that cyphers are merely the sum of their parts (e.g., cardboard, big speakers, onlookers) rather than environments nurtured in dialogic exchanges. Stripped of call and response, of hungry dancers, and will to elevate, it's just a circle. I stick it out for a few minutes, but I am too agitated to stay. This is not what I traveled thousands of miles for.

4

Dancing Global Hip Hop

Negotiating Difference and Tradition in Cyphers

One of breaking's defining qualities is that it draws in people from across various types of differences (e.g., national, gender, racial, age, religion, etc.), and on its surface, that is what the circle in Germany *looked* like. That was not, however, how it felt. What cyphers appear to be on their surface—the things we see like the speakers and the cardboard—loses something essential when its aesthetic sensibilities are ignored. Without call and response as an organizing logic of exchange, we were just a hodgepodge of random people watching cardboard. While up until that point it had not yet occurred to me that someone might not know how to cypher, in looking for them in different places I should have assumed that I would inevitably find one like this: with little evident Africanist thread, no driving spirit behind our circling, nothing that encapsulated why differences in global Hip Hop can get worked on and worked through in cyphers.[1]

Noticeably diverse in its demographics, in many ways breaking is like the Benetton ad of global Hip Hop, dominated by images of multicultural, young, athletic, cool kids dancing together in in-your-face ways that nonetheless can end in handshakes. Those ads fetishized diversity, offering an image of *transcending* difference and glossing over the conflicts, tensions, and frictions of folks actually coming together in practice. This chapter is about global Hip Hop through the lens of cyphers, specifically exploring the ones occupied by dancers from all over the world, and informed by their relationship to Africanist aesthetics as a calibrating force in global Hip Hop. Cyphering encapsulates the ways that difference manifests in discourse and dance, and how it gets negotiated, worked on, and worked through in global Hip Hop.

The "global" is a heterogeneous conceptual frame composed of various interconnected forces that are at once economic, political, social, and cultural.[2] In *Friction: An Ethnography of Global Connection*, anthropologist Anna L. Tsing writes about the global through social projects coming from "spatially far-flung collaborations and interactions," which produce "contingent collaborations" between disparate groups based on overlapping interests, without ever guaranteeing shared goals.[3] That is, just because people come together does not mean that they stop being culturally distinct from one another. Thus, "frictions" inevitably ensue. Cyphers, which often symbolically represent global Hip Hop, capture the "creative frictions" that can arise when people gather in shared practice.[4] And while specific cultural orientations shape how and in what manner people enter the cypher, these rituals nonetheless remain spaces wherein practitioners negotiate difference through dance to get into a shared groove. Africanist aesthetics are central to how cyphers allow breakers to negotiate their differences by grooving together.

Rather than global by itself, this chapter proposes a *global diasporic* frame that explicitly connects Hip Hop to a constellation of Africanist aesthetics in breaking cyphers and their accompanying epistemological lessons. In *The Practice of Diaspora: Literature, Translation, and the Rise of Black Internationalism*, literary scholar Brent Hayes Edwards argues that diasporas are strategic international unities that mobilize distinct groups, "where things are related, as much through their differences as through their similarities."[5] He proposes that diaspora "necessarily involves a process of linking or connecting across gaps—a practice we might term *articulation*."[6] It picks up on the definition of articulation that means "joining up ... as in the limbs of the body, or an anatomical structure,"[7] Edwards's definition of diaspora amplifies the synchronicity of relation and difference. In cyphers, such a synchronicity is precisely where friction can spark *and* where radical energy exchanges can begin.

Within the transnational social field of breaking, diaspora speaks to how Africanist aesthetics mobilize a set of influences that have been historically subject to violent erasure and continue to be aggressively invisibilized. From a global diasporic perspective, though, Africanist aesthetics are evident, circulating, and influential to how people learn to cypher worldwide.

What Is the "Global" in Global Hip Hop?

Among practitioners, a common saying that explains Hip Hop's global reach is that "music is universal." In an article on "translocal style communities," linguistic anthropologist and Hip Hop scholar H. Samy Alim notes that "music as universal" is a meaningful concept among Hip Hop enthusiasts and practitioners because it "reveals a sense of belonging to a community despite differences in linguistic, ethnic, and national identity."[8] Buddha Stretch, renowned Hip Hop choreographer and member of Mop Top Crew, puts his own spin on it, stating, "Music is the universal language; dance is its interpreter."[9] Though logic suggests that a "universal language" would not need an interpreter, his tweak offers a *kinesthetic* interpretation of a sonic mode and dancers' multi-lingual/corporeal capacities.

Within a growing body of literature and documentaries on various regional and national scenes beyond the United States, the global in Hip Hop studies tends to manifest as a collection of sites that align themselves with Hip Hop in distinct and yet familiar ways. This literature demonstrates Hip Hop's expansive reach and offers a unique body of materials with which to consider questions of global connection in general, through a Hip Hop lens. Some work, like cultural anthropologist Ian Condry's *Hip Hop Japan: Rap and the Paths of Cultural Globalization*, deals expressly with globalization. He connects the global to the local through places of momentary performances (e.g., the *genba*, meaning nightclub), an approach I adopt in looking at cyphers. In doing so he shifts from a focus on flows of globalization to expressions or performances of it in local places that transform "borrowed styles" into "domestic versions."[10] A tension in the global cypher arises then when those domestic versions veer away from some of Hip Hop's epistemological foundations.

Japan is a unique example. While there are what music and media scholar Jason Ng calls "cross-cultural intermediaries," subcultural agents who facilitate local-global programming in sites like Tokyo, there is also a competing, more insular Hip Hop scene.[11] In a 2018 online article, writer Tracy Jones contends that Japan's Hip Hop scenes follow two trajectories that do not frequently intersect: "foreign" organized events with a mix of nationalities (including Japanese participants), and "Japanese" Hip Hop events that have a "shut door" policy. The author links that policy to the country's colonial history in Southeast Asia and "Japan's xenophobia and its rejection of multiculturalism."[12] Researching the Japanese scene, Hip Hop scholar Dexter Thomas concurs, stating that "one aspect of Japanese hip-hop that appears to have largely escaped academic attention is the fact that while hip-hop culture is generally assumed to be anti-establishment, Japanese hip-hop is at times explicitly nationalist, or even racist."[13] Describing the scene as "homogenous," Elite Force dancer and choreographer Brooklyn Terry, who has lived in Japan since 2008 and taught a generation of Hip Hop dancers in Tokyo, adds, "For me, that's not what hip-hop is. I was fortunate to grow up in a time when hip-hop was just sprouting in New York. The beauty of hip-hop is that it's never been homogenous. It's always been this and that, all together to create this new thing."[14] The overall commentary suggests that the "domestic version," which took these borrowed styles in service to a nationalist sensibility, created an insularity that then compelled Brooklyn Terry and others to create their own events. Global Hip Hop is not a seamless multiculturalism.

Rather than "borrowing," studies of Hip Hop in Africa and the diaspora emphasize exchange, porous borders, and continued evidence of mutual influence historically over time. In dance scholar Halifu Osumare's study, *The Hiplife in Ghana: West African Indigenization of Hip-Hop*, Hip Hop reinvigorates an ongoing historical exchange between Ghanaians and African Americans. She adopts the phrase "the arc of mutual inspiration" to capture the back-and-forth influence of music and dance, linking this concept to poet and historian Kamau Brathwaite's "bridges of sound."[15] In his poem "Jah," Brathwaite parallels the path of slavers' ships that transported Africans to the Americas during the transatlantic slave trade with the sonic bridges erected by the transport of records and the movement of radio waves that continued to connect the ancestors of this trade to each other through music.[16] Osumare emphasizes how Hip Hop and hiplife (a fusion of Ghanaian twentieth-century highlife and contemporary Hip Hop "beats and styles")[17] are contemporary expressions of African and African diasporic "cross-fertilization," as either arc or bridge, that "transcends the hip-hop 'origin' question" at the root of a borrowing discourse because the question fails to speak to Hip Hop's *circulation* within the African diaspora.[18]

The authors of *Tha Global Cipha: Hip Hop Culture and Consciousness* also invoke Brathwaite's "bridges of sound" specifically to describe the "musical and stylistic borders" between Hip Hop culture and other African diasporic music genres, like reggaeton and dancehall.[19] James Spady, H. Samy Alim, and Samir Meghelli argue that, as metaphors, cyphers encapsulate all of the complexities of the "global-cultural-linguistic-musical flow" of Hip Hop transnationally.[20] Within the context of diaspora, cyphers mirror "bridges of sound" as sites of exchange that also act as structuring forces bridging local places to each other. (This consequently echoes dark matter's structuring capacities, bridging galaxies.) As the global-cultural-linguistic- *movement*-musical flows of Hip Hop branch out rhizomatically, cypher practices in particular build bridges to sites outside of the African diaspora by way of the Africanist aesthetics embedded in them.

Regardless of whether one identifies as part of the diaspora, breaking cyphers are part of an African diasporic continuum of expressive practices that socialize participants into a constellation of Africanist aesthetics. Thus, in practices like cyphering, a global diasporic frame is one that recognizes global Hip Hop *in relation* to the African diaspora. With that said, whether Africanist aesthetics are known or valued (even as Hip Hop sensibilities) is relative, especially when those aesthetics are talked about indirectly and through discourses on movement that consequently are made to bear the weight of other internal frictions.

Old School versus New School: Moves as a Discourse on Difference

Many organized battles are themselves microcosms of negotiations over differences in race, ethnicity, and nationality. Large-scale breaking events tend to be international in attendance, regardless of where they take place. The frictions within global Hip Hop play out in precisely these spaces. Since dance is the common or bridge language at such events, conversations about movement, style, and technique happen more often than discussions about global breaking's internal differences, negotiations with change, and the pull of tradition. Thus, discussions about the movement often stand in for the tensions that inevitably arise across differences.

Gamblerz versus the Mighty Zulu Kingz

One prime example of how movement can hold discourses on difference was the August 2007 Ten-Year Anniversary of Freestyle Sessions in Los Angeles,[21] a two-day event that ended with a final crew battle between the Mighty Zulu Kingz (MZK) and Gamblerz Crew. As I stood among hundreds of sweaty onlookers, craning our necks to see over the crowds to the stage, two ten-member crews took over opposite wings of the stage while the DJ stood behind his deck toward the back, next to a row of judges who had the best view. Those on the stage collectively formed a semicircle, and the audience below completed a kind of cypher, albeit uneven and dual-tiered.

Each crew was formidable in their own way. On one side was MZK, headed by Ness4, who is known for his charismatic and ferocious battle attitude.[22] The crew has members worldwide, but on that day their crew was a racially mixed group of predominately American b-boys, a group of Black, Latino, and one Asian member. In part because of the crew's foundations in New York and their being under Ness's direction, MZK are typically thought of as "old school," meaning they gave as much attention to individual style, toprocking, and burns, as they do to acrobatics and power moves. The strength and prevalence (or lack thereof) of power moves in a dancer's repertoire is one of the deciding factors in whether or not one is considered old or new school.

Opposite MZK was Gamblerz Crew, an internationally renowned group from South Korea. Having won International Battle of the Year in 2004, Gamblerz was consistently one of the top crews in the world for several years running. Though they were once criticized for overemphasizing power moves rather than the dance of breaking, they have since developed a style of a nearly seamless transition between contortionist movement, power moves, acrobatics, well-rehearsed routines, and toprocking—though they retain their signature emphasis on the former approaches. The fusion of styles helps to account for their being labeled "new school." Perhaps nationality plays a role here too, insofar as "new school" at the time also referred to the stylistic development of European and Asian crews, which were heavily influenced by footage that emphasized spectacular moves for the camera rather than the dynamic exchanges of live events.

The language of old and new school is further evidenced in each crew's approach. MZK members brought a sporadic, jagged aggression to their battles. When seasoned with burns, the uniqueness of each member's style, and an incomparable competitiveness, MZK's power was in their capacity to physically express a bravado and intensity that exemplified their demeanor as a crew. They held themselves above their opponents, mocking them at every turn, perhaps to get in their opponents' heads. At times, they used humor to attract the audience and, at other, times their unapologetic attack was enough to garner new fans and turn off others. Whether in a battle or not, MZK explicitly explored modes of vicious attack, performatively displaying fits of frenzied passion and frustration while evoking as much from their spectators. For example, at one point, a b-boy hit the floor with hurried footwork. And as he glided from the center of the stage back to his crew, he pantomimed shooting an arrow at Gamblerz just as another crew member dove forward from behind him as if becoming the arrow. Then he completed MZK's set with an eruption of flips, footwork, and a performative spray of gunshots to the line of Gamblerz in front of him, similar to an execution in an old black-and-white gangster movie. Their energy inspired a mischievous joy.

In contrast, Gamblerz Crew had a more subdued aggressiveness, expressed through their consistent level of talent with comparatively less display of ego. They drew the audience in by letting each member's expertise build anticipation for the next move. Gamblerz capitalized on their range of styles, allowing them to fill the space of the stage and the time of their set. They frequently utilized group routines to bring these elements together. Gamblerz countered MZK's speed by slowing down the pace. Instead of a machine gun attacking an enemy, they put on a show for the audience. They tended more to pique curiosity and a sense of wonder. For example, at one point a breaker propelled himself into a series of spins and flips ending by taking off his hat in time for another member, who was ready for the handoff while doing a one-handed handstand, to take the hat and commence his own set of footwork, only to pass the hat again to yet another member who leapt into a sequence of acrobatics. The audience moved from one performer to another by following the hat until the last breaker finished his set and placed the hat on his head. The routine demanded that attention be paid as if to a story unfolding as the hat was passed, introducing each new breaker. Their performance was more choreographed and was decidedly less aggressive than MZK's. It was also clear that they planned for multiple sets of spectators—judges and audience—and accounted for them all in an effort to entertain and impress rather than dominate in battle.

When the Mighty Zulu Kingz were announced the victors, it surprised more than a few. At this particular battle, the terms of the debate—"old school" and "new school"—reverberated throughout the room. I heard some suggest that MZK won, not because they were better, but because the judges favored an "old school" approach. The judges were the primary target of ridicule by a group of disgruntled attendees. The judges were themselves b-boys with several decades of experience between them, though authority never hinders the unconvinced from questioning the judges' decision. Maybe, some grumbled, the judges needed to learn to appreciate the new school approach. The buzz around the room suggested that a significant contingent of the audience had reached their own conclusion altogether: Gamblerz crew was robbed. And for those who disagreed with the judges' decision, they collectively displayed their discontent by chanting, "Gamblerz! Gamblerz!" after the official decision was announced. Not everyone in the large, open room followed suit, but there was enough support to make their point heard, literally.[23]

These vocal criticisms and debates are typical, as battle cyphers are highly contested spaces wherein aesthetic standards are repeatedly asserted, rejected, or accepted through competition. Winners of battles are not simply determined by what the crowd finds pleasing but an expression of the judges' expertise, which has bearing on breaking culture as a whole. They themselves are not unbiased, and their aesthetic preferences directly influence who wins the money at a battle. Despite their noticeable differences, old and new school are not always clear-cut, especially at this level where both crews exhibit masterful skill. Within the framework of their preferences, judges have a great deal to consider. Can soulful versatility in dancing stand up against a single daring power move? Will contorting your body like a pretzel lose out to toprocking because the latter was more on the beat? How does an impressive power repertoire but weak footwork fare against weak power and impressive footwork? There is one answer to all of these questions: it depends. Judges make decisions based on their tastes, preferences, the principles they hold dear, and a discerning expertise developed after years of practice; yet these decisions are never the *final* word. Breakers and their fans continue to debate and argue over battles for months, particularly online where message boards and video upload sites like YouTube allow anyone with a computer or smartphone to weigh in.

While I certainly have my own opinions about these questions and even on this battle, my analytic interests are in things unsaid that undergird the premise of these arguments in the first place. Those judgments are reflective of more than just differences in dance styles and technique. Aesthetic differences are regularly symbolic of different perspectives on the art of breaking. Whether coming from judges or spectators, an often unspoken aspect of discussions about style are about the tensions between maintaining some sort of tradition alongside its growth and innovation. For example, one judge's critique of Gamblerz was that they used too many routines rather than improvising in a raw exchange. At the same time, the increasing importance of organized battles in the scene undoubtedly shapes how the dance has changed over time, with more and more attention paid to the elements that would best secure a win (e.g., impressing a panel of judges or an audience over battling an opponent). Thus, for judges who recognize that their decisions have broader implications beyond the immediate battle, something specific like the value placed on improvisation in a call-and-response dynamic carries more weight than a spectator may suspect. By extension, the inevitable aesthetic variations produced out of breaking's global context are not simply stylistic, but the locus of concerns about cultural shifts away from breaking's core principles.

Moreover, discussions on moves were also then burdened with the messy, problematic scripts people carry about difference. Critiques of Gamblerz style, for example, were often couched in terms of ethnoracial difference. Over the course of my field research, there were multiple instances when people echoed the xenophobic language of "Yellow peril," suggesting that "they are taking over," in reference to the fact that Korean and Japanese crews had become the world's top-ranked crews. Moreover, Gamblerz along with other East Asian crews have been described as exceedingly technical and precise, dancing without passion or the character expressed through imperfections in form. These critiques bank on stereotypes about Asian people excelling in highly technical arenas. To whatever degree East Asian crews may at one time have overemphasized power moves, *as many international crews did*, it is no longer the case today. Yet Asian stereotypes persist in people's language about difference.

With MZK it was a different story. Some believed the judges' decision reflected national favoritism as the battle was on US soil. While the criticism was that MZK was arrogant and foolishly self-entitled even in the face of certain defeat, this actually often describes aspects of a breaking stance in general as a battle attitude. Members of MZK, though, were being accused of exhibiting a deluded sense of American exceptionalism in terms of believing themselves to be the best despite both past defeats and the growing artistic appreciation for the so-called new school. The underlying idea extends to the American judges who were criticized for being chauvinistic and thus behind the times. Essentially, American b-boys and b-girls become representative of America's imperial power. This critique resonates in a unique way, considering that the majority of MZK members on stage were of Puerto Rican descent, with other Latino breakers, one African American b-boy, and one Asian b-boy. Since Puerto Rico is, in fact, an American colony, this stereotype is ironic at best, and culturally oblivious at worst. It attempts to undermine a sense of American cultural ownership of breaking in a global context when many claim the dance as their own, too. Yet the implication of American exceptionalism crafts all Americans—despite ethnoracial differences—as a single, homogenous group, a blatant disregard for the US's own internal racial and colonial frictions.

While the languages of ethnoracial and national difference are employed to mark distinctions in style, they hit on a more general anxiety about breaking as a global phenomenon. Within these critiques, ethnoracial differences are downplayed and national differences are inflated, but they all play roles in how this battle was interpreted. Though not every battle yields this degree of debate, they all entail layers of meaning wherein difference comes into play.

Negotiating Tradition

Africanist aesthetics reveal another layer of information in the battle between Gamblerz and MZK, beyond the role that improvisation and call and response played in the judges' immediate decision. The recurrence of an "old/new school" debate, sometimes rephrased in terms of conservative versus progressive and other times power versus style, provides insight on that additional layer. In a 1998 article on the subject b-boy Krazy Kujo succinctly discusses the terms of these varied debates: "The debate goes something like this: B-boys who concentrate primarily on power moves say that what they do is more difficult than footwork, and B-boys who concentrate on footwork say that power people can't dance and have no creativity, and that they are just a bunch of wannabe gymnasts."[24] While some call out the overall reductiveness of these debates and conclude that both sides matter,[25] the debate itself and its variations also carry qualities that speak to history, current values, and the future of the culture.

Power versus style seems to have come into prominence in the wake of breaking's worldwide circulation, especially via mass-media outlets that played a pivotal role in what aspects of breaking were adopted and explored and what fell by the wayside.[26] Despite breaking's New York City roots, its exposure on film and television in the early 1980s helped to propel it across the US and internationally, with the most dynamic moves drawing the most attention. Swipes or windmills, backspins, headspins, and other such moves acted as visual soundbites, telling young viewers just how exciting, vibrant, and cool this new dance form was. Some West Coast breakers, like Lil' Cesar of Air Force Crew in Los Angeles, suggest that with little else to go on than the bits and pieces they caught on television or in films, his crew was drawn to the aerial moves of the dance and developed a style based more on power.

Thus, many credit the West Coast with elevating power moves, though this is debatable and not a narrative everyone espouses.[27] If one agrees with this narrative trajectory of breaking's changing aesthetics, funky and original footwork remains largely an East Coast trademark and thus a sign of an old school approach, but it extends to represent an "American" style as power eventually became a more pronounced staple of breaking in Europe and Asia.[28]

Similar to Lil' Cesar's story, generations of breakers outside of the US focused on developing aerial and acrobatic skills, citing a similar attraction to power that they saw in footage, films, stage tours, and so on. This helps account for why "power" became indicative of a newer form of breaking, initially referring to a developing West Coast approach in the 1980s, and then to growing scenes in Europe and Asia through the nineties, as its popularity was waning in the US. The global dispersal of the dance through staged competitions also encouraged a power-versus-style debate. As I understand it (and experienced in the field), practitioners in breaking scenes outside of the US sought out elder American breakers featured in the early circulating footage to learn from, and, upon seeing breaking's evolution, those OGs reasserted the style side of the dance for the sake of its completeness.

Whether old/new school or style/power, in the midst of inevitable change, tradition gets perpetually reasserted and in multiple terms that live across generations. The term "foundation" best captures how breaking continually reorients or attunes itself to its own sense of traditions as an essential dimension of practice. In *Foundation: B-Boys, B-Girls, and Hip-Hop Culture in New York*, ethnomusicologist and Hip Hop scholar Joseph Schloss defines "foundation" as "a concept that combines the physical knowledge of specific movements with a profound historical and philosophical context in which to place those moves."[29] Schloss further writes,

> *Foundation* is a term used by b-boys and b-girls to refer to an almost mystical set of notions about b-boying that is passed from teacher to student. In addition to the actual physical movements, it includes the history of the movements and the form in general, strategies for how to improvise, philosophy about dance in general, musical associations, and a variety of other subjects. The idea that a core b-boy philosophy should be so important that it requires a special term says a great deal about the dance and why it is so significant in the lives of its practitioners.[30]

The adoption of a term whose literal meaning refers to the primary, load-bearing base of a building is powerful. In fact, in conversation with various breakers recovering from serious injuries—everything from torn ligaments to spinal infections—each recounted returning to foundation to relearn the dance and subsequently deepening their relationship to it, valuing it more as a result. Foundation is mystical insofar as it entails a seemingly nebulous set of standards, though I would argue that Africanist aesthetics ground that mysticism in concrete enactments. The type of knowledge passed on from student to teacher as foundation—the "musical associations," improvisation, and philosophies about dancing—necessitates that each generation of breakers renegotiate their relationship to breaking's traditions, thereby reasserting foundation's essentialness to the physical practice. In a global context, what "foundation" means and in how much regard it is held is mixed but enduring.

For some breakers, too much change is a major point of concern when thinking about what the dance will become. How long before Hip Hop culture becomes a sad shadow of its former self? Is it already? Moreover, even in its demise, who makes it in the annals of Hip Hop history? Historical precedence offers multiple examples of erasing Black people, forms of life, and histories when Black expressive cultures become pop cultural phenomena.[31] (Rock 'n' roll is an excellent example.) Foundation conceptualizes an ongoing dialogue with history and tradition from within a practice that also hinges on the expectation that one innovate and be original. Perhaps, then, foundation entails a practice of always circling back to and through tradition as a formative dimension of the change it nurtures. That too, is an Africanist aesthetics. As American studies scholar Gena Caponi states, "The Africanist aesthetic constantly pressures one to innovate within a traditional structure—a rhythmic pattern, for instance—so that each musical event blends history and the contemporary approach."[32]

Though critiques about the judges in the MZK-Gamblerz battle imply that perhaps they just had outmoded ideas, their decisions are wrapped up in foundation. And in a context wherein Hip Hop gets taken up in as many ways as there are rhizomatic offshoots of global Hip Hop, what breakers share across differences is necessarily subject to those differences, which, in cypher exchanges enacts even greater differentiation (see Fig. 4.2). Some of those offshoots amplify or articulate with Africanist aesthetics, and others move in whole new directions, which to some judges is precisely when and where they should intervene. Thus, foundation and cyphering's Africanist

Figure 4.2 International Battle cypher, Floor Lords 25th Anniversary 2006, Boston, MA, 6 August 2006. I encountered a number of breakers from outside the US who travel a circuit of battles along the East Coast of the US during the summers.

aesthetics constantly reassert sensibilities that pressure the expanse of differentiation to reorient to a core set of sensibilities, acting as a cultural compass in an increasingly differentiated performance field.

Dancing Global Hip Hop

Cyphering as a practice always builds in ways to circle back, not only to breaking's traditions but to one's own culture too. Repeatedly, people articulate their commitment to Hip Hop in terms that resonate with their own already present traditions, connecting Hip Hop to new cultural terrains through salient points of aesthetic overlap. Put simply, Hip Hop becomes meaningful for people in part because they interpret it through their own cultural lenses, routing it through notions of already familiar tradition. For example, in the documentary by Vee Bravo and Loira Limbal titled *Estilo*

Hip Hop, MC Guerrillero cites a connection between rhyming couplets in Chilean poetry traditions to rap, not only to explain his connection to Hip Hop but also to deepen a Chilean approach to Hip Hop.[33] A similar sentiment was expressed in another documentary, Benj Bing's *Mongolian Bling*, when epic song vocalist Bayarmagnai explains that practices of "intellectual debates avoiding physically fighting" already existed in Mongolia among the young and old people with challenges like, "*Do you have the bladder to attack me?*" He adds, "If you improvise and enrich those expressions with beats and modern instruments and call that Hip Hop, then I'm 100 percent sure the Hip Hop originated in Mongolia from traditional culture."[34] Historical inaccuracy aside, what he recognizes in his own traditions resonated with what he could recognize in the underlying cultural imperatives of local expressions of Hip Hop in Ulaanbaatar, Mongolia. This happens in dance too.

The following examples demonstrate how Hip Hop's Africanist aesthetics bridge to other cultures through cyphers as ritual points of connection. I argue that notions of how one is *supposed to* cypher return us back to its Africanist aesthetic sensibilities.

Bridging Cultures through Hip Hop's Africanist Aesthetics

During a 2012 trip to Toronto, I spoke with several breakers of various backgrounds who often talked about Hip Hop through terms that connected to their own cultural backgrounds. For example, in a phone interview with Q Rock, an Anishinaabe rapper, b-boy, and graffiti artist from Nipissing First Nation, he had this to say about his first cypher at six years old: "Aww man, I'm Native Indian. My first cypher was called a powwow."[35] When I inquired about the correlation, he first noted aesthetic similarities in the 1970s breaking style to the dances he saw at powwows—there were a lot of "drops and spins."[36] He further elaborated that when he sought out inspiration for making his breaking style more original, he drew on inspirations from Fancy Dancing. And while acknowledging the "totally different" vibes of each site (Hip Hop's energy was more informed by an aesthetic of "cool"), both sites of dancing overlapped because they were about "spirit." That is, in fact, the meaning of his traditional name, Spirit Dancer. He went on: "I was born to dance. I need to dance. It makes my spirit feel balanced. It creates a peace. . . . That's an approach I was taught from birth. I couldn't grass-dance on the concrete. There were dances, though, and I picked the one that was appropriate for me. It was meant to be."[37] Breaking, a dance for concrete, converges with his culture in that both restored balance and peace.

During that same trip to Toronto, b-boy Frostalino remarked that his first experiences with cyphering reminded him of the Portuguese community's gatherings, parades, and public processions in Canada. He hypothesized that perhaps he was preconditioned to appreciate cyphers because of the Portuguese church festivals, "particularly the ones from San Miguel, my island," that he grew up attending.[38] Both cyphers and these processions exuded a strong sense of community that cultivated a bond among the whole. Those festivals featured processions that included brass and drum sections that performed in short spurts, with his father telling him to "listen to the drums. Listen to them play. Watch them play."[39] The story suggested that the aesthetic qualities that spoke to Frostalino's own upbringing in personal and cultural ways laid groundwork for his appreciation for Hip Hop's elements; that perhaps his father prepared him for Hip Hop by teaching him to listen more deeply to the rhythm.[40] Both Q Rock and Frostalino make subtle references to identifiable Africanist aesthetics as resonant points of connection with their own cultural orientations.

B-girl Hanifa Queen of Wolverhampton, England, explicitly connects cyphering with her Jamaican background. In a 2007 Skype interview, she told me about the cypher's relationship to her Jamaican immigrant community in the 1980s.

> As an immigrant, the circle was always there for us. We were in the process of cyphering already. Before b-boying hit the UK, we had cyphers doing our own Jamaican dances. We always had a cypher where each individual would go into the middle. So, the cypher, for us, is not a b-boying practice.
>
> I don't know if you understand about the Black British culture. When I'm saying Black British I mean, like, those who were born of immigrants like myself. People don't realize our culture is completely different from the white British. We are completely different from our own Jamaican family members too. When we're in public with the British, our behavior . . . everything changes just to fit in with them, with the white British culture. In Jamaica being ruled by the British, it was not difficult to fit in [in Britain], but *our culture* didn't fit in with the British. There were no Black clubs back then. We had the Caribbean Center. We had cyphers. So not being able to fit in meant we'd lost a kind of cultural identity and we had to find it back again in the cypher. Because our identity was restored in the cypher.[41]

As a child of immigrants and raised in Britain rather than Jamaica—distinct from both her parents and the white Brits—Hip Hop cyphers allowed her to embody a Jamaican cultural identity in a British context. She points out the capacity for cyphering to *resignify* in and through Hip Hop rather than originate in Hip Hop. Hanifa Queen more explicitly names the blackness of that practice, and how much that lent to her sense of self and perhaps too for other first- and second-generation Jamaican immigrants in Britain. Similar to the others I interviewed, Hip Hop was a new cultural context to encapsulate something that was already there, and that deepened and refreshed her cultural identity. Cyphers resonate with or are interpreted within contexts of already present traditions that bridge Hip Hop to new cultural terrains through salient points of overlap between the two. Which is to say that cyphers can be at once familiar and new. Yet cyphering's anchor in Africanist aesthetic principles remains, such that any correctives in the adopted cultural milieu are to make one's approach *more* Africanist.

While Q Rock, Hanifa Queen, and Frostalino draw attention to the more layered ways their relationship to breaking was already culturally resonant, Filipino American b-boy Profo Won explicitly addresses how those influences are then massaged into a breaking approach. In our 2009 interview, Profo Won talked about the differences in cyphering on a (then) recent trip to Korea and the Philippines with his twin brother, popper Rob Nasty. Profo Won described the differences between the two countries in a manner that gave him room to attest to what Filipino culture already has. For example, he explained that while Korea was "technically advanced"—meaning that they had the technique down and noting how much he was learning from them— the breakers he taught and trained with at the time were more accustomed to formal competitions and were only just starting to explore cyphering for its own sake. To Profo Won, excessive competition stifled freedom in the dance.

In contrast, Profo Won stated that "the Philippines kind of has a vibe, but their technique is not as good."[42] When pressed about what that meant, he specified that, where he was, people did not seem to know the etiquette of cyphers: everybody entered the circle at once and they did not focus on or give energy to the individual in the center. While their approach may have needed tweaking, he felt that they already had the right energy, which he attributed to something already present in Filipino culture in general. He remarked that, not unlike Latinos and African Americans, he was encouraged to dance: "Latinos move their hips. You know? Black people move their hips.... We're [Filipino men are] allowed to express ourselves, through our body.... We move our hips ... like when a mother will teach her little daughter to like, '*Shake your booty girl!*' "[43] He added, "If you're culturally enriched, your dancing will be enriched," implying that Filipino culture was already culturally wealthy in ways that are valued in cyphers.

The hips and the entire pelvic region, including the booty, are charged with meaning and are a source of power in Black dances. In her study *The Black Dancing Body: A Geography from Coon to Cool*, dance scholar Brenda Dixon Gottschild argues that the "buttocks-pelvic region" is central to a bent-legged posture that allows for the ability to isolate "separate parts of the torso (chest, pelvis, shoulders, butt)," and independently articulate the body in multiple directions in response to different rhythms.[44] This ensemble of Africanist aesthetics (a get-low stance, isolations, and polycentric movement to polyrhythms), "draw[s] attention to the pelvis, abdominals, breasts, and buttocks, which, by Europeanist custom and tradition (if not stereotyping), suggest our animal nature."[45] Essentially, to misrecognize Africanist aesthetics through a Europeanist lens means that expressions of power get misread as obscene, hypersexual, and signs of subhumanity.

As well, the power of this region of the body is not the exclusive domain of women. Profo Won attended to masculinity, stating first, "In fact, a man's masculinity is enhanced by his flexibility and capability on the dance floor."[46] He then asked and answered, "Why are men bad dancers? Because we're too macho to move our bodies."[47] Finally, for Filipino men specifically he argued that lessons in dancing happen alongside lessons in being "suave," a "smooth-talker," and romantic. He affirmed that dancing, flexibility, and an ability to move the hips are *also* traits of a virile hetero-masculinity, bringing attention to the need to make the statement in the first place. Profo Won subtly critiqued the stiff bodily ideal of a "macho" masculinity and troubled the gender expression available to cisgender men. Yet he did so by reaffirming a seductive prowess through dance ("'cause to dance is ultimately sexual").[48] Such a reaffirmation implicitly mitigates notions that for men to be physically expressive with the butt and hips is gay, which is one of the ways that their gender expression gets policed and compulsory heterosexuality enforced.[49] In *Sorry I Don't Dance: Why Men Refuse to Move*, Maxine Leeds Craig argues that men shun dancing because of this fear, which undermines the central tenet of hegemonic masculinity: that it be heterosexual. Hip Hop dances, she argues, led to a resurgence of interest in dance for young men because "It is easier for many men to dance when dance is associated with physical intimidation, athleticism, and heterosexuality."[50]

Despite the different ideological and social limitations placed on dancing bodies, breaking still holds the implicit promise to dance one's freedom, at least momentarily. Profo Won refers to breaking as a "tool to freedom" versus the pressure to conform that he associated with East Asian cultures in general and Korea in particular.[51] A type of conditional freedom is a recurring theme in his interview:

> B-boying's a tool to freedom, just like house dancing is a tool to freedom. All of these things are tools for freedom. But we forget that they're tools. And then what we tend to do is go, "The tool is written law." That's when our minds become this [*clasps his hands*]. And to me, that's what competitions kind of do. A cypher is, like I said, it's starting to transcend that. But it takes the right type of mind, the right type of attitude to understand that . . . that transcendentness. Or the transition to that spiritual freedom, you know what I mean?[52]

Cyphering the "right" way and with the right mindset is not meant to be read as conformist or restrictive, but instead as keys to open up cyphering's inherent possibilities. In contrast to the structured finality of competitions, cyphering is an unguaranteed means for moving toward "spiritual freedom" or liberatory and extraphenomenal experiences, as discussed in chapter 1. Transcendence is not a goal in and of itself, but a possibility one moves toward or in the direction of as a result of "the right type of attitude."

Breaking's global diasporic context is absolutely essential to understanding the play of difference here. Africanist aesthetics—whether physically, energetically, or culturally resonant—enable people to identify with other people across differences of nation, race, ethnicity, gender, and generation precisely because these elements make room for someone to refashion their tastes, traditions, and cultural-aesthetic philosophies through cyphering's expressive qualities. As well, they reflect personalized preferences. The variations in styles are highly intertextual and deeply personal, continually referencing that from which they borrow or build upon.[53]

To Be On the One: Cyphering a Funk Sociality

As should be clear by now, the cypher is the locus of a multitude of cultural encounters, each open to the *possibility* of people dancing together in a ritual of restorative creativity. In so doing, cyphers create worlds unto themselves that stage interactions between tradition and change, continually bringing the individual back to modes of sociality activated by foundational aesthetic directives. While cyphering is a collective act, this does not mean that individual expression is less meaningful, especially since individual originality matters so much. Instead, it means that individual expression is contextually meaningful. Or Caponi writes in the introduction to *Signifyin', Sancitfying, and Slam Dunking: A Reader in African American Expressive Culture*, "The virtuosic individual performance is a social act, inspiring the team and the community."[54] Here, individual virtuosity reinvigorates the collective, versus Western glorification of the individual. As social spaces that teach practitioners how to participate in them, cyphering is an embodiment of modes of sociality that route individual practitioners, in all of their diversity, to a collective or group to whom they are then accountable, even if just for that moment in the immediate cypher. Therein are cyphers' possibilities.

Foundation reasserts core breaking philosophies and traditions that carry transgressive modes of sociality through which people connect in expansive ways. These qualities are essential to Hip Hop's capacity for worldmaking, a term that captures how performance and expressive practices broadly are tools to create distinct worlds alongside the one(s) we know. Though *not* about Hip Hop's globality, worldmaking deepens our understanding of how Africanist aesthetics are key to making global Hip Hop. In performance anthropologist Dorinne Kondo's book *Worldmaking: Race, Performance, and the Work of Creativity*, she describes the titular term as evocative of "sociopolitical transformation and the impossibility of escaping power, history, and culture," emphasizing that "performances, either onstage or in everyday life, are replete with possibility arising from, not transcending, power."[55] She looks at how theater can "make, unmake, and remake worlds inside and outside the theater" through a critical use of the tools of its genre.[56] In her work, the elements of a genre—like theater's use of staging and costuming or ethnography's use of form and narrative[57]—become the tools with which people make and remake worlds, and thus fashion transformational changes to their worlds in ways that are already attuned to the conditions of power that shape their lives.

If cyphering's Africanist aesthetics are tools that can "make, unmake, and remake" worlds as Kondo describes, then those worlds "help to keep everybody involved, active, and interdependent,"[58] as Caponi furthers, activating a transgressive sociality and the possibilities therein. That is because breakers do not just interpret the music, they are a physical manifestation of a social relationship to the rhythm. Caponi describes it as finding "the rhythmic center ... [or] a place within the group" of a polyrhythmic environment;[59] that center is felt and heard but not necessarily played. She states that finding that center requires "vigilance and attention to rhythmic relationships" in the polyrhythmic environment, or simply being in the same groove with a rhythm that may not be playing but to which the environment is attuned.[60] She cites multiple terms offered by different ethnomusicologists of African musical genres that capture this dynamic, including "additional rhythm," a "metronome sense," the "hidden rhythm," a "subjective beat," and finally the "invisible conductor" keeping everyone in sync.[61] Sensing the invisible rhythm is part of getting into a groove. With respect to breaking cyphers, I use a concept adopted from funk music, which seems most fitting for breaking: being on the one.

Popularized by James Brown, the phrase "on the one" is a hallmark of funk's funkiness. While some simply think of this as a call for the band to start playing "on the one," it is more than a reference to the beat. In his work *Funk: The Music, the People, and the Rhythm of the One*, radio host and funk historian Rickey Vincent talks about the philosophical import of the rhythmic center:

> A locked, happening rhythm brings everybody together grooving *as one*. Ultimately, to be "on the one," the musical performance is not only emphasizing an ancient rhythmic pattern, it is emphasizing the essential openness toward all participants to the groove. Locked, yet fluid, when everything is "on the one," a harmony among all people is achieved. When George Clinton is heard chanting on stage "On the one, everybody on the one," he isn't trying to get his band on the beat (they are already there), he is savoring the rhythmic lock that has brought the entire house together, as one.[62]

What Vincent terms "an ancient rhythmic pattern" echoes in Caponi's discussion of the hidden rhythm. Describing it as a "a locked, happening" or "locked, yet fluid" harmony, Vincent's phrasing draws out the freedom within the structure. When considered alongside the hidden rhythm, getting into the rhythmic center requires the full sensorium, a sensing-listening-while-watching-and-playing sensibility. Vincent also recognizes that anyone who is compelled to dance is part of the collective, noting that they add "yet another rhythmic contribution to the overall group experience."[63] Viazeen and Poe explained a version of this to me one night after a battle in Los Angeles. As a group of seven or eight of us ate breakfast at a late-night diner, Poe held up one index finger, referring to it as "the beat," then used his other index finger to dance around it. It was a gestural depiction of a sonic-spatial plane within the music wherein he could play, move with and against but never off beat, dancing the hidden rhythm. Viazeen concurred, clarifying that it is a matter of skill, a possibility available to those who really know what they are doing. While breakers do not go around calling for folks to be "on the one," they are encouraged to dance the song and find "the pocket," the rhythmic center or locked happening.

Since cyphers are more than a sum of their parts, kinesthetically getting in sync is generative of more than meets the eye. Finding that rhythmic center opens up another perceptual plane. African dance scholar and choreographer Kariamu Welsh Asante describes it as "something extra" that occurs or exists in a "dimensional sense" that she expressly ties to a rhythmic sensibility.[64] She writes, "There is a plateau feeling, an area perceived as depth that arises out of African dances. The dimensional aspiration speaks to the supernatural in space, the presence beyond the visual presence. The dimensional aspect is characteristic of all the senses in that it is by definition extrasensory. . . . [I]t is not a measured dimension, but rather a perceived dimension."[65] Dimensionality suggests a spatial plane in a realm "beyond the visual" and perceived as a depth in the ritual itself, similar to the spatiality of getting into the rhythmic center. So, rather than a colloquial refrain in a particular musical genre, to be "on the one" is an embodied philosophy about the individual in the collective that entails a dimensional sensory experience activated through dancing that rhythmic center. I am ultimately suggesting that there is a certain relationship between a theory about the individual within the collective and an extrasensory experience of dimensional or spatial depth, though the nature of that relationship is ambiguous.

In a way, Ralph Ellison explored this ambiguity in 1952, in his novel *Invisible Man*. Ellison captures a concern about the individual and the collective when he writes, "Our fate is to become one, and yet many—This is not prophecy, but description."[66] I am particularly fascinated by how "fate," whose definition hinges on the supernatural, correlates to "description," not "prophecy." The protagonist in Ellison's novel, someone who has improvised a life in the bowels of the city, understands this "fate" as observable, not mystical; wherein the inexactness of such language attends to the incalculable dimensions of living this underground existence. (In the end, the titular character contemplates returning above ground, postulating that "there's a possibility that even an invisible man has a socially responsible role to play.")[67]

In an analysis of this same Ellison line, poet and performance theorist Fred Moten draws attention to the punctuation, and the distinct correlative work of a dash over a period or comma. Moten posits an almost spatial depth between the two parts of Ellison's statement. The dash thus acts as a site for improvisational play between the first part, which attends to an understanding of difference, and the second, which registers "a certain understating of totality ... *as a possibility* in the improvisatory break."[68] For Moten, improvisation in the Black radical tradition exceeds definitions that reduce it to acting "without foresight" because it "always also operates as a kind of foreshadowing, if not prophetic, description. . . . [Y]ou need to look ahead with a kind of torque that shapes what's being looked at."[69] Improvisation holds the possibility of making the unforeseen or impossible a reality because it shapes what's coming. For Moten, the dash, as improvisatory, registers the possibility of "prophetic description" in Ellison's formulation. Both thinkers attend to the incalculable by grounding words like "foresight," "fate," and "prophecy," not in the mystic unknown but in lived practice.

The concept of double consciousness further grounds a use of mystic language in the incalculable dimensions of Black life. Coined in 1903 by W.E.B. Du Bois, this term captures the internal struggle of Black life, where we are forced to look at ourselves and measure our value through the eyes of those who hold us in contempt, doubling a sense of self (e.g., Black and American). He also refers to it as being "born with a veil,"[70] a phrasing too often aligned with the statue of Booker T. Washington titled *Lifting the Veil of Ignorance*, wherein that veil needs to be removed. Instead, I draw attention to the African American folk wisdom of "born with a veil" to mean a child born with a caul—rare births wherein a newborn arrives in this world with a thin amniotic membrane covering their face. They are said to be capable of "second sight" and able to communicate with ancestors or the dead. Essentially, those born behind a veil can see beyond the confines of a given reality. Du Bois draws attention to this by referring to being "gifted with second sight"—the incalculable language of the underground, or the margins, or a Black awareness in an antiblack world. Though not necessarily about psychic abilities per se (but why not?), instead this dimension of double consciousness might refer to a kind of prescient understanding of what *is*. That is why he also refers to double consciousness as a source of "power," the guide to our "mission."[71]

Ellison, Moten, and Du Bois all bring in the incalculable through a language that seems to dabble in the mystic or supernatural, but they ultimately ground that language in the realities of Black life and Black cultural practices. This tells me that inexact terms (e.g., dimensional and perceptual depth, being on the one, even foundation) need a global diasporic framework to be understood in concrete rather than mystical ways. Cyphering offers kinesthetic credence to an understanding of global Hip Hop, and is not just a metaphor for it. To paraphrase Poe One in chapter 1, in cyphers that connection *becomes* real.[72]

The type of active participation this implies is about more than technique. And perhaps *that* is the tension in global Hip Hop. Breakers worldwide adopt the culture and reconcile it with their own in the production of breaking identities. And while there is a logical emphasis on how the dance is done, there is a whole dimension of practice that is not easily translatable in instructional videos or studio classes. Practitioners, though, are implicitly and explicitly taught to orient to and through Africanist aesthetics in cyphers, which in turn makes those extra dimensions available though not guaranteed. Yet, in everyday Hip Hop communities, some people recognize a diasporic connection and some do not. This lack of awareness is not accidental but a product of ignorance, denial, or outright racist dismissal of its relevance, especially in a global context where Black cultures are commodified and circulated via channels of racial capitalism and cultural imperialism.

Antiblackness and That Thing That Capitalism Does

Historically, when Black expressive cultures become American pop culture, audiences are encouraged to remain profoundly ignorant of Black histories, and to maintain a cultural distance from Black life. Dance scholar Thomas DeFrantz elaborates on how antiblackness continues to structure the contact between Black dance forms and its diverse practitioners worldwide:

> No matter the ethnicity, race, sexuality, class, location, disability, gender or age of the dancers, black social dances arrive as an effective currency of exchange that allows for both individual expression and forms of group communion.... Contemporary neoliberal currents of exchange push African American social dance forms to global audiences with a forcefulness that evacuates their aesthetic imperatives of regularized, community-based

physical expression, toward terms of engagement that allow it to absorb participants who have *no sustained contact with the corporeal fact of black people in the world*.[73]

Black cultural production and dance in particular circulate along paths made possible by American cultural hegemony in the global marketplace, and furthered by neoliberal capitalist interests that exploit the wealth-creating capacities of blackness, though never to the benefit or freedom of racially subjugated classes. Put differently, the international scope of breaking sets the stage for more heightened forms of cultural appropriation, with no accountability to or responsibility for those who created the forms. DeFrantz makes clear that as a commodity rather than culture, one is encouraged to dissociate Black dances from their historical, social, and aesthetic contexts for the sake of their exchangeability. bell hooks offers pointed words about how commodification shapes ones relationship to blackness: "One could talk about American culture and mainstream culture as being obsessed with blackness, but it is blackness primarily in a commodified form that can then be possessed, owned, controlled, and shaped by the consumer. And not with an engagement in Black culture that might require one to be a participant, and therefore to be in some way transformed by what you are consuming. As opposed to being merely a buyer."[74]

An evacuation of "the corporeal fact of black people in the world" is another facet of an erasure of Africanist aesthetics and the knowledges embedded in them.[75] Postcolonial theorist Gayatri Spivak's concept "sanctioned ignorance" speaks to the idea that society authorizes acceptable absences in knowledge (absences that critical theorist Michel Foucault called "subjugated knowledges") by ignoring them or locating them "low down on the hierarchy" of socially relevant knowledges.[76] The commodification of Black expressive cultures thus widens the gap between practice and the contextualizing histories and knowledges that support that practice, since an ignorance of those things is deemed acceptable if not preferred in their commodity circulation.

Alongside ignorance is a warping of the meaning of freedom in Black social dances. DeFrantz's attention on the politico-economic routes carved out by neoliberal economic policies also operates through neoliberalism's appropriation of the language of freedom, where notions of personal freedoms are collapsed into the freedom of market and trade.[77] In dance, that translates into the freedom to move as one pleases and still call it Hip Hop because, as a buyer, you can consume as you please.[78] During my fieldwork, I have both witnessed and heard countless complaints about how young dancers from around the world correlate moving freely in Hip Hop street dances to being free to do anything and still call it *their* version of Hip Hop, a misunderstanding of the imperative to innovate and no appreciation for the aesthetic imperatives, techniques, and histories that mattered. This is precisely why Kondo says worldmaking cannot transcend, but instead arises from power.[79] The promise of cyphering's transgressive sociality does not transcend difference, but is a literal practice of dancing in consistent exchanges with others, negotiating the differences that shape one's practice, and knowing that things can play out in good and ugly ways.

A Politics of Soulfulness: Rokafella

> Hip Hop has managed to save a lot of people from the oppression, from loss, from drug addiction, from all these things, you know. Drugs. Wars. It's such a good release.[80]
> —Rokafella, personal interview, September 2006

There is, undoubtedly, political power in the sheer number of lives touched by Hip Hop. And if, in broad terms, the political simply refers to the means by which people struggle to achieve particular social ends, then Rok's comment is apropos of Hip Hop's political potentiality particularly at the scale of the everyday, the personal wars people fight, and the lives already saved. At their heart, my interests in global connection and shared culture across differences are interests in the political possibilities for the people who live Hip Hop culture, practice it, and teach it to their children. In this section, I offer a closer and extended analysis of an especially rich and nuanced phone interview in September 2006 with Rokafella, an Afro–Puerto Rican b-girl from Spanish Harlem who has been breaking since the early 1990s. We talked about breaking's appeal across differences, and the tensions and stakes of the day-to-day dynamics of living a breaking life in that context.

Her perspective on global Hip Hop is well captured in two sentiments. One was on racial difference: "Racially I think, we can always say, 'Oh, white people can't dance.' But there are white people who can, and they're dope, and we give them props, and we allow them in. Now, if we have to speak about this dance and where it comes from, they have to be able to know that it's an

African diasporic tradition."[81] The other was on national difference: "And it doesn't matter if you're Arabic, or French, or Chinese. This dance has a way of just allowing you to be. As long as you're good."[82] In both cases, the openness of the form and its seeming accessibility come first, followed immediately by something conditional that is vital to participation.

The conditionalities that Rok names are wrapped up in breaking's Africanist aesthetics and the dance's relationship to blackness. At one point in the interview, Rok addressed the complicated ways race matters to breaking by recounting an exchange she had with a young, white b-girl and her mother. I quote at length to capture her full comments.

IKJ: So, when you started dancing, was there a sense that—was there a lot of tension around, racially, who should or shouldn't be doing whatever in Hip Hop?

ROK: Racially. See now, this is something that . . . It's, it's . . . I don't know. I don't even know sometimes if it applies when it comes to breaking because it really is about the soul of the dance. I was having a conversation with [a young white b-girl]. Because I was telling her, you know, "You being white, that's never gonna go away. This being a Black dance, that's never gonna go away either. You have to first become well versed at, is acknowledging the fact that slavery or oppression of a European country on their colonies, you have to be able to acknowledge that *that* shit was wrong. And that it's still wrong. So that, you know, when conversations come up, you can honestly say, 'Yes, that was wrong. *And* that has nothing to do with me.' Because that isn't even your generation. It's not your mom's or your grandmother's generation. We're talking eons, oh my gosh, of imperialism. But for you to acknowledge it helps me perceive you as an ally. And the fact that you renounce your privilege in this society is, is . . . is helpful. What is *also* helpful to you is to become a soulful dancer. You have got to study this dance and be good, without a doubt. And always contribute back to the people who created it, back to the people who teach you. Because you have to give back to the communities [and not just] be able to take away from it." And I explained that to her.

Unfortunately, her mom doesn't believe that, doesn't understand that. And I don't even know how to have a conversation with her. Because when she [the daughter] lost that competition, she [the mom] was like, "Oh you know, my daughter's white and that's why she didn't win." And I would one day like to address her mom and say, "You're gonna have to let that go 'cause your daughter isn't actually that good. Yes, she can do headspins; yes, she can do all the power moves. But dancing wise and the soul of it, it's not there. And she needs time." I needed time.... I could rock house, I could rock rap dancing, you know I could do salsa, I could do African. But this dance when I started, the first three or four years: not yet. And even in my fifth and sixth years! I had the moves, but I was still trying to navigate the soulfulness of it.... If that was me, and I come from this, and I have an African diasporic background, *you've* gotta work. And she and her mother have to analyze that.[83]

Rokafella's initial hesitancy to talk about race quickly gave way to a generous response, despite my own struggle to ask the question well. While sequence and setting are omitted, Rok recounted two parallel examples of precisely the ways that race comes into conversations about style, and the inevitable points of tension born out of the impossibility for movement on its own to bridge the gaps between us. Though it might appear that Rokafella simply reiterated the power-versus-style critique, her reference to soulfulness moved beyond that binary. Being good is more than knowing moves. Rokafella's emphasis on a deeper study of the dance, or perhaps deeper study *as a dimension of the dance*, means understanding that history plays a part here, too.

At the same time, Rokafella is not suggesting that blackness alone is the key. For one, her critical use of blackness is much more nuanced than the mother, who accused the judges of so-called reverse racism. The mother seems to acknowledge that race can matter, but only relative to her own perceived victimization. When Rok initially named breaking a "Black dance" that will always be so, she both marked it as African diasporic and as a product of world Black histories, inclusive of but not exclusive to US African Americans. She named histories of Black people in various countries in opposition to white (European and American) histories of imperialism, capitalist expansion, and social and political privilege. The multiplicity of meanings of blackness in her discussion disrupts passive assumptions of a monolithic group. Second, despite having already labeled it a Black dance, Rok herself could not simply master breaking's nuances, clarifying that her dance background in diasporic genres may have helped but were not enough. Rokafella's use of Black was political, ethnoracial, and diasporic, all of which commingle in her ideas of a deeper study moving toward soulfulness. Her notion of soulfulness is the linchpin to understanding the complexity of Hip Hop as a global culture because it necessitates an interplay between things that do and don't "apply" to the dance. It was a recurring theme in our interview.

In answer to my initial question, Rok elaborated on the complicated stakes of connecting across racial differences, and what role historical knowledge can play at that time in the mid-2000s:

ROK: If you are borrowing from this be able to acknowledge that and say, "Yes I am." You know? And I think a lot of times the Europeans don't have a clue. And the Japanese, I mean the Asians don't have a clue. . . .
IKJ: Not learning the history?
ROK: They're not learning the history. They're not looking to the sociopolitical, the economical edge to this. They're not. And I think even me telling her this is something that's coming post-civil rights, I don't think she knew that. So we have to, at some point, just be able to speak about these things. And not put, I don't want to say put white people or Asian people in their place. Just let them know what our place is in this. And yes, you can be the best dancer, but are you helping my community express themselves, as educated, as skillful, as humans, as equal people in *this* American society? No, you're not. You come in, you get what you want, you go back to your country. And then, when you go back to your country, you forget about who we are . . . because now you're holding competitions, and you're in all the media and you're—you know what I'm saying? . . .

But it takes bringing the other nations to this realization. It's difficult, because that's not why they get into it. Actually nobody, me neither! I did not get into it as a form of resistance, as a form of revolution. I didn't. I got into it because I like to dance. And maybe subconsciously, that was my way to rebel against society. Maybe. I'm a woman, I'm a person of color. My parents are immigrants. So maybe subconsciously it is a way to rebel against the rigid forms of society. . . . And it's hard. It's hard to blame people not from these ethnicities; or even people from this ethnicity. If I take [some Black people] and talk to them about being Black, about Africa, about Europe, about the Asian side, whatever, I don't think they're interested. You know what I'm saying? Our Black people, they're not interested because there's like this apathy. Like, "What the fuck am I gonna do about that?" You know? And it's real!

. . . And that's what I mean. I don't think that racism, or racial, or anything like that applies to the cypher. I don't think it applies to this dance.

The mainstream wants to [say] it's a Black person dance and we can praise the white person that has been so exceptionally driven. We can praise him but it's a Black dance. That's just the mainstream, again warping what this is. It's weird.[84]

Rokafella named a complex interplay of underlying racial politics within a seemingly apolitical dance culture. Her comments were revealingly circular, oscillating between the inapplicability of race and its inescapable qualities. Her back and forth perhaps signaled the ways that, as sociologist Howard Winant writes, "Despite the best efforts ... to render race invisible, it keeps exerting significant sociopolitical 'gravity' ... in an increasingly internationally networked culture."[85] Breaking is not about race, yet it is about racism, at least in part.

Moreover, its global context is increasingly something that requires negotiation. For example, it matters that Hip Hop culture is a product of the benefits and failures of the post-civil rights era. She argued that an ignorance of relevant histories, particularly of the people who developed the culture and of the social conditions that set the stage for Hip Hop, reiterates a long-standing pattern of cultural appropriation and perhaps a misguided form of participation. It becomes evident that there is privilege in operating without an awareness of others' oppressions; only some people have it while others do not. Yet apathy also acts as a kind of refuge from the burden of awareness. There is no single explanation for the lack of a deeper historical perspective on breaking across groups.

The things that "do/do not apply yet matter" may be better understood through what Cornel West describes as the "cannot *not know*" of the realities that shape Black lives, and by extension Black expressive cultures. West writes,

> The concrete, everyday response to institutionalized terrorism—slavery or Jim-Crowism—was to deploy weapons of kinetic orality, passionate physicality, and combative spirituality to survive and dream of freedom. . . . Black cultural practices emerge out of an acknowledgement of a reality they cannot *not know*—the ragged edges of the real of necessity; a reality historically constructed by white supremacist practices in North America during the age of Europe. These ragged edges—of not being able to eat, not to have shelter, not to have health care—all of this is infused into the strategies and styles of black cultural practices.[86]

West's phrasing amplifies the unavoidable realities, historically and today, that inform Black expressive practices. How well they are *known* is probably relative, but the "cannot *not know*" is a different kind of baseline. I hear echoes of Rok's sensibility here, that the things that do/don't apply reflect an awareness of unavoidable truths, capturing the ambiguity of knowledge that she cannot opt out of even if disbelieved or ignored. Such realities matter to the dance precisely because they contextualize the sociopolitical conditions of breaking and Hip Hop, the "ragged edges" of an outlaw sensibility.

Despite the impossibility of totally renouncing one's privilege, Rokafella recognized how Hip Hop lent itself to working through other structures of power. Breaking's life-sustaining qualities are a driving force behind the sentiment. She elaborated:

> If you look at it from cultural perspectives and stuff, [Hip Hop is] life-sustaining, it gives them a home, a new take on, the feeling of, "I am somebody." And I think that we can see that as a whole and almost everybody can feel that way—like it is a collective identity—then I think we can kinda start to heal the wounds that we've been carrying for such a long time, for generations, you know: that women will always be gendered; that men are usually oppressive. We can kind of come to the point that we're at a happy medium. We're both struggling; we're both trying to fight off these stereotypes. You know, just trying to exist and make families, and be at peace. I think maybe things can be different, but that's like a huge, *huge* utopian type of undertaking. I just feel like at this moment in time we just kind of come together and talk, so that they can see what we've been through, so we can know what they've been through. You know, trying to come back together.[87]

Her attention to gender stereotypes was an examination of the perpetuation of divisions within Hip Hop. The goal of mutual understanding echoed her call for allies and historical awareness cited earlier. That is, whether in reference to colonialism, racism, or a gender divide, Rokafella's cultural and political work within the breaking community has moved toward her "*huge* utopian type of undertaking." For example, during my field research in the mid-2000s, Rokafella hosted a series of "B-Girl Sit-Downs," open forum conversations among practitioners to cultivate a site for dialogue led by but not exclusive to women practitioners (not just b-girls). Examples of these sit-downs are featured in her film *All the Ladies Say*.[88] That platform served to engage what is not part of breaking, but not *not* part of it either. Thus, it is not simply that "when we talk about this dancing community we're talking about skills." Soulfulness offers insight on how to understand what exists beyond skills.

Soulfulness is not genetic, yet it is expressly tethered to diasporic aesthetics, epistemologies, histories, peoples, and cultures. I was especially struck by Rokafella's use of "navigate," as if it were a dimensional space or a terrain to explore as opposed to a goal or an achievement. Perhaps too, soulfulness is Rok's language for Welsh Asante's dimensional sense. To traverse the soulfulness of the dance is to discover its hills and valleys in a kind of exploration of the unchartered territory of your own practice. Getting to a soulful place in one's dancing is an ongoing journey. A deeper study into history and culture is a dimension of being more soulful dancers. Recurring terms in our interview—like "utopian," "freedom," "peace," and "life-sustaining"—capture the height of breaking's possibilities when folks strive toward soulfulness versus just moves.

Conclusion

Breaking cyphers have something to say about our interconnected world, and a global diasporic lens makes that apparent. The constellation of Africanist aesthetics featured in this chapter—including those embedded in foundation, the invisible conductor, getting on the one, and dimensionality—signal a kinesthetic sensibility that is all about the individual in the collective, the one and the many. Somewhere in there, between a commitment to the practice and a decision to deepen that practice by learning more about the people, cultures, and political-historical contexts from which the dance comes, the opportunity to move toward the "cannot *not know*" of Black life reveals even deeper dimensions of these aesthetics of survival and liberation. Since cyphers can, but do not always, lead to new planes of perceptual-kinesthetic understanding (unpacked further in chapter 1), this suggests that the sensibilities they teach live in the body in substantive ways. Ultimately, hope for Hip Hop to become a more overt political movement is galvanized and invigorated in cyphers because they attend to embodied connection across differences, not just discursive ones.

In *Close to the Edge: In Search of the Global Hip Hop Generation*, sociologist Sujatha Fernandes explores the lived differences between the multiple, sometimes conflicting local Hip Hop scenes in different parts of the world—Chicago, Caracas, Havana, Sydney—asking what of that political hope actually survives the inevitable tensions of difference (e.g., deepening national identities and differential economic or political privileges). What she finds is that "creating a broader fellowship that would unite hip hoppers across racial lines requires more than rhetoric of international alliances and cultural borrowings. It depended on the existence of spaces of mutual interaction and experiences within the working-class areas and diasporas where collaborations could be realized."[89] Fernandes shifts her expectations about the nature of the political, arguing instead that, while Hip Hop did not propagate a singular movement, its strength was in "the myriad of local forms of expression that made it possible."[90] In her study she highlights working class and rural-urban collaborations as well as international ones, calling forth the necessary presence of different kinds of Others as part of the cypher.

What practice tells us is that the everyday ways, the trained-into-the-body ways, the sweating-on-each-other-in-cyphers ways that connect people across differences actually establish ground for horizontal exchanges that, at their heart, resonate with the type of coalitional politics that underlies Fernandes's hope.[91] Such a politics locates its potentiality in the capacity for Hip Hop to make room for the local scene to see itself in there too. For example, in Jacqueline Shalloum's 2008 documentary *Slingshot Hip Hop*, members of the Palestinian Hip Hop group DAM recognize a connection to African American sociopolitical struggles via a Tupac music video. They credit Tupac and the visual representations of structural ghettoization for moving them past a "bling"-centric rap music, stating, "It looked like he'd filmed it in our hometown, Lyd. Even though we didn't know English and we didn't get the lyrics, we made the connection."[92]

Activist and prison abolitionist Angela Davis's term "intersectionality of struggles" captures a similar sense of connection, but one animated by planetary struggles against racism, homophobia, and transphobia.[93] Davis's concept activates points of mutual understanding specifically based on sociopolitical positionality within intersecting structures of power. For example, she gives an example of Palestinian activists sharing information about protesting violent, military-armed police with activists in Ferguson, Missouri, who were protesting the police killing of Michael Brown, as an example of an intersectionality of struggles.[94] In a way, it is a recognition of another's "cannot *not know*" (e.g., of state violence) that registers as a willingness to take up other people's struggles because they are connected to and have bearing on one's own. This enables a political interconnectedness that can push us toward a more just world.

At the scale of the dance circle and on any given day, cyphers can do *some* of that work. There are, of course, no guarantees, but it is through practice, not decree, that their possibilities are activated. There is no set formula, no checklist, but rather a doing *and* an intentional deepening of knowledge in a holistic practice. Perhaps, then, cyphers are telling us *a* strategy, *a* way to "make/unmake/remake" worlds beyond the circle.

Coda

Cyber Cyphers and Africanist Aesthetics

I started this research in 2005 wanting to understand cyphers on a philosophical level and wondering why circle practices were so ubiquitous in the African diaspora. (I sat with the idea for two years before starting the research.) I grew up experiencing circles largely through Hip Hop cyphers, and breaking cyphers in particular always drew me into their gravitational sphere. Learning about Africanist aesthetics only deepened my appreciation because it meant that what I experienced in cyphers—the joy, connection, desire, release—were born out of a technology my ancestors used, tools of spirit, survival, and liberation that still work. Something like foundation, which continually reasserts Africanist aesthetics, does so in a way that remains connected to the sociopolitical and cultural realities that shape Black expressive practices like Hip Hop (see Fig. C.1).[1] And, as I have demonstrated thus far, when enacted in concert, Africanist aesthetics open up spaces where spirit entered, identities were reaffirmed, life strategies were learned, connections made, souls healed, and new social paths were formed. Thus, I end this book with another set of possibilities, a somewhat undercooked analysis that I share as an invitation for others to carry further.

Ultimately, the full story of breaking's cyphering practices and the life of Africanist aesthetics in global Hip Hop includes a lesser acknowledged undercurrent of the overall research: the internet, social media, and digital technology. From the minute I joined Myspace in 2006 (solely to find breakers to interview btw), social media platforms were key to my research. YouTube videos broadened my exposure to archival material, and following dancers on social media kept me in a loop with people and events worldwide. By 2020, these forms of connection were all the more important in light of the global pandemic. What follows, then, is just the beginning of exploring cyphering and Africanist aesthetics in an online context. It is not

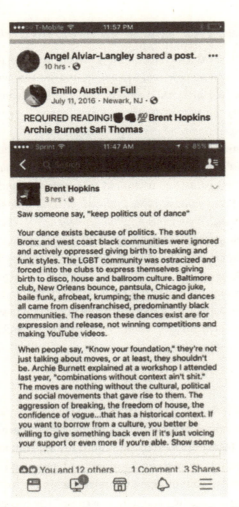

Figure C.1 Screenshot of multiple reposts about foundation, Facebook, 11 July 2016. The pertinent, missing, final word is "respect." Foundation matters across Hip Hop genres. The people in this post alone are known for DJing, popping, breaking, house, and Hip Hop social dances.

an exhaustive consideration of social media practices nor a deep dive into cypher videos, but instead a speculative look at the digital arena with the hope that this offering further demonstrates the expansive possibilities of studying Hip Hop dances.

* * *

"The Social Life of Social Media" (December 2010, Brooklyn, NY)

I arrive at b-girl Neva's apartment for a gathering in honor of her birthday. Her small apartment is warm and welcoming, and the dozen or so of us share food, sweets, laughter, and casual conversation. By all accounts it is a low-key and fun gathering. I await the dancing, which I assume is inevitable, but then everything changes. Someone asks if folks have seen footage of a particular battle—some have, some haven't—and an invitation gets extended to watch it. Even though a couple of people opt to help out in the kitchen instead, most everyone except me gathers on or around the couch surrounding one laptop screen. I sit across from them to take in the whole scene. I don't want to be in research mode in such an obvious way, but I cannot help it. They check out clip after clip, critiquing and deconstructing the dancing. I am fascinated by their studied appreciation, and the intimacy of their relationships to special clips. Some state that they watch certain videos over and over again, and others chime in about doing the same. In their collective enthusiasm, one mentions a different video, perhaps of a different genre of dance altogether, and they quickly transition to it. This goes on most of the rest of the night, and it occurs to me that watching together, like this, is more significant to community than I had realized.

* * *

My memory of Neva's party sat with me unexpectedly. There was little for me to write about in terms of live dancing, but there was obviously something important happening, something familiar and practiced that suggested, perhaps, that I needed to reimagine my relationship to the digital space. As performance theorist Marcela A. Fuentes writes, "The physical and the digital are intertwined and feed on each other."[2] That entanglement was evident in this experience at Neva's, and it made me wonder, how do cyphering's Africanist aesthetics fare online?

Such a question immediately brings me to choreographer, writer, composer, and educator D. Sabela grimes's blog (culled from his MA thesis), "SOCIAL| *DANCE*| MEDIA."[3] Grimes explores the "Crank That (Soulja Boy)" online dance phenomenon in the 2000s, and makes a case for the virtual continuation of cyphers. He argues that Black social dancing has always navigated its mediation (e.g., vinyl, radio, internet) to innovate in "predictably unprecedented" ways.[4] Rather than getting mired in questions about the song's artistic merit or the limits and losses of the online platform, grimes examines the Soulja Boy phenomenon as an example of the transmission of Black dance online, which he situates within a longer lineage of Black social dance practices or "move/meant (moves encompassing meaning beyond the oral/lyrical content)."[5] As a result, he offers a reimagined digital space:[6]

> In the virtual world what's produced in both the official and instructional videos is a two-dimensional split cipha. The circle is cut into halves, the arcs are flattened into straight lines that are crossed, and their intersection becomes the point of connection on the world-wide-web, a *URL* (Uniform Resource Locator). The content of the circle is diffused. As presently commonplace as it may seem to post video content online this sort of cultural diffusion is unique, eventful and predictably unprecedented.[7]

grimes disentangles cyphers from their live contexts, redefines shared space through the URL, and expands the time frame of a recorded experience posted online indefinitely (or perhaps until the video is no longer available). When the video displays an arc of people, there is an implicit call to viewers facing the screen to respond and participate by recording and posting their own videos or commenting on the post, thus becoming a part of that cypher. Though we may experience the footage on a flat screen, a call-and-response communicative strategy is still at work, ensuring that "the dance circle/cipha is experienced [by viewers] as a unified field of interaction."[8] Yet, as with cyphers, there is also a choice in how one participates. For example, I am left to decide whether to ignore the aural-kinesthetics of the dancing and solely focus on the mechanics of the body by keeping the sound off.

I also experience a *version* of "being there live," or perhaps an extension of it because online practices are in a perpetual present. Digital media allows people to enter the cypher long after it happened. In a 2021 talk on his practice titled "Blk Haptics—Experiences Aesthetics + Feedback in Performance Technology," interdisciplinary artist André Zachary described the digital arena as a "relational space beyond the corporeal," noting too that it is also "durational" and "more of a negotiation of what you can do with time in the digital space."[9] Perhaps this shift in temporal orientation offers another opening, another potential point of suggestive overlap with cyphers.

* * *

"A Diasporic Cyber Cypher" (August 2017, Long Beach, CA)

Out of habit I open my Facebook feed and quickly scroll through, half paying attention. I scroll and scroll, then stop. A clip begins to play automatically: a slim, young dancer saunters onto an empty stage, face conveying composed confidence. Suddenly arms begin to project in and out in distinct angles, limbs flexed in unexpected directions. Their precision is exceptional! I quickly turn on the volume to hear this voguer's dancing as they swing around effortlessly, then dramatically drop to the ground. My reactions mimic the crowd in the clip: supportively yelling (except to a screen) or looking to others for confirmation of shared appreciation (except I'm alone in my bedroom). The short clip whets my palate.

Scroll, scroll. A snippet of a battle with b-boy Smurf. He makes a face at his opponent that seems more like he's teasing a small child. Then fifteen seconds into "Give It Up, Turn It Loose," he tugs up his shorts and springs his compact tattooed body into a power combination. "When was this?"—LA Breaker's thirty-fifth anniversary, forty minutes ago on the other side of the city! "Damn." I should've sucked it up, made my way through traffic. Who else did I miss? I need to go tomorrow; last chance.

Scroll, scroll, scroll . . . A classic! Whitey's Lindy Hoppers in the most well-known clip from Hellzapoppin'. *1941, black-and-white film, upbeat jazz, incredible. Breakers love this clip. It's so Hip Hop: the drums come first, one of the musicians spits a rhyme, a loose almost-circle forms, and then an explosive lindy routine begins, unrelenting to the fast-paced jazz. Playful, skillful, awe-inspiring. This one comes across my feed almost monthly.*

Scroll, scroll, a posted memory of an FB friend (whom I've never met IRL), footage of breakers I don't know, from a country that I've never visited, familiarly starting to throw down in a battle. . . . The juxtaposition of clips is fleeting, and this iteration of my FB feed cannot be duplicated. But for a few minutes, it feels special, like a cypher.

* * *

In a manner of speaking, I participated in a cypher: I praised, talked back to the performance, clapped, moved my body to the music, and registered the Africanist aesthetics across practices. Admittedly, my affective response to that cyber cypher (or cypher-like experiences online) could not feed back into the already recorded danced moment in the same way; yet my "loving" it helped get the algorithm to amplify the post. Though a happenstance product of algorithmic curation, brief moments like these suggested new ways of considering Africanist aesthetics in an online context.

This cyber cypher experience, made so by the juxtaposition of clips in my encounter of them, echoed qualities of a visual technique that filmmaker Arthur Jafa uses in his work. In a 2013 talk between bell hooks and Jafa, he spoke of his five-year process of making the four-minute film *Apex*, a rhythmic, quick-paced barrage of images that both overwhelms the senses and is evocative of a range of emotional responses based on what you are able to process.[10] Purposeful not to call it curatorial,[11] at that time he referred to it as "organizing images," a phrase that is decidedly accessible as a practice, and deeply respectful of the labor in crafting the sequence of images. *Apex* began by compiling images using Adobe Bridge software and then turning that process into a kind of compressed time-lapse of those images.[12] He remarked, "I've never done anything in my life that's calibrated to this level."[13] Jafa later adopted filmmaker John Akomfrah's term "affective proximity" to describe an overarching visual technique that attends to the juxtaposition of imagery from different contexts that are positioned in such a way as to produce "a certain kind of contextual dissonance."[14]

I am drawn to affective proximity because it captures some degree of what I experienced as a diasporic cyber cypher. As well, unspoken in the name itself, is a particular project around blackness. Specifically, Jafa states that his "overriding ambition [is] to make a black cinema that has the power, beauty, and alienation of black music," adding, "But increasingly I became interested in dance, African-American social dance. I was trying to think through what is happening when people actually dance."[15] In the published excerpts of a conversation between Jafa and Black feminist theorist of visual culture and contemporary art Tina Campt, Jafa details the multidimensionality of blackness and the complexity that is already evident in Black music and social dance:

> So I was really trying to think through what's going on when black people dance. On a phenomenological level, what's going on? I came up with the two things that black Americans are acutely sensitive to. One is rhythm. Everybody's familiar with the idea that black people have an acute sensitivity to rhythms. But there's another thing that people have a harder time putting their hands on, which is an acute sensitivity to what I term vectors, or spatial arrays. . . . So there's this acute sensitivity to space. And I started saying, "Oh, black people can predict the future"—and that sounds really

crazy, but what I mean is that they have this acute sensitivity to vectors and trajectories... setting up a series of vectors and then breaking them.... It's really about flow—flow through figures.[16]

Jafa uses Michael Jackson as an example, noting, "He looks like he's going in one direction but he's actually going in another direction."[17] He ultimately expresses an appreciation for multiple trajectories at once: the anticipated direction, the actual direction, the projected trajectory of both, and preparedness of another unexpected shift or change. (Or a prescient understanding of what is.) What Jafa sees as vectors or trajectories is a perceptual awareness that seems predictive but is really a sensibility about flow that gets continually exercised, like a muscle, in Black music and social dance.

Jafa's observations about angles, vectors, and the multiple trajectories that are active (or activated) simultaneously reflect the workings of an ensemble of Africanist aesthetics, particularly asymmetry as balance, angularity, an aesthetic of cool, and the "get down" stance. In her book *Jookin': The Rise of Social Dance Formations in African-American Culture*, Katrina Hazzard-Gordon writes about asymmetry as balance, stating, "In the African esthetic, balance is achieved through the combination of opposites," which she recognized "as well... in break dancing."[18] In Western definitions of asymmetry, a "lack" of symmetry is literally defined as a lack of equality or equivalence.[19] In Africanist terms, balance is key, not symmetry. And balance necessitates bringing together different angles and energies, opposites and adjacents: the angularity of limbs, the flexed foot alongside the pointed toe. Vectors get at the epistemological implications of a kinesthetic sensibility acutely activated through Black social dances. This is what Jafa hopes to cultivate through film.

Jafa attempts to tap into the sensibilities embedded in Africanist aesthetics by "worrying that note" of dissonance produced by the arrangement of images. As Aria Dean explains in "Worry the Image," a 2017 review of Jafa's work, "The term is a mutation of a 'worried note,' a synonym of 'blue note,' a note played or sung at a slightly different pitch than is standard in Western scales and notation. Worried notes are common in blues, jazz, and other black musical genres. They evince black music's tendency to treat sound as unstable, unlike the exacting constructions of Western harmony."[20] A blue note, particularly in how it troubles a certain understanding of harmony, seems like a sonic counterpart to asymmetry as balance. Both concepts prioritize the power of the unstable and the unexpected produced by a social arrangement of contrasts that undermine Western convention. Jafa recognizes such an arrangement in Black music and dance, and crafts a similar sensibility in a film like *Apex*. I see the arrangement of contrasts in cyphering, and even in cyber cyphers. (And as tempting as it is to further explore the theoretical implications of *that*, I have to stop here.)

As this brief exploration barely scratches the surface of where the analysis could go, cyphering and Africanist aesthetics continue to create unforeseen possibilities online. While Jafa's focus is on creating a visual technique, my own cyber cypher experience makes me ask, can Africanist aesthetics offer strategies for watching? When algorithms make the arrangements, where is the wiggle room to intervene when we are decidedly not the ones in control? And how do those algorithms amplify or invisibilize Africanist aesthetics?

Outro

Cyphers matter because the day-to-day ways that we live, talk to, and dance with one another are intimate interventions in the world. Whatever energy we commit to those exchanges is up to us. For me, writing about tools of survival and liberation in the midst of Covid-19 and its ongoing aftermath, social distancing practices, and sheltering has been a life raft. I learned that we all have a part to play in our various cyphers to keep the energy flowing. This book is my offering to the cypher.

I chose the dark matter metaphor precisely because it is "a reminder of how much we don't know about the universe."[21] The dark matter of cyphers represents the sheer possibility of the force of Africanist aesthetics, and all that they can reveal and teach us about what we do not yet know or recognize in global Hip Hop. And while I end with more questions than answers, perhaps that is how best to end the book, at a place of possibility.[22] Because what if Black aesthetics are liberation aesthetics for everyone? Seems to me they can be, but it requires active participation, a deeper study, confronting antiblackness, and a willingness to get dirty and continue to build in exchanges with others.

Acknowledgments

I am deeply appreciative of everyone who has, at some point in time, helped me bring this project to completion. While academic work can feel solitary and isolating, all the names that follow attest to the importance of community in making this project possible. (With apologies to anyone I may have inadvertently overlooked.)

My family has remained steadfastly supportive. Thank you Carole Hopkins, C. Danny Johnson, T. Hasan Johnson, RaKhem Ajani Johnson, Garrett Johnson, Pat Johnson, and George Hopkins. As well, my chosen family: Crizella Wallce, H. Saron Anglon, Charnjeet "Mini" Bhogal, Chaylon Blancett, Sadio Jonas, Rich Blint, Ted Sammons, and Gloria Kim.

I am grateful to my advisers, Fred Moten and Dorinne Kondo. I cannot articulate how grateful I am for developing this work under your guidance, and I know that I am a stronger scholar for it. I also thank formal and informal mentors, particularly Ruthie Wilson Gilmore, Lanita Jacobs, Karen Shimakawa, Priya Srinivasan, Candice Jenkins, Jayna Brown, and Rosemarie Roberts.

Thank you friends and colleagues for supporting the work or me along the way: Takiyah Nur Amin, Edwina Ashie-Nikoi, Marlon Bailey, Melissa Blanco Borelli, Karen Bowdre, Cornelius Byrd, Derrais Carter, Dasha Chapman, Ananya Chatterjee, Jian Chen, Wendy Cheng, Michelle Commander, Sybil Cooksey, Aaron Dailey, Yvonne Daniel, Thomas DeFrantz, Meiver De la Cruz, T. J. Desch-Obi, Norman Francis, Jens Giersdorf, Artisia Green, Tina Ehsanipour, Aracelie Esparza, Chris Farrish, Carol Garza, Brenda Dixon Gottschild, Perla Guerrero, Jesus Hernandez, Emily Hobson, Nicole Hodges-Persley, Dan Hosang, Jasmine Johnson, Adanna Jones, Raha Jorjani, Nisha Kunte, Viet Le, Delroy Lindo, Sharon Luk, Belinda Lum, Erica Maceda, Susan Manning, Angela Marino, Jeffrey McCune, Xhercis Méndez, Zoila Mendoza, Mireille Miller-Young, Krista Miranda, Royona Mitra, Raquel Monroe, Sionne Neeley, Halifu Osumare, Onye Ozuzu, Mark Padoongpatt, Felicia Perez, Elliott Powell, Jade Power Sotomayor, Reina Prado, Prarthana Purkayastha, Anton Smith, SA Smythe, Anthony Sparks, Jennifer Stoever,

Devon Turner, Tree Turtle, Gretel Vera-Rosas, Maria Villaseñor, Terrion Williamson, Kim Woodring, S. Ama Wray, and Simone Zeefuik.

A special thank you to those who helped elevate my writing and thus the project. Much appreciation to Ashon Crawley for your critical feedback and challenging questions, Kyle Livie for giving feedback on the writing since the dissertation, and Luisa Giulianetti and Liz Keithley for your early guidance as both a writer and a teacher.

A special thanks to Stacey "BLACKSTAR" Robinson for the amazing art work on the cover.

I especially thank the team of graduate student who helped in the final stages of editing the manuscript: Ïxkári Estelle, MiRi Park, and Lindsay Rapport; and Manuel Macias for compiling the bibliography. In addition, I thank all of the graduate students that I have worked with at UC Riverside and beyond. Though I cannot name you all, opportunities to learn from your developing insights have been especially gratifying to my experiences at UCR.

To my colleagues at UC Riverside, I deeply appreciate being part of a supportive intellectual environment: Kelly Bowker, Xóchitl Chávez, Colette Eloi, Maria Firmino-Castillo, Xiomara Forbez, Donatella Galella, Irvin Gonzalez, Robert Hernandez, Rickerby Hinds, Tammy Ho, Emily Hue, Brandon J, Anusha Kedhar, Kelli King, Anthea Kraut, Makeda Kumasi, Aleca LaBlanc, Maiko LeLay, Sophia Levine, Kendall Loyer, Denise Machin, Luis Lara Malvacias, taisha paggett, Cuauhtémoc Peranda, Liz Przybylski, Jose Reynoso, Wendy Rogers, Judith Rodenbeck, Jacqueline Shea Murphy, Setsu Shigematsu, Joel Smith, Stephen Sohn, Melissa Templeton, Linda Tomko, and Ni'Ja Whitson. As well, I thank the members of the Blackness Unbound Collective for helping me navigate the university: taisha, Ni'Ja, João Costa Vargas, Ayana Flewellen, Anthony Jerry, Natasha McPherson Vorris Nunley, and Dylan Rodriguez.

I extend appreciation to Norman Hirschy and the editorial staff of Oxford University Press for their patience and support. Thank you for your labor.

To the amazing dancers, practitioners, artists, Hip Hop heads, and thinkers who introduced me to a new world, thank you: Aby, Aiko, Asia1, Batch, Brian Polite, Buddha Stretch, Don Tony, Emiko, Ephrat, Hannifah Queen, House, iona brown, Joanna Cruz, Ken Swift, Kwikstep, Little Cesar (the very first breaker to agree to speak with me), Macca, Miss Little, Ness4, Neva, Poe One, Poppa Smurf, Rokafella, Teena Marie, Toni Blackmon, Trac2, Tweet Boogie, Viazeen, Yarrow, and Ynot. Last, though certainly not least,

I want to make a special shout out to my Hip Hop scholar crew, collaborators, and friends. You make me feel like I'm part of something bigger. Thank you Amanda Adams-Louis, Serouj Aprahamian, Adisa Banjoko, Naomi Bragin, Lynnée Denise, Martha Diaz, Moncell Durden, Mary Fogarty, Kyra Gaunt, d. Sabela grimes, grace shinhae jun, Kuttin' Kandi, Jessica Pabón-Colon, MiRi Park, Emery Petchaur, Raquel Z. Rivera, Marcella Runnell-Hall, Joseph Schloss, and Shanté Paradigm Smalls.

Completion of this project was in part supported by the Ford Foundation Dissertation Fellowship, New York University's Provost Diversity Postdoctoral Fellowship, the A Diverse East Tennessee State University initiative and especially Dr. Keith Johnson (thank you for your support!), and the Woodrow Wilson Career Enhancement Fellowship.

Notes

Being There

1. Poe One told me of the conscious decisions he made to maintain the flow of open cyphers. As an event organizer, he considers the room's layout, the lighting, the floor, and the music as all important to cyphering. MC and b-boy Triple7 and b-boy Krazy Kujo both agree that the lighting needs to be low to promote a sense of intimate focus that enables the ability to tune out the rest of the room in order to focus one's energy on the music and the floor. Music is especially important, needing to be loud enough to pulsate through the body so breakers can literally *feel* the beat. Smooth floors, wide open spaces, and nonstop music enable marathon-like continuity. In combination, these factors can foster or hinder the presence of cyphers. Poe One, personal interview, 6 March 2007; Triple 7, personal interview, 3 October 2006; Krazy Kujo, personal interview, 4 September 2006.

Preface

1. Fred Moten's discussion of the aesthetics of the Black radical tradition is a poignant reminder of what *could be* in how we understand cyphers. He writes, "That black radicalism cannot be understood within the particular context of its genesis is true; it cannot be understood outside that context either. In this sense, black radicalism is (like) black music. The broken circle demands a new analytic (way of listening to music)." Rather than a straight line, cyphering's relationship to its historical context is more like a broken circle, hearkening back to a historical previous-ness that resonates despite the break. Along the lines of Moten's statement about Black radicalism and Black music, breaking cyphers (as embodied expressions of the music) demand a new analytic. I'm inspired by the possibility. Fred Moten, *In the Break: The Aesthetics of the Black Radical Tradition* (Minneapolis: University of Minnesota Press, 2003), 24.

Introduction

1. Brenda Dixon Gottschild, *Digging the Africanist Presence in American Performance: Dance and Other Contexts* (Westport, CT: Praeger, 1996), xiv.
2. Gottschild's use of Africanist aesthetics, she notes, is more along the lines of how Toni Morrison writes of them versus Melville Herskovits. For Gottschild, Africanist

aesthetics "designate the vitality and energy of a lively aesthetic that is characterized by the privileging of process or experience over product or thingness." Gottschild xv n.
3. Gottschild 2.
4. Cedric Robinson, *Black Marxism: The Making of the Black Radical Tradition* (Chapel Hill: University of North Carolina Press, 1983), 171. He also describes it as "an accretion, over generations, of collective intelligence gathered from struggle" (xxx). Robinson demonstrates how resistance was regarded as a group activity that went against expectations, historically manifesting in three ways: returning (e.g., suicide, revolt on slave ship), marronage (recreating Africa), and open rebellion. Citing Gerald Mullin on Blacks in eighteenth-century Virginia, he writes, "Africans, assuming that resistance was a group activity, ran off with their own countrymen, and American-born slaves including mulattoes" (169). In the context of that struggle, Robinson gives particular attention to religious expressive practices (e.g., obeah, myal, vodun) as "frustrated" expressions of the Black radical tradition unrealized in rebellion that nonetheless signal Africanist epistemological orientations with various qualities. "When its actualization was frustrated, it became *obeah, voodoo, myalism, pocomania*—the religions of the oppressed as Vittorio Lanternari put it. When it was realized, it could become the Palmares, the Bush Negro settlements, and, at its heights, Haiti" (169). The metaphysical in Robinson's assessment is enacted by way of material means, and thus becomes a material force in how people organize themselves and act collectively.
5. Robinson 73. Robinson states specifically that "it was the ability [for enslaved Africans] to conserve their native consciousness of the world from alien intrusion, the ability to imaginatively re-create a precedent metaphysic while being subjected to enslavement, racial domination, and repression. This was the raw material of the Black radical tradition, the values, ideas, conceptions, and constructions of reality from which resistance was manufactured" (309).
6. Fred Moten, *In the Break: The Aesthetics of the Black Radical Tradition* (Minneapolis: University of Minnesota Press, 2003), 18.
7. See Su'ad Abdul Khabeer, *Muslim Cool: Race, Religion, & Hip Hop in the United States* (New York: New York University Press, 2016); Nitasha Sharma, *Hip Hop Desis: South Asian Americans, Blackness, & a Global Black Consciousness* (Durham: Duke University Press, 2010); H. Samy Alim, *Roc the Mic Right: The Language of Hip Hop Culture* (London: Routledge Press, 2006); Marc Lamont Hill, *Beats, Rhymes, & Classroom Life: Hip-Hop Pedagogy and the Politics of Identity* (New York: Teachers College Press, 2009).
8. Osumare 61.
9. Barbara Christian, "The Race for Theory," *Cultural Critique* 6 (1987): 51–63.
10. Jessica Nydia Pabón-Colón, *Graffiti Grrlz: Performing Feminism in the Hip Hop Diaspora* (New York: New York University Press, 2018), 32.
11. Early written and photographic representations of Hip Hop culture focused on popular publications like the *New York Times*, the *Village Voice*, and *Time*; niche market publications like *Latino NY* and *Right On! Magazine*; and dance journals. I gathered these materials from the dance holdings at the New York City Performing Arts Library at the Lincoln Center, and the general holdings at the Schomburg Center

for Research in Black Culture, the special collections at the Center for Puerto Rican Studies at CUNY Hunter College, and the Harvard Hip Hop Archives. I was especially impressed by and appreciative of select holdings at Cornell University's Hip Hop Collection, which, though not focused on dance, offered access to previously private collections from figures like Crazy Legs (Rock Steady Crew president) and Charlie Ahearn (director of the 1982 film *Wild Style*), and was the only site that provided formal access to these types of holdings. Otherwise, access to personal archives came by way of one-on-one relationships (for example, Lil' Cesar showed me footage from the first Radiotron event), which did not often result in my having copies of that material. While archival research was not central to what is presented in this book, it informed how I even understood this project. I hope to publish an article that speaks directly to this aspect of my research in the future.

12. Though convention would have me use one name per person, convention among breakers is a common-sense use of shortened versions of practitioner names (e.g., Rokafella, Rok) or variations that breakers choose for themselves (e.g., Alien Ness, Ness4). I expect readers to pick up on these obvious variations without additional explanation.

13. Diana Taylor, *The Archive and the Repertoire: Performing Cultural Memory in the Americas* (Durham: Duke University Press, 2003), 3.

14. Taylor contrasts the repertoire with the archives—repositories of recorded (usually as text) history, knowledge, and memory—arguing that the repertoire should compel the same degree of legitimacy through different means. She goes on to challenge standards, contending that archives are also mediated, and thus meaning changes depending on their use.

15. I opt for "OG" (a shortening of "original gangsta") over "pioneer," which carries obvious colonial vestiges.

16. Common questions included "Do you remember your first circle?" "What did your parents think of your dancing?" "Is there cypher etiquette?" "What are the necessary elements to a cypher?" The age range of interviewees has been from nineteen to fifty, with over thirty of them in their thirties.

17. In the introduction to *Foundations* Joseph Schloss wonderfully unpacks the very limited discourse attached to Hip Hop in mainstream references, in comparison to its broader meaning for cultural insiders as both community and art forms. See Joseph Schloss, *Foundation: B-Boys, B-Girls, and Hip-Hop Culture in New York* (Oxford: Oxford University Press, 2009). Several other works delve into Hip Hop as a culture, but also shift emphasis to rap music. See Steven Hager, *Hip Hop: The Illustrated History of Break Dancing, Rap Music, and Graffiti* (New York: St. Martin's Press, 1984); David Toop, *Rap Attack #3: African Rap to Global Hip Hop*, 3rd ed. (London: Serpent's Tail, 2000); Tricia Rose, *Black Noise: Rap Music and Black Culture in Contemporary America* (Hanover, NH: Wesleyan University Press, 1994); Jim Fricke and Charlie Ahearn, *Yes Yes Y'all: Oral History of Hip-Hop's First Decade* (Oxford: Perseus Press, 2002); Jeff Chang, *Can't Stop Won't Stop: A History of the Hip-Hop Generation* (New York: St. Martin's Press, 2005).

18. Dance scholar and b-boy Serouj Aprahamian notes that "b-boying" is a "new school" term, advanced in the 1990s. Its then proponents have since begun to openly discuss why the language shifted in the first place, undermining any notion that "b-boying" is somehow more authentic than "breaking." Serouj Aprahamian, "'There Were Females That Danced Too': Uncovering the Role of Women in Breaking History," *Dance Research Journal* 52.2 (August 2020): 52–53.
19. Chang 117. Specifically practitioners referenced it as a *cocolo* (English-speaking Black person) dance. For a discussion of the first generation of Black breakers, see Serouj Aprahamian, "Going Off: The Untold Story of Breaking's Birth," PhD diss., York University, Dance (2021).
20. People like Aby and Batch of The Bronx Boys/Girls Rocking Crew insist that the dance be called "rocking," despite overlaps with "the rock dance"—a style that predates breaking and from which breaking gets elements of its toprock—which too gets called rocking.
21. See Mark Katz, *Groove Music: The Art & Culture of the Hip-Hop DJ* (Oxford: Oxford University Press, 2012), 1.
22. Herc incorporated Jamaican dancehall elements such as giant speakers and short rhymes on the mic (which evolves into MCing). For further reading see Rose; Chang; Schloss, *Foundation*; Katz.
23. According to Trac2, between 1975 and 1977 the dance was called "rocking" and dancers referred to themselves as "*beat* boys," because as far as the dancers were concerned, they danced to the beat, as there was yet no common understanding of a "breakbeat." Trac2 suggests that "break-boy" comes from a DJ's perspective since "the break" is a musical term. Trac2 is the only informant who used beat-boy in this way. With that said, since "break" is also a street term among African Americans with multiple social meanings, it is clear that people understood these terms differently, depending on their perspective.
24. *Freshest Kids*, dir. Israel (2002), QD3 Entertainment.
25. Different Hip Hop elements had different mainstream trajectories. In the early 1980s, graffiti was being recognized in the downtown New York visual and performance art scene, while the music industry was only beginning to recognize rap music's commercial potential.
26. *Wild Style*, dir. Charlie Ahearn, Submarine Entertainment (1983); *Style Wars*, dir. Tony Silver and Henry Chalfant, PBS (1982); *Flashdance*, dir. Adrian Lyne, Paramount Pictures (1983).
27. This list includes television features, documentaries, feature films, foreign films and documentaries, and movies that are not about Hip Hop but feature some its elements. This number then represents a minimum.
28. These are two distinct genres sometimes lumped together under the misnomer "poplocking." Unlike breaking, locking is a bouncy, exuberant dance that was developed in the very early 1970s in Southern California by Don "Campbellock" Campbell, who says he stumbled across his distinct style of dance through his unsuccessful attempts at doing the Funky Chicken. According to Moncell "Ill Kosby" Durden—a locker,

dance historian, and documentary filmmaker—Campbellock has also recited the story in reference to the Funky Robot rather than the Funky Chicken.

Popping developed in the early to mid-1970s in Fresno, California, credited to "Boogaloo Sam" Solomon, who innovated a powerful style that stressed the pulsating contractions of the muscles, in sometimes fluid and sometimes staccato movements to the rhythms of funk music. For some, popping is an umbrella term for a multitude of styles coming from all over California, and for others "Funkstyles" is a more appropriate catchall for the different dances of which popping is but one. Other styles include ticking, hitting, and strutting, boog style (or boogaloo), and more. On the East Coast, where only snippets of popping were seen on TV, it became known as "electric boogie"; in the UK, it was popularized under the term "smurf." Popping is also the source of a number of popular social dances, like the robot and the moonwalk. I feel compelled to add that what we think of as the moonwalk, made popular by Michael Jackson in the early 1980s, is actually the backslide. The public's admiration of and fascination with Jackson's capacity to move in exciting and new ways came from African American and Latino communities in Central and Southern California. As it hit the mainstream through Jackson, he was often credited with inventing or perfecting the move, and the dancers like Poppin' Taco, who was one of his main teachers, received little attention.

The popularity of the term "pop-locking" in eighties eventually led to a style that ultimately merged these two genres, suggesting that such a dance actually came into being. Whether one attempts to correct this type of misinformation or not, pop-locking persists as an actual dance, even among Hip Hop heads.

29. Jihad, personal interview, 2 April 2004; Trac2, personal communication, 28 July 2006; Krazy Kujo, personal interview, 4 September 2006; Triple7, personal interview, 3 October 2006; Brooklyn Terry, personal interview, 13 October 2006; Anna of Fraggle Rock Crew, personal interview, 16 March 2007; Aby, personal interview, 18 March 2007; Ness4, personal interview, 9 August 2006; Poe One, personal interview, 3 January 2007; Leanski, personal correspondence, 29 June 2006; Genesis, personal correspondence, 26 July 2006; Slinga, personal interview, 14 August 2006.

30. I've chosen to use the term "embodied knowledge," a term that circulates in dance studies. Embodied knowledge allows us to focus on the body itself as a medium of transmission, even in the absence of spoken language. Yvonne Daniel, *Dancing Wisdom: Embodied Knowledge in Haitian Vodou, Cuban Yoruba, and Bahian Candombleé* (Urbana: University of Illinois Press, 2005), 52, 265.

31. "Cipher, *n.*," *OED Online*, July 2009.

32. W. E. B. Du Bois, "Sociology Hesitant" [1905], *boundary 2* 27.3 (Fall 2000): 41.

33. Felicia Miyakawa, *Five Percenter Rap: God Hop's Music, Message, & Black Muslim Mission* (Bloomington: Indiana University Press, 2005).

34. The Nation of Islam has been called the "Lost-Found" Nation of Islam in reference to the idea that Islam, to them, is "the Black man's" true and original religion that was once "lost" and then reintroduced by the Nation's founder, W. D. Fard. The "Lost-Found lessons" were teachings Clarence 13X (founder of the Nation of

Gods and Earths) learned from Elijah Muhammad. They are said to be modeled on the catechism of Masons, and are arranged in a question-and-answer format. Ted Swedenburg, "Islam in the Mix: Lessons of the Five Percent," paper presented at the Anthropology Colloquium, University of Arkansas, 19 February 1997.

35. *The Book of the Five Percenters Edition #195* (Monticello, NY: Original Tenets of Kedar, 1991), 348.
36. During and part of the popularity of Black nationalist signifiers in 1990s Black pop culture and rap in particular.
37. MC cyphers are the most well known of the Hip Hop cyphers, but graffiti writers and Hip Hop dancers of all kinds have their versions too. There have yet to be treatments of cyphers in the other elements of Hip Hop except MCing. While her focus is on the Los Angeles freestyle MC scene in general, Marcyliena Morgan expands on battling and improvisational lyricism that happens in cyphers. See Marcyliena Morgan, *The Real Hip Hop: Battling for Knowledge, Power, & Respect in the LA Underground* (Durham: Duke University Press, 2009).
38. While this echoes notions of competition in capitalist terms of fueling technological innovation, the motivation differs. Rather than a profit motive that fuels hoarding and property rights, in cyphers (especially when they are not battles) the intent is to collectively build its energy.
39. See also Rose; and Joseph G. Schloss, *Making Beats: The Art of Sample-Based Hip-Hop* (Middletown, CT: Wesleyan University Press, 2004).
40. In *More Brilliant Than the Sun* (London: Quartet Books, 1998), Kodwo Eshun argues that the collage of beats created by technology and the textural-sonic overlay of scratches, rhymes, and the vocal and instrumental chorus had a multisensorial impact:

> Your perception ... switches from hearing individual beats to grasping the pattern of beats. Your body is a distributed brain which flips from the sound of each intensity to the overlapping relations between intensities. Learning pattern recognition, this flipflop between rhythmelody and texturhythm drastically collapses and reorganises the sensorial hierarchy. For the 90s rhythmatician the body is a large brain that thinks and feels a sensational mathematics throughout the entire surface of its distributed mind.... The kinaesthete overrides that premodern binary that insists the dancefloor is all mindless bodies and the bedroom nothing but bodiless minds. (21–22)

Eshun draws attention to "sensorial hierarchy" that Hip Hop compels, one wherein kinesthetics reign supreme. He suggests that the music itself collapses any perceived distinction between verbal mind and the body, a hierarchy at the heart of Western Enlightenment thought that claims the mind as superior to the body (i.e., "I think therefore I am"). Eshun reformulates that idea, positioning the verbal mind as only one part of a whole body-distributed perceptual system ("the body is a large brain that thinks and feels") that overrides an ideology of binaries otherwise reinforced in Western societies. Put another way, the textural complexity of the music itself prompts a sensorial response that undermines a mind-body division. The patterns generated from the overlay of sonic textures tap into more than one's hearing; the music stimulates intelligences throughout the body. When practitioners began to stay down on the ground with increasingly energetic, punchy, and acrobatic moves, it coincided with the increasingly complex music. Eshun elaborates that the body's physical response is a means of interpreting the music's impact on our person—the foot taps, the head bobs. We mutter along to the lyrics in hypnotic appreciation. Eshun contrasts this with what he calls "cerebral music," such as "Abstract beatz, math rock, intelligent Techno, proper Drum'n'Bass," that celebrates the sheer mathematical complexity of the beat alone rather than a visceral response to the music and the many ways a body can react—a *sense*-ational mathematics. Breaking is a full-bodied response to Hip Hop.

41. Cleis Abeni, "Improvisation in African-American Vernacular Dancing," *Dance Research Journal* 33.2 (Winter 2001): 43–44.
42. Jacqui Malone, *Steppin' on the Blues: The Visible Rhythms of African American Dance* (Urbana: University of Illinois Press, 1996), 28.
43. One b-boy, Ness4, remarked in an interview that he preferred to break primarily to music that had a "car chase" quality because he preferred a style that was urgent and confrontational like that music. Imani Kai Johnson, "Music Meant to Make You Move: Considering the Aural Kinesthetic," *Sounding Out! Sound Studies* blog (12 June 2012), https://soundstudiesblog.com/2012/06/18/music-meant-to-make-you-move-considering-the-aural-kinesthetic/ (last accessed 11 July 2021); Ness4, personal interview, 9 August 2006.
44. Nketia has one chapter dedicated to the "Interrelations of Music and Dance." J. H. Kwabena Nketia, *The Music of Africa* (New York: Norton, 1974).
45. Wilson goes through a variety of musical, religious, work-oriented, and performance-based practices. In other words, his focus is on whenever stylized and rhythmic movement is constitutive of music-making practices. Olly Wilson, "The Association of Movement and Music as a Manifestation of a Black Conceptual Approach to Music-Making" [1977], *More Than Dancing: Essays on Afro-American Music and Musicians*, ed. Irene V. Jackson (Westport, CT: Praeger, 1985), 9–23.
46. Cornel West, "Black Culture & Postmodernism," *Remaking History*, ed. Barbara Kruger and Phil Mariani (Seattle: Bay Press, 1989), 87–96; Kyra D. Gaunt, *The Games Black Girls Play: Learning the Ropes from Double-Dutch to Hip-Hop* (New York: New York University Press, 2006), 93.
47. Gaunt 4.
48. Drawing on the capacity for dance-music gestures to carry histories, DeFrantz points to Black social dance's communicative capacity to index and evoke aspects of Black life not commoditized and sold to white audiences. Thomas F. DeFrantz, "The Black Beat Made Visible: Hip Hop Dance and Body Power," *Of the Presence of the Body: Essays on Dance and Performance Theory*, ed. Andre Lepecki (Middletown, CT: Wesleyan University Press, 2004), 64–81.
49. Ashon Crawley, *Blackpentecostal Breath: The Aesthetics of Possibility* (New York: Fordham University Press, 2017).
50. Crawley argues that the choreosonic captures an intervention of Black expressive practices, as mutually constituted by both music and dance, producing indeterminate

meanings that are inherently "aphilosohical and atheological." See Crawley, chapters "Shout" and "Noise."

51. Crawley 149.
52. Crawley 134–38, 146–58.
53. Joseph G. Schloss, "'Like Old Folks Songs Handed Down from Generation to Generation': History, Canon, & Community B-Boy Culture," *Ethnomusicology* 50.3 (Fall 2006): 411–32.
54. bell hooks, "An Aesthetic of Blackness: Strange and Oppositional" [1990], *Lenox Avenue: A Journal of Interarts Inquiry* 1 (1995): 65–66.
55. Gottschild xiv.
56. Aside from that which is revealed in readings on specific practices like capoeira, the ring shout, and bomba, other sources that address Africanist aesthetic qualities broadly include Gottschild, *Digging*; Brenda Dixon Gottschild, "Crossroads, Continuities and Contradictions: The Afro-Euro-Caribbean Triangle," *Caribbean Dance from Abakuá to Zouk: How Movement Shapes Identity*, ed. Susanna Sloat (Gainesville: University Press of Florida, 2002), 3–10; Gena Caponi, ed., *Signifyin(g), Sanctifyin', & Slam Dunking: A Reader in African American Expressive Culture* (Amherst: University of Massachusetts Press, 1999); Robert Farris Thompson, "Hip Hop 101," *Droppin' Science: Critical Essays in Rap Music & Hip Hop Culture*, ed. William Eric Perkins (Philadelphia: Temple University Press, 1996), 211–19; Robert Farris Thompson, "An Aesthetic of the Cool: West African Dance," *African Forum* 2 (1966); Robert Farris Thompson, *Flash of the Spirit: African & Afro-American Art & Philosophy* (New York: Vintage Books, 1983); Katrina Hazzard-Donald, "Dance in Hip Hop Culture," *Droppin' Science: Critical Essays in Rap Music & Hip Hop Culture*, ed. William Eric Perkins (Philadelphia: Temple University Press, 1996), 220–35; Katrina Hazzard-Donald, *Jookin': The Rise of Black Social Dance Formations in African-American Dance* (Philadelphia: Temple University Press, 1992); James Snead, "On Repetition in Black Culture," *Black American Literature Forum* 15.4 (Winter 1981): 146–54; DeFrantz, "Black Beat"; Thomas DeFrantz, *Thomas DeFrantz: Buck, Wing, and Jig* www.youtube.com/watch?v=A34OD4eA17o (last accessed 31 October 2016); Malone; Henry Louis Gates, "The 'Blackness of Blackness': A Critique of the Sign & the Signifying Monkey," *Critical Inquiry* 9.4 (June 1983): 685–723; Marta Moreno Vega, "The Ancestral Sacred Creative Impulse of Africa & the African Diaspora: Asé, the Nexus of the Black Global Aesthetic," *Lenox Avenue: A Journal of Interarts Inquiry* 5 (1999): 45–57; Zora Neale Hurston, "Characteristics of Negro Expression," *"Sweat": Written by Zora Neale Hurston*, ed. Cheryl A. Wall (New Brunswick, NJ: Rutgers University Press, 1997), 55–72; Kariamu Welsh Asante, "Commonalities in African Dance," *African Culture: The Rhythms of Unity*, ed. Molefi Asante and Kariamu Welsh Asante (Trenton, NJ: African World Press, 1985), 77–78; John Storm Roberts, *Black Music of Two Worlds: Africa, Caribbean, Latin, & African-America Traditions* (Belmont, CA: Wadsworth / Thomas Learning, 1998); Rickey Vincent, *Funk: The Music, the People, & the Rhythm of the One* (New York: St. Martin's Griffin, 1996); Nketia; LeRoi Jones, *Blues People: Negro Music in White America* (New York: Harper Perennial, 1963); Cleis Abeni, "Improvisation in African-American Vernacular Dance," *Dance Research Journal* 33.2 (Winter

2001): 40–53; Christina Fernandes Rosa, *Brazilian Bodies & Their Choreographies of Identification: Swing Nation* (New York: Palgrave Macmillan, 2015); Wilson; Dick Hebdige, *Cut 'n' Mix: Culture, Identity and Caribbean Music* (New York: Methuen, 1987); Gaunt; Crawley; Johnson.
57. Gottschild, *Digging* 2.
58. Gottschild, *Digging* xiii–xiv.
59. Gottschild, *Digging*.
60. Physicists hypothesize that dark matter (and dark energy) make up to 95 percent of the universe, which throws a huge wrench in already established understanding of how the universe works. Think about that. As illustrated in a short video by Jorge Cham, it is like discovering that after a couple of centuries scientists have only been studying the tail of an elephant before realizing that there is an entire beast they've overlooked. They also hypothesize that dark matter may scaffold the connection between galaxies, accounting for their unexpected star formations. Such studies suggest the possibility that dark matter has a weblike or filament shape that may even flow like water, generating interactions between these galaxies. Paul Rincon, "Team Finds 'Proof' of Dark Matter," *BBC News*, 21 August 2006, Web, 21 August 2006; Stephen Battersby, "Giant Ropes of Dark Matter Found in New Sky Survey," *New Scientist*, 21 February 2008, Web, 13 November 2008; "X Marks the Spot in Dark Matter Web," *New Scientist*, 29 February 2008, Web, 13 November 2008; "Nearby Galaxies Are Chock-Full of Dark Matter," *New Scientist*, 4 June 2008, Web, 13 November 2008; "Dark Matter 'Bridge to Nowhere' Found in Cosmic Void," *New Scientist*, 15 September 2008, Web, 13 November 2008; "Dark Matter May String Together Starry Necklace," *New Scientist*, 17 September 2008, Web, 13 November 2008; Rachel Courland, "Astronomers Find Universe's Dimmest Known Galaxy," *New Scientist*, 18 September 2008, Web, 13 November 2008; Rachel Courtland, "Is Dark Matter a Wimp or a Champ?," *New Scientist*, 9 September 2008, Web, 13 November 2008; Louis E. Strigari, Savvas M. Koushiappas, James S. Bullock, Manoj Kaplinghat, Joshua D. Simon, Marla Geha, and Beth Willman, "The Most Dark-Matter-Dominated Galaxies: Predicted Gamma-Ray Signals from the Faintest Milky Way Dwarfs," *Astrophysical Journal* 678 (10 May 2008): 614–620; Lotty Ackerman, Matthew R. Buckley, Sean M. Carroll, and Marc Kamionkowski, "Dark Matter and Dark Radiation," California Institute of Technology CALT-68-2704 Report, arXiv:0810.5126v1 [hep-ph] (28 October 2008 onward); Jorge Cham, "True Tales of Dark Matters: A Conversation with Daniel Whiteson & Jonathan Feng," www.phdcomics.com, 27 April 2011.
61. Ackerman et al.; Stephen Battersby, "Dark Matter May Shine with Invisible 'Dark Light,'" *New Scientist*, 31 October 2008, Web, 4 November 2008.
62. Leonard Susskind, "Dark Matter and Dark Energy," video, *The Black Hole War*, The Public Forum, Commonwealth Club of California, 12 August 2008, https://www.youtube.com/watch?v=3SiGujnfDVc.
63. Many Black physicists, like Chanda Prescod-Weinstein, dispute the use of "dark matter" as a metaphor for blackness. Prescod-Weinstein specifically argues for an Afropessimist bent to dark matter, whereas I opt for an exploration of possibility. This is not a counterargument but instead leans on the concept's yet-to-be-discovered

qualities. Chanda Prescod-Weinstein, *The Disordered Cosmos: A Journey into Dark Matter, Spacetime, & Dreams Deferred* (New York: Bold Type Books, 2021).

64. I was first introduced to this Dumas short story by Fred Moten, who gave a talk on University of Southern California campus presenting a draft of what would be published as "The New International of Rhythmic Feel/ings," *Black and Blur: Consent Not to Be a Single Being* (Durham: Duke University Press, 2017); Henry Dumas, "Will the Circle Be Unbroken?," in *Echo Tree: The Collected Short Fiction of Henry Dumas*, ed. Eugene B. Redmond (Minneapolis: Coffee House Press, 2003), 104–15.

65. Dumas 108.

66. Dumas 110.

67. Dumas 107.

68. This is in contrast to the physics of dance, a physics-based area of inquiry that engages physics principles in their studies of dancers in motion.

69. There are a number of theories and schools of thought that might address aspects of what I couch in "dark matter." Maurice Merleau-Ponty's approach to a phenomenology of perception and its critique of Cartesian duality in favor of embodiment immediately comes to mind. Victor Turner's "communitas," experienced in a liminal state during rites of passage where a heightened sense of community forms among all of the participants regardless of rank, could be part of this exploration. Émile Durkheim's notion of "collective effervescence," which describes the exultant state felt among those who congregate during religious ceremonies (or carnivals, sporting events, and the like) also comes to mind. Other possibly connected theories that echo in my use of dark matter also include Judith Butler's use of "psychic life," a psychic or interior sense of self that is formed in relation to the social world. Sally Sommer's definition of "vibe," depicting the "powerful sense of liberation" experienced in the mix of house dancers in the delicate balance of a club, is an apt correlative as well. Even the Yoruban concept of *asé*, as written about by Marta Moreno Vega, echoes in how I will employ "dark matter" in this work. The specificity of each of these concepts makes them potentially useful at points, and inapplicable at others. Rather than spend much time arguing for or against their value, I opt to focus on breakers' conceptualizations of their experiences without obligating them to fit any particular preexisting concepts. Maurice Merleau Ponty, *Phenomenology of Perception* [1945], 2nd ed., trans. Colin Smith (New York: Routledge, 2010); Victor Turner, *The Ritual Process: Structure & Anti-structure* (Chicago: Aldine, 1969); Émile Durkheim, *Elementary Forms of Religious Life* [1912], trans. Karen Fields (New York: Free Press, 1995); Judith Butler, *The Psychic Life of Power: Theories in Subjection* (Stanford: Stanford University Press, 1997); Sally Sommer, "C'mon to My House: Underground House Dancing," *Ballroom, Boogie, Shimmy, Sham, Shake: A Social & Popular Dance Reader*, ed. Julie Malnig (Chicago: University of Illinois Press, 2009), 285–301; Maya Deren, *Divine Horseman: Voodoo Gods of Haiti* [1953] (New Paltz, NY: McPherson, 1984).

70. In other uses of dark matter in Black studies, the term gets invoked differently in each text. Some develop the theoretical implications in its use, some do not. The following are ones that I have come across during the course of my research: Sheree R. Thomas's *Dark Matter*, 2 vols. (New York: Aspect Warner Books, 2000, 2004), on African

diasporic speculative fiction; Simone Brown, *Dark Matters: On the Surveillance of Blackness* (Durham: Duke University Press, 2015).
71. Some of the other works that do not necessarily reference dark matter but still use physics (or the sciences in general) as points of entry to deeper discussions about race, blackness, feminism, etc., include Michelle M. Wright, *The Physics of Blackness: Beyond the Middle Passage Epistemology* (Minneapolis: University of Minnesota Press, 2015); Denise Ferreira da Silva, "1 (life) ÷ 0 (blackness) = ∞ − ∞ or ∞ / ∞: On Matter beyond the Equation of Value," *e-flux* 79 (February 2017); and Zakiyyah Iman Jackson, "'Theorizing in a Void': Subliminality, Matter, & Physics in Black Feminist Poetics," *South Atlantic Quarterly* 117.3 (July 2018): 617–48.

Dark Matter

1. *The Three Stooges* refers to an American vaudeville comedy trio, active from the 1920s through the 1970s, who turned their antics of slapstick and physical comedy into multiple short films and a television series.
2. Ness4 suggests that one of the necessary components of cyphers is "hungry dancers." Without them, there is no cypher. The energy grows more intense the more dancers who desire to step into it. Ness4, personal interview, 9 August 2006.

Chapter 1 Dark Matter & Diaspora

1. Jay-Z, *Decoded* (London: Virgin Books, 2010), 11.
2. Fred Moten's discussion of Nathaniel Mackey's phrase, "Words don't go there," echoes aspects of how breakers discuss the extraphenomenal in cyphers (41–42). While Moten's discussion focuses on meaning-making in the gap between legible utterance and sound, comparatively, my work hinges on the not-quite-fitting comparisons meant to capture some aspect of breakers' experiences. Many of my informants struggled to fully articulate the gravity of their experiences and opted for narratives that offer the most accessible point of entry for listeners, and they do so in the most legitimizing or respected terms, though these comparatives often fall short. They convey a meaning that adequately represents aspects of an experience, yet that which is elusive in the experience often remains so. In this way, Moten's footnoted discussion of the phrase "words don't go there" carries what he calls "the double absence: the disappearance of the performance that is not recorded; the loss of what the recording reduces or occludes by embodying an illusory determinacy and representativeness" (265 n. 31). That is, not only does the narrative or discourse (recording) fail to capture the referenced experience (unrecorded except in memory), but that the narrative chosen also loses qualities of the experience by packaging it in illusory terms to represent it. Fred Moten, *In the Break: The Aesthetics of the Black Radical Tradition*

(Minneapolis: University of Minnesota Press, 2003); Nathaniel Mackey, *The Bedouin Hornbook* (Los Angeles: Sun & Moon Press, 1997).
3. Ness4, personal interview, 9 August 2006.
4. Emiko, personal interview, 18 September 2006.
5. Krazy Kujo, personal interview, 4 September 2006.
6. Dark Marc, personal interview, 11 August 2006.
7. Machine, personal interview, 30 August 2007.
8. Kwikstep, personal interview, 8 August 2007.
9. Brenda Dixon Gottschild, "Crossroads, Continuities, and Contradictions: The Afro-Euro-Caribbean Triangle," *Caribbean Dance from Abakuá to Zouk: How Movement Shapes Identity*, ed. Susanna Sloat (Gainesville: University Press of Florida, 2002), 9.
10. Alma Concepción, "The Challenges of Puerto Rican Bomba," *Caribbean Dance: From Abakuá to Zouk* (Gainesville: University Press of Florida, 2002), 168–69.
11. Gottschild 9.
12. Cases made for more direct capoeira influences on breaking in New York City in the early 1980s are cursory and disputable. With that said, the blog site *Breaking and Capoeira* features a growing collection of digital archival resources and analytic perspectives on the historical relationship between breaking and capoeira, making the case that it warrants greater attention. At the same time, breaking is a dance that has always evolved by borrowing from other movement practices, so I would argue that the connection to capoeira is not evidence of direct lineage or origin but rather evidence of diaspora in action. The sense of connection between Hip Hop and capoeira is not new. Hip Hop scholar Joseph Schloss draws particular connections between b-boying and various African martial arts. Like myself, he's clear to note similarities and overlaps but does not argue for a one-to-one correlation or origin narrative to breaking, though they are related. I argue that Africanist elements of Hip Hop culture likely come by way of the active reworking of cultural imperatives inherited from more immediate expressive practices that already possess Africanist sensibilities. Such traditions continue to live in the cultural lives of the range of people of the African descent who collectively created Hip Hop culture. See Joseph G. Schloss, *Foundations: B-Boys, B-Girls, and Hip-Hop Culture in New York* (New York: Oxford University Press, 2009). See Jelon Vieria, "The Influence of Capoeira on Breaking in the 1970s," *Breaking and Capoeira* blog (February 2019), https://www.breakingandcapoeira.com/2019/02/the-influence-of-capoeira-on-breaking.html.
13. John Storm Roberts, *Black Music of Two Worlds* (New York: Praeger, 1972), 6; J. H. Kwabena Nketia, *The Music of Africa* (New York: Norton, 1974), 217, 224; Roger D. Abrahams, *Singing the Master: The Emergence of African-American Culture in the Plantation South* (New York: Penguin, 1992); Janheinz Jahn, *Muntu: African Culture and the Western World*, trans. Marjorie Grene (New York: Grove Weidenfeld, 1961); Kathryn Linn Geurts, *Culture and the Senses: Bodily Ways of Knowing in an African Community* (Berkeley: University of California Press, 2002).
14. H. Samy Alim, "Hip Hop Nation Language," *Language in the USA: Themes for the Twenty-First Century*, ed. Edward Finegan and John R. Rickford (Cambridge: Cambridge University Press, 2004), 402.

15. That exchange is improvisational, made evident in moments of incongruity between the center dancer and the lead drummer, which anthropologist Halbert Barton notes as counter to Europeanist expectations of synchronicity and conformity to choreography. Halbert Barton, "The Challenges of Puerto Rican Bomba," *Caribbean Dance: From Abakuá to Zouk* (Gainesville: University Press of Florida, 2002), 184; Concepción 169; Jade Power-Sotomayor, "Corporeal Sounding: Listening to Bomba, Listening to Puertorriqueñxs," *Performance Matters* 6.2 (2020): 43.
16. Power-Sotomayor 47.
17. Ashon Crawley, *Black Pentecostal Breath: The Aesthetics of Possibility* (New York: Fordham University Press, 2017): 103.
18. Power-Sotomayor 47.
19. Dance scholar Cristina Rosa's writing at moments exemplifies an aural kinesthetic analysis, far better than I ever could. When discussing samba for example, she writes,

> In samba dancing, different parts of the body participate in the construction of multi-meter arrangements by either following the audible score or by layering new rhythmic patterns above the main riff. While musicians play with musical instruments, dancers produce rhythmic patterns by "playing" with their own isolated body parts in dialogue with the ground/gravity. As a result, both musicians and dancers produce syncopated rhythms, which bounce back and forth, through call-and-response interactions between seeing and hearing. (77)

This short excerpt acts both as movement analysis and musical description. Rosa skillfully depicts and describes movement that is music, laying out a multidimensionality made possible precisely because these are aural-kinesthetic practices. The dancer is part of the music-making environment as a rhythm instrument, or a kinesthetic and visual riff. The description speaks to so many African diasporic practices. Cristina F. Rosa, *Brazilian Bodies and Their Choreographies of Identification* (New York: Palgrave Macmillan, 2015).
20. Rosa 102–3.
21. Rosa 115–16.
22. H. Samy Alim, *Roc the Mic Right: The Language of Hip Hop Culture* (New York: Routledge, 2006), 81.
23. Rosa makes this point particularly with regards to "capoeira angola," a version of capoeira said to be a more traditional form than "capoeira regional." (102).
24. H. Samy Alim, *Roc the Mic Right: The Language of Hip Hop Culture* (New York: Routledge, 2006), 81.
25. The berimbau replaced the drums as the primary instrument in the early nineteenth century. Thomas Desch-Obi, "Combat & the Crossing of the *Kalunga*," *Central Africans and Cultural Transformations in the American Diaspora*, ed. Linda M. Heywood (Cambridge: Cambridge University Press, 2002), 184–85.
26. Thomas Desch-Obi, *Fighting for Honor: The Story of African Martial Arts in the Atlantic World* (Charleston: University of South Carolina Press, 2008).
27. Though I will focus on a few different secular and sacred practices, it is also worth noting that Joseph Schloss draws on martial arts as well in examination of breaking, including capoeira, Angolan *engolo*, Igbo wrestling in modern-day Nigeria, and

ladja in Martinique. In his discussion of these same practices, T. J. Desch-Obi makes clear that all of these martial arts take place in circle practices and are connected to practices of the *kalunga* line. See Desch-Obi, *Fighting*; Desch-Obi, "Combat"; Schloss; and John Lowell Lewis, *Ring of Liberation: Deceptive Discourse in Brazilian Capoeira* (Chicago: University of Chicago Press, 1992).

28. Lewis 191, 193, 195.
29. Lewis 78, 84.
30. Desch-Obi adds specificity to Lewis's small but unelaborated point that capoeira is connected to African evocations of the spirit world. While Desch-Obi explicitly acknowledges the cultural legacies and ancestral and spiritual capacities of capoeira angolan rodas, Lewis's focus on the visible physical environment permits him to only briefly mention the heightened sensory dimension that is in accordance with practitioners' physical exertion. He never expands on the named "liberating mental sensations," to which the body's physical limits correspond. What Lewis captures are descriptive pieces of a larger experience, "a sense of flight" not evident in the details of the physical plane of activity, which is his focus. See Desch-Obi, "Combat"; Desch-Obi, *Fighting*; Lewis.
31. Robert Farris Thompson, *Flash of the Spirit: African and Afro-American Art and Philosophy* (New York: Vintage Books, 1983); Desch-Obi, "Combat"; Desch-Obi, *Fighting*.
32. Desch-Obi, "Combat" 354.
33. Qtd. in Thompson 108. Thompson goes on to state, "The four disks at the points of the cross stand for the four moments of the sun, and the circumference of the cross the certainty of reincarnation" (108).
34. There are three styles of capoeira: Angola, regional, and *contemporanea*. Lewis 84.
35. Desch-Obi, "Combat" 358.
36. Desch-Obi's work goes on to detail the ways that the inverted positions of capoeiristas in Angolan style capoeira echoes similar practices among the Kongolese, an orientation indicating entrance into the spirit world that was believed to be inverted. Desch-Obi, "Combat" 354–55.
37. Barbara Browning, *Samba: Resistance in Motion* (Bloomington: Indiana University Press, 1995), 108–9.
38. Sterling Stuckey, *Slave Culture: Nationalist Theory and the Foundations of Black America* (New York: Oxford University Press, 1987), 11–13.
39. Michael A. Gomez, *Exchanging Our Country Marks: The Transformation of African Identities in the Colonial and Antebellum South* (Chapel Hill: University of North Carolina Press, 1998), 114, 118.
40. Over time, ring shouts went from expressions of ancestral or polytheistic spiritual forces to a conversion practice to Christianity. Funerals, revivals, harvest time, and prayer meetings were also occasions for ring shouts. Historian Albert Raboteau argues that at their height, shouts were "the essence of religion" and essential to conversion. As one shout participant proclaimed, "The Spirit of God works upon people in different ways. At campmeeting there must be a ring here, a ring there, and a ring over yonder, or sinners will not get converted" (qtd. in Raboteau 69).

Commenting on this same comment—which was originally published in AME bishop Daniel Alexander Payne's autobiography—Gomez notes specifically that Payne's point of contention was that "he disagreed that human beings were in a position to proscribe such movement," despite it having been deemed necessary (Gomez 270). Albert Raboteau, *Slave Religion: The "Invisible Institution" in the Antebellum South* (Oxford: Oxford University Press, 1978); see also Gomez 266–69.

41. Crawley 103.
42. Crawley 103. Through an exploration of what he refers to as "perhaps unverifiable relation *between*" the word "shout" and the Arabic-Islamic word *saut*, African American and religious studies scholar Ashon Crawley opens space for the consideration of this counterclockwise movement's ties to the Afro-Arabic tradition of circling the Kaaba during pilgrimages to Mecca. Though my research led me toward Kongolese cosmologies rather than Islamic practices, both of these tracks suggest that the counterclockwise movements in African diasporic ritual circles are embodied practices that carry deeper meanings, connecting the diaspora to spiritual practices (96–99).
43. Crawley 103.
44. I am purposefully invoking Ashon Crawley's notion of "otherwise possibilities" here, but will develop it further in chapter 4. Crawley describes his use of "otherwise" in this way: "Otherwise . . . announces the fact of infinite alternatives to what *is*. And what *is* is about being, about existence, about ontology. But if infinite alternatives exist, if otherwise possibility is a resource that is never exhausted, what *is*, what exists, is but one of many. Otherwise possibilities exist alongside that which we can detect with our finite sensual capacities" (Crawley 2).
45. Crawley 103–4.
46. Crawley's discussion of shouts as otherwise social organizations is not itself about the extraphenomenal, yet it expands how we can think of the possibilities of the extraphenomenal as part of an otherwise sensibility.
47. Lewis 74.
48. Barton 192.
49. Qtd. in Concepción 170.
50. Alex LaSalle, "Bambula," *Güiro y Maraca* 11.2 (Summer 2007): 15.
51. LaSalle 11.
52. LaSalle 15.
53. Raquel Z. Rivera, "New York Afro-Puerto Rican and Afro-Dominican Roots Music: Liberation Mythologies and Overlapping Diasporas," *Black Music Research Journal* 32.2 (Fall 2012): 9.
54. Rivera 13.
55. While I don't know that I would land on the word "goal," much of Brown's discussion of the Òrìṣà Paradigm falls right in line with discussion thus far. Note how the circle is an organic dimension of a purposeful act of opening up to the spiritual realm:

> During the improvisational movement, dancers conjure up their own movement style and foot patterns but stay in the basic rhythmic structure of the accompanying music. Some dancers appear to experience euphoria as they carve out their personal movement expressions while out on the dance floor.

> When dancers are really showing off their skills, this solicits emotive responses from observers. Highly skilled dancers draw a crowd that encircles them as they continue to perform. The euphoria becomes contagious, and participants and observers seem to enter an emotional realm that passes through a spiritual threshold as they enter into a euphoric experience. Thus, the Òrìṣà Paradigm claims that ritualizing the African-derived dance performatives (to include and/or bring about ecstatic dancing), cultural practices, mythological characters, and folkloric practices accompanied by music, song, and drama significantly assist the individual's ability to open himself or herself up to the spiritual realm: that is the goal, and it is purposeful. (64–65)

Though she is writing about vernacular jazz dancing, one can easily recognize breaking, bomba, or capoeira in her descriptions. Benita Brown, "The Òrìṣà Paradigm: An Overview of African-Derived Mythology, Folklore, and Kinesthetic Dance Performatives," *Myth Performance in the African Diasporas: Ritual, Theatre, and Dance*, ed. Benita Brown, Dannabang Kuwabong, and Christopher Olsen (Lanham, MD: Scarecrow Press, 2014), 53–70.

56. Brown 65.
57. Silky Jones, personal interview, 10 August 2006.
58. Aby, personal interview, 18 March 2007.
59. Float, personal interview, 28 May 2007.
60. Mikhail Bakhtin, *Rabelais and His World*, trans. Helene Iswolsky, 2nd ed. (Bloomington: Indiana University Press, 1984[1964]).
61. Hartman writes, "'Stealing away' designated a wide range of activities, from praise meetings, quilting parties, and dances to illicit lovers and family on neighboring plantations" (66). See Saidiya Hartman, *Scenes of Subjection: Terror, Slavery, and Self-Making in Nineteenth Century America* (New York: Oxford University Press, 1997).
62. Norman King and Jane Ripley, "Steal Away Home: The Spirituals as Voice of Hope," *Phenomenon of Singing* 7 (2013): 74–80.
63. Hartman 66–67.
64. Hartman 69–70.
65. Hartman 78.
66. Poe One, personal interview, 3 January 2007.
67. He goes on to describe familiar critiques of the problems with capitalist exploitation, commercialization, and hypermaterialism, all of which he says evidence Hip Hop's antichrist energy. Triple7, personal interview, 3 October 2006.
68. KRS-ONE, "The Milk and the Meat: An Essay on Christ," *Bronx Biannual* 1 (June 2006): 145–58.
69. Poe One, personal interview, 3 January 2007.
70. Poe One, personal interview, 3 January 2007.
71. Miss Little, personal interview, 27 November 2006.
72. Miss Little, personal interview, 27 November 2006.
73. Aby, personal interview, 18 March 2007.
74. Pia, personal interview, 17 August 2012.
75. As much as funk music inspires Aby's transport to a different time and place, Pia's vehicle is an instrumental piece by Clint Mansell featured in the 2000 film *Requiem for a Dream*.

76. Jaekwon, personal interview, 17 August 2012.
77. Stuart Hall, "Negotiating Caribbean Identities," *Postcolonial Discourses: An Anthology*, ed. Gregory Castle (Oxford: Blackwell Publishers, 2001[1995]), 284.
78. Despite this rupture, African cultural influence on the Americas persisted through the people. Hall writes, "Africa, the signified which could not be represented directly in slavery, remained and remains the unspoken unspeakable 'presence.' . . . It is the secret code with which every Western text was 'reread.' It is the ground-bass of every rhythm and bodily movement." Stuart Hall, "Cultural Identity & Diaspora," *Identity: Community, Culture, Difference*, ed. Jonathan Rutherford (London: Lawrence & Wishart, 1990), 230.
79. Thomas F. DeFrantz, "Unchecked Popularity: Neoliberal Circulations of Black Social Dance," *Neoliberalism and Global Theatres*, ed. Lara D. Nielsen and Patricia Ybarra (New York: Palgrave Macmillan, 2012), 130.
80. This conversation spanned two different dance chat rooms including a Dance.net conversation thread titled "Africa to Hip Hop the Connection Made Clear," originally posted on 15 December 2006, http://www.dance.net/topic/5683709/1/Hip-Hop/african-to-hip-hop-the-connection-made-clear.html and the now defunct MrWiggles.biz conversation thread titled "Some People in This Community Are beyond Confused," originally posted on 20 December 2006, http://p076.ezboard.com/fmrwigggleshiphopfrm1.showMessageRange?topicID=13367.topic&start=1&stop=20.
81. Brenda Dixon Gottschild, *Digging the Africanist Presence in American Performance: Dance and Other Contexts* (Westport, CT: Praeger, 1996), xiv.
82. Viazeen, personal interview, 7 July 2007.
83. Gottschild, *Digging* 8; Viazeen, personal interview, 7 July 2007.
84. Brent Hayes Edwards, *The Practice of Diaspora: Literature, Translation, and the Rise of Black Internationalism* (Cambridge: Harvard University Press, 2003), 11. Edwards picks up on the definition of articulation that means "joining up . . . as in the limbs of the body, or an anatomical structure"—a formulation central to cultural studies scholar Stuart Hall's discussion of race and social dominance. Stuart Hall, "Race, Articulation, and Societies Structured in Dominance," *Sociological Theories: Race and Colonialism* (Paris: UNESCO, 1980), 328.
85. Earl Lewis, "To Turn as on a Pivot: Writing African Americans into a History of Overlapping Diasporas," *American Historical Review* 100.3 (June 1995): 765–87; Juan Flores, *The Diaspora Strikes Back: Caribeño Tales of Learning and Turning* (New York: Routledge, 2009), 71.
86. Primarily kung fu, karate, taekwondo, or aikido.
87. Eric Pellerin traces b-boying's 1970s and 1980s legends to the popularity of kung fu movies in the US. He incorporates comments from members of Star Child La Rock, New York City Breakers, Floormasters, Rock Steady Crew, and Ghetto Original Productions. Pellerin also has a forthcoming article on the same topic in the *Oxford Handbook on Hip Hop Dance Studies*, ed. Mary Fogarty and Imani Kai Johnson. Eric Pellerin, "The Impact of Kung Fu Movies on Bboying," 13 October 2008, http://koreanroc.com.
88. Bruce Lee, *Tao of Jeet Kune Do* (Valencia: Black Belt Communications, 1975), 3.
89. Krazy Kujo, personal interview, 4 September 2006.

90. I remain indebted to Latinx literary scholar Dr. Aracelie Esparza for introducing me to this language during the dissertation.
91. In "Cultural Identity and Diaspora," Stuart Hall writes that "*Presence Africaine* is the site of the repressed." Stuart Hall, "Cultural Identity and Diaspora," *Colonial Discourse and Post-colonial Theory: A Reader*, ed. P. Williams and L. Chrisman (London: Harvester Wheatsheaf, 1994), 398.
92. Desch-Obi, *Fighting* 157, 166–73; Desch-Obi, "Combat" 361.
93. Desch-Obi disputes origin narratives that propose that capoeira began among shackled slaves who learned to defend themselves while their hands were chained together. He argues that most bondsmen were shackled by their legs and not their hands and that "even ritual forms of *capoeiragem* would have been prohibited, not to mention the fact that many of techniques would have been impossible to execute." Desch-Obi, "Combat" 360–61.
94. Paul Harvey, "'These Untutored Masses': The Campaign for Respectability among White and Black Evangelicals in the American South, 1870–1930," *Journal of Religious History* 21.3 (October 1997): 315; Stuckey 94; Raboteau 68–69; Gomez 269–70.
95. Isar P. Godreau, "Folkloric 'Others': *Blanqueamiento* and the Celebration of Blackness as an Exception in Puerto Rico," *Globalization and Race: Transformations in the Cultural Production of Blackness*, ed. Kamari Maxine Clarke and Deborah A. Thomas (Durham: Duke University Press, 2006), 184.
96. Godreau 180.
97. See Imani Kai Johnson, "Black Culture without Black People: Hip Hop Dance beyond Appropriation Discourse," *Are You Entertained? Black Popular Culture in the Twenty-First Century*, ed. Simone C. Drake and Dwan K. Henderson (Durham: Duke University Press, 2020), 191–206; DeFrantz.
98. Gottschild, *Digging* 3.
99. As dance scholar Brenda Dixon Gottschild argues,

> All texts are intertexts. That is, forces, trends, languages, movement, modes—texts, in other words—of previous and contemporary societies influence us, live within and around us, and form the threads through which we weave our "new" patterns. They are the anonymous, unauthored codes of the culture. . . . Africanisms shape processes or the way that something is done, not simply the product or the fact that it is done. Concomitantly, a theory of Africanisms parallels a theory of intertextuality, which seeks to deal with the how or the process-phenomenon of the living text, rather than the text as product.

Whether articulated as intertextual or syncretic, Gottschild shows that "previous and contemporary societies" live in the way that movement is done. I adopt her approach to Africanisms, highlighting the common approach to circle practices as processes of channeling God, or one's past, or each other's energies. These qualities are recognizable through diaspora. My approach to this analysis is not meant to shut down other connections but to acknowledge an aspect of breaking culture that remains underexplored. Gottschild, *Digging* 3–4.

Superheroes Among Us

1. KR3Ts dance troupe led by choreographer Violeta Galagarza. See www.kr3ts.com.

Chapter 2 Battling in the Bronx

1. By now, Hip Hop is credited to multiple lines of origin, including formative cultural inheritances from Jamaica and Puerto Rico, African Americans on the East and West Coasts, and West African culture. See David Toop, *Rap Attack #3: African Rap to Global Hip Hop*, 3rd ed. (London: Serpent's Tail, 2000); Tricia Rose, *Black Noise: Rap Music and Black Culture in Contemporary America* (Hanover, NH: Wesleyan Press, 1994); Jeff Chang, *Can't Stop, Won't Stop: A History of the Hip-Hop Generation* (New York: St. Martin's Press, 2005); Raquel Z. Rivera, *New York Ricans from the Hip Hop Zone* (New York: Palgrave Macmillan, 2003); Joseph G. Schloss, *Foundation: B-Boys, B-Girls, and Hip-Hop Culture in New York* (New York: Oxford University Press, 2009); Robert Farris Thompson, "Hip Hop 101," *Droppin' Science: Critical Essays on Rap Music and Hip Hop Culture*, ed. William Eric Perkins (Philadelphia: Temple University Press, 1996), 211–19; Jeff Chang, ed., *Total Chaos: The Art and Aesthetics of Hip-Hop* (New York: BasicCivitas Books, 2006); James G. Spady, H. Samy Alim, and Samir Meghelli, *The Global Cipha: Hip Hop Culture and Consciousness* (Philadelphia: Black History Museum Publishers, 2006).
2. Schloss 125.
3. Schloss 125.
4. In the 1970s and today, it was not unlikely that practitioners were schooled in multiple Hip Hop expressive practices (including Graff, DJing, MCing, and other street dance genres like popping, locking, rocking, etc.). "Popping: is an umbrella term for several different funkstyles (e.g., roboting, tutting, boogaloo, ticking), but it also falls under the rubric of Hip Hop. Popping was born in California, developed out of Bay Area and Central and Southern California social dances, and innovated by figures like Boogaloo Sam. Showcased on nationally syndicated shows like *Soul Train* that featured California social dances, they were adopted by New York youth who incorporated them into a burgeoning cultural movement now called Hip Hop. I will on occasion use "street dances" (meaning specifically Hip Hop street dances) as a catchall for breaking, which is typically associated with Hip Hop, and funkstyles that are now associated with Hip Hop culture. See Naomi Elizabeth Bragin, "Black Power of Hip Hop Dance: On Kinesthetic Politics," PhD dissertation, University of California Berkeley, 2015, 46–47.
5. Andrew Hewitt, *Social Choreography: Ideology as Performance in Dance and Everyday Movement* (Durham: Duke University Press, 2005), 6.
6. Hewitt 21, 30.
7. My emphasis. Goran Sergej Pristaš, "Andrew Hewitt: Choreography Is a Way of Thinking about the Relationship of Aesthetics to Politics," *Frakcija* 42 (2007): 45.

8. While there are different works about social choreography in analyses of dance (mainly the waltz), Cox's discussion more aptly suits the context of my research.
9. My emphasis. Aimee M. Cox, *Shapeshifters: Black Girls and the Choreography of Citizenship*. (Durham: Duke University Press, 2015), 29.
10. Cox 29–30.
11. Cox 30.
12. Thank you to Manuel Macias, doctoral student in Critical Dance Studies, University of California, Riverside, for directing me to this helpful citation. Anurima Banerji, *Dancing Odissi: Paratopic Performance of Gender and State* (London: Seagull Books, 2019), 30–32.
13. Cleis Abeni, "Improvisation in African-American Vernacular Dancing," *Dance Research Journal* 33.2 (Winter 2001): 43–44.
14. The aural-kinesthetic speaks to the simultaneity of music and movement in social dance cultures. Imani Kai Johnson, "Music Meant to Make You Move: Considering the Aural-Kinesthetic," *Sounding Off! Sound Studies* blog (18 June 2012), http://soundstudiesblog.com/2012/06/18/music-meant-to-make-you-move-considering-the-aural-kinesthetic/.
15. Bragin 16.
16. See Rose; Chang, *Can't Stop*; Schloss; Imani Perry, *Prophets of the Hood: Politics and Poetics in Hip Hop* (Durham: Duke University Press, 2004).
17. The documentary *Flyin' Cut Sleeves* is named after this item of clothing, referencing how wearing it showcased one's affiliations. *Flyin' Cut Sleeves*, dir. Henry Chelfant and Rita Recher (Mvd Visuals, 1993).
18. Chang, *Can't Stop* 121.
19. They settled on requiring teens to get permits from city hall to dance, but refused to acknowledge any correlation to what multiple articles note was a reduction in gang activity at the height of breaking's popularity. Robert Goldberg, "'All-American City' Puts the Freeze on Break Dancers," *Wall Street Journal*, 1 May 1984; Wesley G. Hughes, "Ban on Break Dancing Up for Vote: San Bernardino Council Faces Youthful, Other Opposition," *Los Angeles Times*, 5 May 1984; "San Bernardino Revises Proposed Break-Dance Law," *Los Angeles Times*, 6 May 1984.
20. Monica Evans, "Stealing Away: Black Women, Outlaw Culture, and the Rhetoric of Rights," *Critical Race Theory: The Cutting Edge*, ed. Richard Delgado (Philadelphia: Temple University Press, 1982), 268.
21. Perry 104.
22. Richard Severo, "Bronx a Symbol of America's Woes," *New York Times*, 16 October 1977; Lee Dembart, "Carter Takes 'Sobering' Trip to South Bronx," *New York Times*, 6 October 1977; Joseph P. Fried, "The South Bronx, U.S.A.," *New York Times*, 7 October 1977; Staff Writer, "The Trip to the Bronx," *New York Times*, 6 October 1977.
23. Evelyn Gonzalez, *The Bronx* (New York: Columbia University Press, 2004).
24. The Cross Bronx Expressway cut through South Bronx neighborhoods and killed local businesses, dispersing residents to different parts of the city (Rose 30–33; Chang, *Can't Stop* 10–13; Gonzalez 121). See also Ric Burns's "New York: The City and the World Episode Seven: 1945 to Present" (1999); Rose's chapter titled "'All Aboard

the Night Train': Flow, Layering, and Rupture in Postindustrial New York"; Chang's chapter titled "Necropolis: The Bronx and the Politics of Abandonment"; Gonzalez's chapter titled "The South Bronx."

25. In *Can't Stop, Won't Stop*, Jeff Chang writes that in the South Bronx alone, between 1973 and 1977 there were thirty thousand documented incidents of arson, thus contributing to the national image of the South Bronx as a "war-zone" (15). Howard Cosell's on air proclamation, "The Bronx is burning!," during the 1977 World Series at Yankee Stadium (where he could see the smoke and flames of the five-alarm fire burning the abandoned Public School 3 east of the stadium) painted that picture for a national audience (10). Despite the nationwide economic crisis and the citywide problems, it was the South Bronx that became "a symbol of America's woes," according to a 1977 article in the *New York Times*. The sentiment was echoed in other articles as well. See Severo; Dembart; Fried; Staff Writer.
26. "The lag between when the landlord stopped paying taxes, providing services, and collecting rents and when the city acquired, demolished, and finally wiped the structure from its books often varied from years to overnight. At each stage of the process, landlords, tenants, and squatters could and often did burn their buildings.... Other city policies encouraged arson. In 1969, the city installed a less reliable fire alarm system and shut down firehouses where they were most needed" (Gonzalez 125). In a PBS documentary about the Bronx, filmmakers note that in their research, *no one was ever convicted of arson in the Bronx despite the sheer volume of arson cases*. See *Decade of Fire*, by Vivian Vasquez Irizarry, Gretchen Hildebran, and Julia S. Allen (PBS, 2019).
27. Community organizations like Advocates for Children (AFC), a nonprofit educational advocacy organization, put particular focus on those families and children living in the "welfare hotels" and relocation buildings for poor, newly homeless families. Though proposed as temporary locations wherein families could get back on their feet and create new homes elsewhere, more than a decade after the 1977 New York blackouts and President Carter's subsequent visit to the South Bronx, homeless hotels were still being emptied. AFC issued a "Testimony on Progress Made by New York City in Emptying the 'Welfare Hotels' and Relocating Homeless Families" at a congressional hearing on May 8, 1989. AFC noted its progress in housing eight hundred families the previous year, but drew attention to the offset of such progress—the inefficiency of quick moves that "caused more disruption and hardship, often leaving families stranded." Advocacy for Children, "Testimony on Progress Made by New York City in Emptying the 'Welfare Hotels' and Relocating Homeless Families," Press Release, 8 May 1989.
28. Moncell "ill Kozby" Durden, dir., *Everything Remains Raw: Hip Hop's Folkloric Lineage* (https://www.youtube.com/watch?v=-F-j5aXs_o4).
29. Qtd. in Durden.
30. Mr. Wiggles, 2007, interview with Moncell Durden, VHS recording.
31. *City of God*, dir. Fernando Meirelles and Kátia Lund (2002).
32. Trac2, personal communication, Manhattan, 28 July 2006.
33. As described by Mr. Wiggles. See *Freshest Kids*, dir. Israel (QD3 Entertainment, 2002).

34. Trac2, personal communication, 28 July 2006; Trac2 and Kwikstep, video-recorded interview with author and Moncell Durden, Boston, 26 May 2007; Trac2, personal interview, 28 July 2007.
35. To Trac2, breaking's four elements are top rocking, drops, floor work, freezes. Other dancers conceptualize the genre's parts differently, specifying footwork, air moves, or spins, all of which are part of Trac2's use of "floor work." This particular point is still applicable to other genres, like popping, in broader terms of appropriate technique.
36. "Gypsy" is a pejorative for the Romani people and is associated with criminality and poverty. In Trac2's discussion, he uses it euphemistically in reference to the fact that they are also nomadic communities. Thus, I opt to shift to the language of nomadism, replacing his term to capture the sentiment behind his use (i.e., in reference to a nomadic lifestyle) than insult a particular group.
37. Trac2, personal communication, 28 July 2006.
38. Jessica Nydia Pabón-Colón, "Writin', Breakin', Beatboxin': Strategically Performing 'Women' in Hip-Hop," *Signs* 43.1 (2017): 181.
39. Trac2, personal communication, Manhattan, 28 July 2006.
40. Perry 111.
41. Gerald Vizenor, *Manifest Manners: Narratives on Postindian Survivance* (Lincoln: Nebraska University Press, 1999), vii.
42. Serouj Aprahamian, "Going Off! The Untold Story of Breaking's Birth," PhD dissertation, York University Graduate Program in Dance Studies, 2021.
43. Aby, personal interview, video recording, 18 March 2007.
44. In response to an earlier draft of this chapter, Ashon Crawley offered the following insight: "One can move as oneself but not *by* oneself, moving collectively into the Other thing that is constantly already here with you (i.e. the concept of the metaphor as not just invisible; it's here, it's material, and the invisible as material)." While my analysis in this chapter runs in a slightly different direction, this thought has been especially important to my thinking throughout the book. Moreover, the idea of moving collectively toward and with the Other as a material force in the Bronx feels especially resonant with the community response to the film *Fort Apache: The Bronx*, during this era in the early 1970s. It is an easy example both of depictions in American pop culture of the Bronx as a place to be feared and the collective action activated in the wake of the filming. Community-based protests raged against its filming and even subsequent showings on television because it was rife with stereotypes. The Committee Against Fort Apache (CAFA) was formed 5 March 1980 with the following purpose and goals: "to actively engage in community opposition and resistance to the on-going denigration of Black and Puerto Rican people by the multi-national corporations that control one of the major means of mass communications. In this instance we are referring to Time, Inc. and 20th Century Fox, who are respectively the producer and distributor of 'Fort Apache, the Bronx'" (Diana Perez, Nilda Rodriguez, and Richard Perez, "Committee Against Fort Apache (CAFA)," Funding Request North Star, 25 November 1980, Series V, Box 8, Folder 7, Lourdes Torres Papers, Center for Puerto Rican Studies, CUNY Hunter College). As part of their campaign, they

joined forces with the Black United Front, who were protesting *Beulah Land*. A member of CAFA actually wrote a protest song titled "The Fort Apache Bop" and published it in *Latin N.Y.* magazine, noting that it should be "sung to the music of the Sugar Hill Gang," which is to say in the vein of rap music (Serrano 37). Since "Rapper's Delight" by the Sugar Hill Gang was one of the first popular rap songs and sung over Chic's "Good Times," that the credit went to the former rather than the latter speaks to the ways that rap suited them as an expression of the collectivity activated in protest. In this example, the collectivity is formed in a place that is othered and among the "Others" who are "constantly already here with you." See Raymond Serrano, "A Community Stands Together and Makes Nation-Wide News," *Latin N.Y.* (n.d.): 34–37; Perez, Rodriguez, and Perez.

45. As an Africanist aesthetic, a return to the collective or a glorification of the whole is especially meaningful in diasporic expressive cultures. In the introduction to *Signifyin(g), Sanctifyin', & Slam Dunking: A Reader in African American Expressive Culture*—a collection exploring the points of convergence between dance, music, athletics, oral expression, and their influence on American culture—Gena Caponi notes: "*(1) Rhythmic and metric complexity; (2) Individual improvisation and stylization; (3) Dialogic interaction or call-and-response; (4) Active engagement of the whole person and the whole community; (5) Social commentary or competition through indirection and satire; and (6) development of a group consciousness or sensibility—the invisible conductor.*" Caponi offers six principles of African ritual circles, a set of "remarkably consistent" principles that emerge across practices. She writes, "Each of these African aesthetic principles aids in the process of developing and maintaining an interactive and interdependent social community." For example, rhythm and multiple meters stage an active group engagement; call and response structures a multivalent social exchange; the principle of improvisation within tradition maintains a tensioned balance between the group and the individual. Gena Caponi, "The Case for an African American Aesthetic," *Signifyin(g), Sanctifyin', & Slam Dunking: A Reader in African American Expressive Culture*, ed. Gena Caponi (Amherst: University of Massachusetts Press, 1999), 10–12.
46. Aby, personal interview, video recording, 18 March 2007.
47. He told me that he had started out trying to learn how to break, which he saw first and was excited by as "a new dance" that he wanted to be part of. He even notes having a signature freeze, a "pledge of allegiance" gesture with a salute. But he was mesmerized by popping. Cartoon, personal interview, 28 September 2006.
48. Bragin 54.
49. Bragin 54.
50. Bragin 53.
51. Cartoon, personal interview, video recording, 28 September 2006.
52. In the documentary *Underground Dance Masters*, popping OG Popin' Pete comments about his older brother, popping innovator Boogaloo Sam, teaching him in the same way, starting first with his arms. See *Underground Dance Masters: Final History of a Forgotten Era*, dir. Thomas Guzman-Sanchez (2015).

53. Drama and theater scholar Jacqui Malone concurs with Gottschild, also noting that when the butt is involved, it tends to get read in overly sexualized ways. I expand on this point in chapter 4. See Brenda Dixon Gottschild, *The Black Dancing Body: A Geography from Coon to Cool* (New York: Palgrave Macmillan, 2003), 104; Jacqui Malone, *Steppin' on the Blues: The Visible Rhythms of African American Dance* (Urbana: University of Illinois Press, 1996).
54. Qtd. in Malone 34.
55. Bragin 47.
56. Bragin 43. That is literally what the ritual teaches. As Abeni reminds us, improvisation is composition within the ritual's structures.
57. See https://www.kipsbay.org/missionandhistory.
58. Baby Love, personal interview, video recording, 29 June 2007.
59. Baby Love remarks that though Lady Rock could dance, she "never took it to the next level of step that I did with the Rock Steady Crew." Baby Love, personal interview, video recording, 29 June 2007.
60. Baby Love, personal interview, video recording, 29 June 2007.
61. Rose 48.
62. Baby Love, personal interview, video recording, 29 June 2007.
63. "Elsewhere: Randy Martin on Performing the Changing City," https://movementresearch.org/publications/critical-correspondence/elsewhere-randy-martin-on-performing-the-changing-city).
64. Randy Martin, "A Precarious Dance, a Derivative Sociality," *TDR: The Drama Review* 56.4 (Winter 2012): 63, 72.
65. Martin 73; my emphasis. Martin proposes the kinesthetic in contrast to a society of the spectacle (Guy Dubord) wherein people are increasingly isolated from one another, relating more through spectacles and commodity exchange than relationships. Martin activates the kinesthetic because it "render(s) the spectacle internal to performance." Hence, it models a sociality that shifts social relations from their capitalist terms of being mediated by objects and external forces to being relationships through practice (Martin 73).
66. Caponi 9–10.
67. Brenda Dixon Gottschild, "Crossroads, Continuity, or Contradiction: The Afro-Euro-Caribbean Triangle," *Caribbean Dance from Abakuá to Zouk: How Movement Shapes Identity*, ed. Susanna Sloat (Gainesville: University Press of Florida, 2002), 9.
68. Kwikstep, personal interview, video recording, 8 August 2008.
69. Sometimes spelled "babalawo," this figure is recognized in Yoruba-based spiritual systems in Latin America, including Cuban lucumí and Brazilian candomblé. There are many sources that delve into the intricacies of this figure. One such source is Baba Ifa Karade, *The Handbook on Yoruba Religious Concepts* (Newburyport, MA: Weiser Books, 1994).
70. Rose 73, 89.
71. Joseph G. Schloss, *Making Beats: The Art of Sample-Based Hip-Hop* (Middletown, CT: Wesleyan University Press, 2004), 3.
72. Schloss 138–39.

73. Cox 30.
74. Nicole Hodges-Persley, "Sampling," *Reading Contemporary Performance: Theatricality across Genres*, ed. Meiling Cheng and Gabrielle H. Cody (London: Routledge, 2016), 260.
75. Kwikstep and Trac2, personal interview, 26 May 2007.

Crossing the Line

1. Speedy Gonzales is itself an update of the Go-Go Gomez character in the old *Dick Tracy* cartoon. Though considered problematic and conceived of in racist stereotypes, many Mexican Americans embrace the Speedy character for his ingenuity and hints of anti-imperialism, though I doubt those particular German breakers were invoking the latter meaning. See Gustavo Arellano, "Column: Why Do So Many Mexican Americans Defend Speedy Gonzales?," *Los Angeles Times*, 12 March 2016, https://www.latimes.com/california/story/2021-03-17/speedy-gonzales-cancelled-hollywood-mexican-americans.

Chapter 3 Badass B-Girls Dancing the Dissonance

1. Qtd. in Martha Cooper and Nika Kramer, *We Be*Girlz* (New York: powerHouse Books, 2005), 57.
2. Their reticence in providing details meant that such information was not meant for me to disclose, but simply to better understand their positionalities and priorities. That background informs my overall understanding of breaking as a community.
3. Cooper and Kramer 113. In my 2007 interview with Aruna, she stated, "It got me to a point where I was experiencing the culture as an adult. So that means to me that you are much more interested in the background of it, that you're much more . . . how do you say this? Uh, not by accident. You're not there by accident. This is like a choice that you made. . . . I had like a lot of career options within that field of schooling that I had. But I *chose* to be in Hip Hop, so that means to me in my—I had to prove my, my parents, my family, my friends that my choice was legitimate you know. That that was, th-that's not something like, 'Oh I like it *now*.' No, this is something that I want to do. And I think I did that." Aruna, personal interview, 1 July 2007.
4. Matthew Ming-tak Chew and Sophie Pui Sim Mo, "Towards a Chinese Hip-hop Feminism and a Feminist Reassessment of Hip-hop with Breakdance: B-Girling in Hong Kong, Taiwan and China," *Asian Studies Review* 43.3 (March 2019): 16.
5. As I have argued in previous work, b-girls' claims to femininity contrasts with expectations that they solely or mainly identify with and through "female masculinities" (as discussed by Halberstam) like the tomboy, though certainly it is a familiar and available reference. As I previously wrote, "Like tomboys, b-girls stake claim to a freedom of expression that pushes the boundaries for gender performativity. . . .

Yet the category of tomboy does not fit b-girls entirely. From eight years of research on breaking communities in North America and Europe, I have come to understand b-girling through femininity rather than masculinity. In fact, most of the b-girls that I have met claim femininity, even when they operate outside of social expectations of what femininity is supposed to be." Imani Kai Johnson, "From Blues Women to B-Girls: Performing Badass Femininity," *Women and Performance* 24.1 (2014): 19; Judith Halberstam, *Female Masculinity* (Durham: Duke University Press, 1998).

6. Dance scholar and b-boy Serouj Aprahamian reiterates this point, acknowledging that, despite studies suggesting that dance writ large is viewed as a "feminine" practice, breakers approached that dance differently: "Just as young men in The Bronx did not view their dancing as a 'feminine' activity—as it is often stigmatized in dominant Western discourse—neither did young women who were 'going off' and burning see themselves as performing 'masculinity.'" See Aprahamian, "'There Were Females That Danced Too': Uncovering the Role of Women in Breaking History," *Dance Research Journal* 52.2 (August 2020): 45.

7. Johnson 16.

8. Hortense Spillers, "'Mama's Baby, Papa's Maybe': An American Grammar Book," *Diacritics* 17.2 (Summer 1987): 67.

9. Tara Crichlow and Stacey Earsman, "B-Girls Worldwide," "Cypher-Rock: A Virtual Hip Hop Dance Listening Cypher," special issue of *Conversations across the Field of Dance Studies* 41 (October 2021).

10. I think there is an inexact overlap with Latina feminist performance studies scholar Jessica Pabón-Colón's project, itself an extension of a call from Hip Hop feminist Joan Morgan, for a feminism that "fucks with the grays." See Jessica Nydia Pabón-Colón, *Graffiti Grrlz: Performing Feminism in the Hip Hop Diaspora* (New York: New York University Press, 2018), 43.

11. Jessica Nydia Pabón-Colón, "Writin', Breakin', Beatboxin': Strategically Performing 'Women' in Hip-Hop," *Signs* 43.1 (2017): 181; Aprahamian 53.

12. Aisha Durham, Brittney C. Cooper, and Susana M. Morris, "The Stage Hip-Hop Feminism Built: A New Directions Essay," *Signs* 38.3 (Spring 2013): 721–37; Eisa Davis, "Sexism and the Art of Feminist Hip-Hop Maintenance," *To Be Real: Telling the Truth and Changing the Face of Feminism*, ed. Rebecca Walker (New York: Anchor Books, 1995), 127–41; Joan Morgan, *When Chickenheads Come Home to Roost: My Life as a Hip-Hop Feminist* (New York: Simon & Schuster, 1999); Gwendolyn Pough, "Do the Ladies Run This . . . ? Some Thoughts on Hip-Hop Feminism," *Catching a Wave: Reclaiming Feminism for the 21st Century*, ed. Rory Dicker and Alison Pipemeier (Boston: Northeastern University Press, 2003); Aisha Durham, "Hip Hop Feminist Media Studies," *International Journal of Africana Studies* 16.1 (Spring–Summer 2010): 117–40; Gwendolyn Pough, Elaine Richardson, Aisha Durham, and Rachel Raimist, eds., *Home Girls Make Some Noise: Hip-Hop Feminism Anthology* (Mira Loma, CA: Parker, 2007); Whitney A. Peoples, "Under Construction: Identifying Foundations to Hip-Hop Feminism and Exploring Bridges between Black Second-Wave and Hip-Hop Feminisms," *Meridians* 8 (2008): 19–52; Shanté Paradigm Smalls, "The Rain Comes Down: Jean Grae and Hip Hop Heteronormativity," *American*

Behavioral Scientist 55.1 (January 2011): 86–95; Durham, Cooper, and Morris; Johnson.

13. For example, ethnomusicologist Kyra Gaunt's *The Games Black Girls Play: Learning the Ropes from Double-Dutch to Hip-Hop* bridges work on music and movement by looking at the cultural contributions and ongoing impact that Black women and girls have had on Hip Hop's music and rhythms, through the titular embodied games and their uncredited contributions. In her study of women graffiti writers titled *Graffiti Grrlz: Performing Feminism in the Hip Hop Diaspora*, Pabón-Colón contextualizes women graffiti writers' "feminist masculinity" to capture the masculinist nature of graffiti performed in such a way that does not perpetuate misogyny. And in terms of street dances, gender gets marked in bodily comportment, dress, particular moves, and in gestures. In "Techniques of Black Male Re/Dress: Corporeal Drag and Kinesthetic Politics in the Rebirth of Waacking/Punkin'," dance scholar Naomi Bragin argues that the sexy and confident femininity that cisgender women embody in these dances draws on the radical embodiment of femininity by the Black queer men who innovated them, thereby "corporeal[ly] drag[ging]" ciswomen into a queered femininity. Kyra D. Gaunt, *The Games Black Girls Play: Learning the Ropes from Double-Dutch to Hip-Hop* (New York: New York University Press, 2006; Pabón-Colón, *Graffiti Grrlz*; Naomi Bragin, "Techniques of Black Male Re/Dress: Corporeal Drag and Kinesthetic Politics in the Rebirth of Waacking/Punkin'," *Women and Performance* 24.1 (2014): 61–78.
14. Mary Fogarty, "Breaking Bad: New Bgirls," *Dance Current*, March–April 2015, 39.
15. What Pabón-Colón calls dominant Hip Hop masculinity "represented as a stubborn independence, a stoic singularity, an autonomous subjectivity that reads as tough and callous..., simultaneously celebrated and criticized for the oppressive power it wields over women (be they straight, queer, cis, or trans)" (Pabón-Colón, *Graffiti Grrlz* 72).
16. Marlon Bailey, *Butch Queens Up in Pumps: Gender, Performance, and Ballroom Culture in Detroit* (Ann Arbor: University of Michigan Press, 2013), 44. Much appreciation to taisha paggett for reminding me of the importance and necessity of naming this connection to the ground already laid by LGBTQI people.
17. Ming-tak Chew and Pui Sim Mo, "Towards a Chinese Hip-hop Feminism and a Feminist Reassessment of Hip-Hop with Breakdance: B-Girling in Hong Kong, Taiwan and China," *Asian Studies Review* 43.3 (2019): 10.
18. Chew and Mo 16.
19. Such works explore hegemonic and subordinate or marginalized femininities, what sociologist and women's studies scholar Mimi Schippers calls "pariah" femininities—nonidealized femininities that disrupt or contend with a compliance to patriarchy. Mimi Schippers, "Recovering the Feminine Other: Masculinity, Femininity, and Gender Hegemony," *Theory and Society* 36.1 (February 2007): 85–102; K. D. Pyke and D. L. Johnson, "Asian American Women and Racialized Femininities: 'Doing' Gender across Cultural Worlds," *Gender and Society* 17.1 (2003): 33–53; R. W. Connell and James Messerschmidt, "Hegemonic Masculinity: Rethinking the Concept," *Gender and Society* 19.6 (December 2005): 829–59. See also Tricia Rose, *Black Noise: Rap Music and Black Culture in Contemporary American* (Hanover, NH: Wesleyan University

Press, 1994); Nancy Guevara, "Women Writin' Rappin' Breakin'," *Droppin' Science: Critical Essays on Rap Music and Hip Hop Culture*, ed. William Eric Perkins (Philadelphia: Temple University Press, 1996), 49–62.
20. Schippers 95.
21. Schippers 95. My emphasis.
22. See Eliana Dockterman, "More Female Heroes in Hollywood? Yes, but Not Nearly Enough," *Time*, 23 December 2016, https://time.com/4599585/hollywood-female-action-heroes/; Seth Mlawski, "Why Strong Female Characters Are Bad for Women," blog on OverthinkingIt.com, https://www.overthinkingit.com/2008/08/18/why-strong-female-characters-are-bad-for-women/; Schippers 95.
23. Alien Ness, *The Art of Battling: Understanding Judged Bboy Battles* (self-published, n.d.). As there are no page numbers in this text, I will specify the headers noted in the table of contents under which one can find the cited information.
24. Aprahamian 44.
25. Alien Ness, Part 1, "Explanation of Terms Used." See also Rachael Gunn, "'Don't Worry, It's Just a Girl!': Negotiating and Challenging Gendered Assumptions in Sydney's Breaking Scene," *Journal of World Popular Music* 3.1 (2016): 66.
26. He gives an example of a freeze "done with such swiftness and perfection that no one saw it coming." Alien Ness, Part 3, "Understanding Burners."
27. See Alien Ness; also Joseph Schloss, *Foundation: B-Boys, B-Girls and Hip-Hop Culture in New York* (New York: Oxford University Press, 2009), 133.
28. Burns allow one to both conserve energy and grab the attention of crowds and judges. Hence their usefulness in clinching a win. See Alien Ness, Part 3, "Understanding Burners."
29. The rock dance sometimes called uprocking is a dance predating breaking that performs a range of rhythmic, pantomimed forms of attack against an opponent standing across from the dancer. Breaking's toprock style is adopted from uprocking, a dance developed in the Bronx and Brooklyn in the early 1970s.
30. Even in its earliest iterations burning carried this meaning: "Although burning was most often performed upright—and was not as acrobatic as breaking would later become—the dance during this period was known for its confrontational use of everything from comedic to offensive gestures, such as the miming of weapons or alluding to sexual inuendo" (Aprahamian 45).
31. Posted by Tai. "Bgirl Vendetta vs Bgirl A-Plus," https://www.youtube.com/watch?v=g7m5pkFV0ng (accessed 7 November 2020). Start at 2:34 to catch it.
32. Visit *Rock Dance History: The Untold Story of Up-Rocking*, directed by Jorge "Popmaster Fabel" Pabón.
33. "Rock Dance History: The Untold History of Up-Rockin' = Papo Luv on 'Outlaw' Sisters That Rock," http://www.youtube.com/watch?v=AR_MULaVMg0 (accessed 28 October 2020).
34. Qtd in Aprahamian 44. Aprahamian cites a YouTube video interview with Disco Daddy.
35. L. H. Stallings, *Funk the Erotic: Transaesthetics and Black Sexual Cultures* (Urbana: University of Illinois Press, 2015), 10–11.

36. Stallings xv, 10. My emphasis.
37. Robert Farris Thompson, "An Aesthetic of the Cool: West African Dance," *Africa Forum* 2.2 (Fall 1966): 85–102.
38. Signifyin' is not just a verbal practice. It manifests in performance as well. See n. 42.
39. Armin Schwegler, "Black Ritual Insulting in the Americas: On the Art of 'Vociferar' (Colombia), 'Vacilar' (Ecuador) and 'Snapping', 'Sounding' or 'Playing the Dozens' (U.S.A.)," *Indiana* 24 (2007): 107–55; Lawrence W. Levine, "The Ritual of Insult," *Black Culture and Black Consciousness: Afro-American Folk Thought from Slavery to Freedom* (New York: Oxford University Press, 1978), 345–58; Sally Price and Richard Price, *Afro-American Arts of the Suriname Rain Forest* (Berkeley: University of California Press, 1981), 169, 175–76; Roger D. Abrahams, The Man-of-Words in the West Indies (Baltimore: Johns Hopkins University Press, 1983); Raquel Z. Rivera, *New York Ricans from the Hip Hop Zone* (New York: Palgrave Macmillan, 2003); Kenneth Bilby, "Playful Insults in Aluku: Guianese Maroon Variations on an African and Diasporic Theme," paper presented at "Contesting Culture: Battling Genres in the African Diaspora," CUNY Baruch College, 2 May 2008; Elijah Wald, *The Dozens: A History of Rap's Mama* (New York: Oxford University Press, 2012).
40. Schwegler 110.
41. Schwegler 115. See also Ernie Adolphus Smith, "The Evolution & Continuing Presence of the African Oral Tradition in Black America," PhD dissertation, University of California, Irvine, 1975. In it, Smith includes a "Glossary of Oral Expressive Styles" that included sixty entries, fifteen, or 25 percent, of which entailed physical movement or have gestures affiliated with them as a central dimension of the term's meaning. Smith was an early thinker around the term "Ebonics," which did not simply mean "ebony phonics" but was intended to capture a sense of the embedded Africanist dimensions of African American language practices. Smith's emphasis on language further supports movement as a fundamental dimension of Africanist epistemologies in action.
42. Citing Robin D. G. Kelley, Aprahamian concurs that the neglect of women in such studies is evidence of social scientists' infatuation with and pathologizing of poor, inner-city Black men. Aprahamian writes, "In the realm of cultural expression, this has resulted in scholarly generalizations that reduce complex articulations of creativity and joy to masculine survival strategies for ghetto life. Women are commonly excluded from such narratives, as they do not fit the masculinized image of resistance to urban destitution and deprivation." See Aprahamian 46; and Robin D. G. Kelley, *Yo' Mama's Disfunktional! Fighting the Culture Wars in Urban America* (Boston: Beacon Press, 1997), 33.
43. Abrahams xvi; Schippers 95.
44. Abrahams 2.
45. Johnson 23.
46. Saidiya Hartman, *Wayward Lives, Beautiful Experiments: Intimate Histories of Riotous Black Girls, Troublesome Women, and Queer Radicals* (New York: Norton, 2019), 256.
47. In contrast to nomadism in chapter 2—which was about the necessity of connecting to others who practiced to expand breaking networks and test one's level—Hartman's

use of errantry was an already criminalized mobility that thwarted the design of the law to regulate Black women's intimate lives.
48. Hartman 256.
49. My understanding of Desch-Obi's work in this area comes from being on multiple panels with him over years, as he has developed these ideas, and in multiple drafts of his forthcoming book, *Hombres y Mujeres Históricos: Grima and the Afro-Colombian Struggle* (ICESI University Press [Editorial Universidad Icesi]). Conference panels include the National Endowment of the Humanities Summer Workshop "Black Aesthetics and African Centered Cultural Expressions: Sacred Systems in the Nexus Between Cultural Studies, Religion and Philosophy," Emory University, Atlanta, GA, 2014; the panel "Badass Women: Feminine Elements in the Africanist Aesthetics of Battling," National Council for Black Studies Conference, Los Angeles, CA, 14 March 2015; and the Association for the Study of the Worldwide African Diaspora, Charleston, SC, 6 November 2015.
50. Desch-Obi.
51. Desch-Obi offers a parallel example from the Kongo region, looking at a weapon called the twin blades of power, "a pair of elaborate machetes that were gendered male and female." He notes that "even the most feared, the most politically powerful and iconically potent weapons of western Africa were often linked on a cosmological level to the female principle, highlighting the fact that combat in pre-colonial Western Africa was not conceptualized as exclusively male, even when all the physical combatants were biologically male." He goes on to consider these principles as necessarily inhabitable by anybody, and in fact needing to be in balance rather than a dichotomy inhabitable only by certain bodies.
52. Producing what Gunn refers to as "unisex" style because "b-boys and b-girls have access to the same movement vocabulary" (65).
53. See Alien Ness.
54. In the documentary *The Freshest Kids: A History of the B-Boy*, they feature footage of the 1999 B-Boy Summit in Venice Beach, California, during which police in full riot gear are called to suppress the event. They treat the dancers and the proliferation of cyphers like a riot. As the police formed a human barricade, walking in an intimidating line—batons prepared to strike, and steadily pushing the crowd off the beach and promenade toward the streets—Crazy Legs (Rock Steady Crew) took to the concrete. In the space between the barricade of officers and the increasingly frustrated, confused, and angry crowd of dancers and spectators, Crazy Legs dropped to the ground and hurled himself in a quick series of revolutions, coming up to his feet, and ending by throwing the dick at the police. The breakers behind him cheered. See "Crazy Legs Bboy Summit Police Raids and Brutality," a clip from *The Freshest Kids* (dir. Israel, 2002), http://www.youtube.com/watch?v=h0YDrWZlz-I (accessed 5 March 2018).
55. In some cases, some b-boys expressed the sentiment that to battle a b-girl is beneath them, an insult, or an easy win. Though it was never clear to me how frequent or rare it is, the extreme of this is when a b-boy won't battle a b-girl because he feels encumbered. In a personal interview with Ness4, he said that he does not battle

b-girls because he "can't win." He alluded to the idea that his approach in a battle against a b-girl might fault him more than help him, and anything less than his best would make him vulnerable to a loss anyway. One infamous Ness example is known as the condom burner, where mid-battle he unfurled a condom and dropped it at the feet of b-girl Nadia, eliciting laughter from the *thousands* of spectators at a battle (which, in the video looked to be at least 80 percent b-boys). He says he used "our biggest weapon" to "cripple" that crew's most "dangerous" element, b-girl Nadia. Brina, referred to in the article as Mama Zulu, watched the battle, noting that Ness "really embarrassed her so that she wouldn't come out again." While certainly my reflection on this example demonstrates the "no win" situation Ness described, in the literal battle *it worked*; and no one faulted him for it. And while it may have been a calculated gamble, it would always be more harmful to her. In any case, to *not* battle a b-girl is especially problematic in a culture that thrives on competition and confrontation. See Helen Simard, E. Hodac, Brina Martinez, and L. Martinez, "The Inner Workings of Crew Politics: A Discussion with the Mighty Zulu Kingz," *Proceedings of the Canadian Society for Dance Studies Conference* (Montreal: QC, 2012), 9.

56. B-girl and researcher Gunn concurs: "If they are too close to me, I mime humping my opponent or bringing their face down to my crotch. If a b-boy mimes giving me the cock, I pretend to bite it off or make a face of disgust to undermine their action through humour. . . . I see the practice of burns and the sparring that often ensues as a space to deplete its potency" (71).

57. This is a commonplace retort against b-girls. Ansley Joye James addresses it and the range of feelings and responses to sexualized burns and specifically "throwing dick" in her MA thesis titled "A Battle of Repression: Hip Hop Bgirls, Burns and Gestural Languages 1970 to 2010," Florida State University, 2011. In it she reaches a conclusion opposite mine, questioning whether breaking offers women opportunities beyond mimesis of masculinity, and whether it can actually be a viable practice that opens the possibilities of what she cites in Schloss's *Foundations*: "the power to redefine themselves and their history, not by submission or selective emphasis, but by embracing *all* of their previous experiences as material for self-expression in the present moment" (44). James argues that the practice of throwing the dick proves Schloss's statement as mere myth. I, however, see Schloss's conjecture as viable when we pay attention to the repertoire of Africanist aesthetics practiced in sexualized burns. There, b-girls throwing the dick highlights the liminality that James herself names as potentially offering something beyond mimesis of masculinity.

58. Emiko, personal interview, 18 September 2006.

59. Emiko, personal interview, 18 September 2006.

60. Shout out to MiRi "Seoulsonyk" Park, b-girl and graduate student in World Arts and Culture at UCLA, for bringing this point to my attention. Sports science scholars Tonja Langnes and Kari Fastin explain: "This means that becoming involved in the subculture of breaking involves adopting and internalizing the subculture's ideas, objects and practices so that the individual is identified and accepted as a breaker. This identification and acceptance does not happen once, but is a continuous process."

Tonje F. Langnes and Kari Fasting, "Identity Constructions among Breakdancers," *International Review for the Sociology of Sport* 51.3 (2016): 352.

61. Emiko, personal interview, 18 September 2006.
62. Part of the moment is shaped by the fact that Emiko did not let his attempt to undermine her run interrupt her flow, even as she took the time to put him in his place. Typically, the concern is that sexism hinders experimentation, as Fogarty stated, and flow. Gunn and Scannell write, "Perhaps the biggest discouragements to the B-girl are those entrenched cultural techniques and expectations that impede the capacity of 'flow' as the formulation of self-expression." Rachael Gunn and John Scannell, "Overcoming the Hip-Hop Habitus," special issue, "Shifting Sounds: Musical Flows" (2012 IASPM Australia/New Zealand Papers), ed. Oli Wilson and Sarah Attfield, *Journal of World Popular Music* 3.1 (2016): 53.
63. She stated in our interview later that when she overthinks it, she does not do well. So when she dances, she commits to showing her character, being silly, and having fun.
64. Another, perhaps long-overdue consideration is of philosopher and gender theorist Judith Butler's analysis of matter, gesture, and gender. Butler's approach to gender performativity in *Bodies That Matter: On the Discursive Limits of Sex* argues that gestures cannot be understood without also understanding how the crucial coupling of power and discourse together give precedence to the reiterative gesture. That is to say that a gesture's meaningfulness rests on the ways that its repetition reinforces its hegemonic meaning; and such gestures are among the ways that people perform gender. Popular burners like throwing the dick can enact this nexus of power and discourse, which reproduces the binary's control by reasserting discourses that exclude b-girls. But as discussed earlier, there is always a counterattack or an improvisation that can disrupt it. The dark matter metaphor resonates with the influence of the improvised disruptive gesture (which has no certain meaning) over the traditional or hegemonic one. Gunn notes that b-girls are "invited" to "'experiment' with the body's affective capacities, and exposes breakdancing as a salient site to increase the regulated repertoire of bodily expression." Rachael Gunn, "The 'Systems of Relay' in Doing Cultural Studies: Experimenting with the 'Body without Organs' in B-Girling Practice," *Continuum* 30.2 (2016): 183.
65. Thomas DeFrantz, "Hip-Hop Habitus v.2.0," *Black Performance Theory*, ed. Thomas F. DeFrantz and Anita Gonzalez (Durham: Duke University Press, 2014), 234.
66. Brenda Dixon Gottschild, "Crossroads, Continuity, Or Contradiction: The Afro-Euro-Caribbean Triangle," *Caribbean Dance from Abakuá to Zouk: How Movement Shapes Identity*, ed. Susanna Sloat (Gainesville: University Press of Florida, 2002), 10.
67. Gottschild 9–10.
68. Gottschild 9–10.
69. DeFrantz 234–36.
70. Gunn and Scannell 56–57.
71. Gunn and Scannell 56.
72. Fogarty 37.
73. Rokafella, personal interview, 7 September 2006.
74. Rokafella, personal interview, 7 September 2006.

75. My emphasis. DeFrantz 235.
76. I look to Ashon Crawley's notion of "otherwise possibilities," as already existing practices that affirm alternative modes of sociality and being that both critique a normative world and act as a site of radical challenge to it. In addition, his concept of *centrifugitivity* is a reflection of a logic of expanding out while inviting in—of extending the connection to otherness outward by way of practices that also draw practitioners into the folds of Black culture, I am also inspired by Crawley's repeated formulations of relation as operative in practice. See "Otherwise Movements," *New Inquiry*, 19 January 2015, http://thenewinquiry.com/essays/otherwise-movements/; "Otherwise, Ferguson," *Interfictions Online* 7 (October 2016), http://interfictions.com/otherwise-fergusonashon-crawley/; "Against the Normative World," *New Inquiry*, 9 April 2015, http://thenewinquiry.com/features/against-the-normative-world/. He fully discusses this concept in his work *Blackpentacostal Breath: The Aesthetics of Possibility* (New York: Fordham University Press, 2017).
77. For a thorough discussion of Glissant's relevance to Hip Hop studies, see Travis Harris, "Can It Be Bigger Than Hip Hop? From Global Hip Hop Studies to Hip Hop," *Journal of Hip Hop Studies* 6.2 (Winter 2019): 17-70.
78. Or *chaos-monde* (French for chaos-world), which speaks to the proliferation of connections through difference. In Hip Hop's take on Glissant's formulation of "*chaos-monde*," Harris writes, "This 'chaos is not chaotic,' rather it is a cipha." Édouard Glissant, *Poetics of Relation*, trans. Betsy Wing (Ann Arbor: University of Michigan Press, 1997 [1990]): 138; Harris 57.
79. Glissant 138-39.
80. Glissant 79.
81. Joseph Holloway, ed., *Africanisms in American Culture* (Bloomington: Indiana University Press, 1990), 12; Evelyn O'Callaghan, *Women Writing the West Indies, 1804-1939: "A Hot Place, Belonging to Us"* (London: Routledge, 2004), 167-68; Kokahvah Zauditu-Selassie, "Dancing between Two Realms: Sacred Resistance and Remembrance in African American Culture," *Journal of Interreligious Studies* 23 (May 2018): 62.
82. Zauditu-Selassie, n. 58, 46-67. In Western body language discourse, this gesture is sometimes called a superman stance, but the meaningfulness of the gesture is not exclusive to that particular pop cultural reference.
83. Thomas F. DeFrantz, "The Black Beat Made Visible: Hip Hop Dance and Body Power," *Of the Presence of the Body: Essays on Dance and Performance Theory*, ed. André Lepecki (Middletown, CT: Wesleyan University Press, 2004), 64-81.
84. Her then trainer and now husband Kwikstep told her that while he liked her curves, she would need to lose some of them to be a better breaker. Unpublished Field Notes, "Diary of European Trip inc Int'l BOTY Notes 10-05 to 10-22-06."
85. Writing on American b-girls in the 1980s and 1990s, Tricia Rose notes how "most girls were heavily discouraged from performing break-moves because they were perceived by some male peers as 'unsafe' or 'unfeminine.' Female breakdancers sometimes executed moves in conventionally feminine ways, to highlight individuality and perhaps to deflect male criticism. Again, women who performed these moves

were often considered masculine and undesirable or sexually 'available.'" In my 2014 badass femininity article, I noted discourses about upper-body strength used to suggests that b-girls "lack" the appropriate body, versus what came down to a matter of training in skills to discipline a body to the form. Rose 48-49; Johnson 18, 24.

86. Gunn, "'Don't Worry" 62.
87. Qtd. in Chew and Mo 9.
88. Pabón-Colón, "Writin'" 180.
89. This language about b-girls needing to lose their curves implies an ideal body. In contrast, though, in her work on aging bodies in breaking, Mary Fogarty writes, "In breaking practice, b-boys and b-girls do not regard body type as the 'perfect body' or ideal shape. In fact, unlikely bodies are given 'respect' and 'props' for their skills, which are often body-type related. Taller b-boys and b-girls are given props for being able to do what traditionally has been conceived of as a shorter person's dance form." In this same vein, curvier does not detract from anyone's potential athleticism, strength, and agility. Given Fogarty's insight about the respect given to "unlikely" or atypical breaking bodies, at least as long as they express an "enthusiastic and dedicated" approach—for example, the noticeably older (e.g., Krazee Grandma) or disabled ("some of the best b-boys and b-girls in the world would be categorized as having a 'disability' in their society")—then why the discourse about "losing one's curves"?

Admittedly, the question of an ideal body type was not a consistent point of discussion in my interviews. Thus, in light of Fogarty's studied intervention, I propose that even within her argument there are nonetheless traditions or assumptions about what a quintessential breaking body is. In fact, in my interviews with Toronto-based breakers conducted in 2012, in answer to a question about whether there was such a thing as an ideal body type, the most applauded answer was "Spiderman" because he was compact, agile, and strong. (The lone b-girl in this small group of four or five breakers later expressed her disappointment that no one proposed a b-girl equivalent, like Wonder Woman, for example.) It is not a coincidence then that breakers tend to be physically small in stature, lean, muscular, and necessarily strong for better maneuverability and control, especially while balancing on fingers, forearms, elbows, butts, shoulders, and the sides of a foot. When applied to b-girl's bodies, these expectations translate into a loss of curves, particularly in the hips and breasts. It suggests that despite an *acceptance* and even appreciation for different body types in breaking, there are still assumptions that follow when one recognizes how "true" breakers (to echo Trac2 in chapter 2) are typically thought to be b-*boys*.

I can appreciate how having "less curves" meant embodying the music differently. Breaking is such an exuberant dance form that. In the handful of breaking classes that I took, I recognized how I actually experienced the rhythm of the music in my body differently precisely because my breasts or belly would register a bounce, for example, milliseconds *after* my feet and hands, which threw off my sense of my own rhythm. I was not sure how to deal with it. Had I stuck with it, learning to break in my body and accounting for my curves would undoubtedly have to become a dimension of my style. Mary Fogarty, "'Each One Teach One': B-Boying and Ageing," *Ageing and Youth Cultures: Music, Style and Identity* (London: Bloomsbury, 2012), 53–65.

90. Black Pearl, personal interview, 21 October 2006.
91. Black Pearl, personal interview, 21 October 2006.
92. Stuart Hall writes, "Perhaps instead of thinking of identity as an already accomplished fact, . . . we should think, instead, of identity as a 'production,' which is never complete, always in process, and always constituted within, and not outside, representation." Stuart Hall, "Cultural Identity & Diaspora," *Identity: Community, Culture, Difference*, ed. J. Rutherford (London: Lawrence & Wishart, 1990), 222–37.
93. Perhaps some would consider it ironic that, despite my case for Hip Hop's Africanist aesthetics, one can perform them while still acting racist, but they would be wrong precisely because those aesthetics circulate in ways that are persistently divorced from Black life. Consider, for example, how Brenda Dixon Gottschild opens her seminal work *Digging the Africanist Presence* by recounting a brief exchange with a white student uncertain as to whether they should take Gottschild's course, Black Performance from Africa to the Americas. Gottschild's poignant response, "Honey, you're taking it right now; you've been taking it all your life!" reminds us that (to state the obvious) these aesthetic lessons are taken up every day across communities because they are a part of what gets called "American culture," which then circulates around the world along paths of American cultural hegemony, alongside global antiblackness, and divorced from the communities that birthed them, as dance scholar Thomas DeFrantz has repeatedly reminded us. Thus, there is no guarantee that Africanist aesthetics are recognized by or are meaningful to people in the same way. Brenda Dixon Gottschild, *Digging the Africanist Presence in American Performance: Dance and Other Contexts* (Westport, CT: Praeger, 1996); DeFrantz 2004, 2014; Thomas DeFrantz, "Unchecked Popularity: Neoliberal Circulations of Black Social Dance," *Neoliberalism and Global Theatres: Performance Permutations*, ed. Lara D. Nielsen and Patricia Ybarra (London: Palgrave Macmillan, 2012), 128–40.
94. Hanifa Queen, personal interview, 22 May 2007.
95. *Redder Than Red: The Story of B-Girl Bubbles*, dir. Martha Cooper and Nika Kramer (We B*Girlz Productionz!, 2005).
96. The filmmakers were also behind the *We B*Girlz!* book.
97. Awad Ibrahim, *The Rhizomes of Blackness: A Critical Ethnography of Hip-Hop Language, Identity, and the Politics of Becoming* (New York: Peter Lang, 2014), 193.
98. Ibrahim 2.
99. DeFrantz, "Hip-Hop Habitus" 234–36.

Chapter 4 Dancing Global Hip Hop

1. Of course, not all of the circles at IBOTY were like the one described in the opening of this chapter. The after-parties were geared toward cyphering, but the cyphers I did see at IBOTY were dominated by Americans and veteran European breakers. Cyphering did not seem to be a prominent part of breaking culture in Europe in 2006 as it was in the US. In a 2006 interview with Dark Marc, of Ghost Crew, he explained that in

Norway, because members of his crew lived so far apart from each other, even their practices together were infrequent. At the time, several breakers I met in Germany spoke of cyphering on a monthly basis at best, or every few months for others. In a 2012 interview, Jaekwon, a Taiwanese b-boy who grew up in Germany, would explain to me that in his experience, Europeans practiced, competed at competitions, and performed on stage, but did not cypher as frequently as dancers do in the States. Dark Marc, personal interview, 11 August 2006; Jaekwon, personal interview, 17 August 2012.

2. In her article "The Global Situation" and book *Friction: An Ethnography of Global Connection*, anthropologist Anna L. Tsing cautions against invoking the global without attending to its diversity. In her work, the global is a concept that speaks to certain kinds of social projects, ones that come from "spatially far-flung collaborations and interactions." Such "contingent collaborations" proceed due to overlapping interests, yet never guarantee shared goals. This is what allows for conversation across differences that are often couched in ideas of an almost utopic interconnection. Yet Tsing argues that something substantive can be born in the tensions of "creative frictions" brought forth by the inevitable differences in interests of such collaborations. In other words, just because people come together does not mean that they stop being culturally distinct from one another; and that distinction can be productive within the context of something shared. See Anna L. Tsing, "The Global Situation," *Cultural Anthropology* 15.3 (August 2000): 327–60; and Anna L. Tsing, *Friction: An Ethnography of Global Connection* (Princeton: Princeton University Press, 2005).

3. Tsing, *Friction*; Tsing, "Global Situation."

4. Tsing, *Friction*.

5. Brent Hayes Edwards, *The Practice of Diaspora: Literature, Translation, and the Rise of Black Internationalism* (Cambridge: Harvard University Press, 2003), 11.

6. Edwards 11. I also read the diasporic as "overlapping" in the manner of historian Earl Lewis, or, as Juan Flores once described, as "mutually interlocking diasporas." Earl Lewis, "To Turn as on a Pivot: Writing African Americans into a History of Overlapping Diasporas," *American Historical Review* 100.3 (June 1995): 765–87; Juan Flores, *The Diaspora Strikes Back: Caribeño Tales of Learning and Turning* (New York: Routledge, 2009), 71.

7. *The American Heritage Dictionary*, 3rd ed. (Boston: Houghton Mifflin, 1993).

8. H. Samy Alim, "Translocal Style Communities: Hip Hop Youth as Cultural Theorists of Style, Language, and Globalization," *Pragmatics* 19.1 (2009): 107.

9. While I have heard Buddha Stretch say this on multiple occasions, this is a phrase that he puts in his bio and even has written on his resume. See https://www.peridance.com/facprofile.cfm?FID=1248&name=Buddha_Stretch (accessed 12 February 2022).

10. *Genba* organize local interactions and global participation. Condry uses nightclubs (*genba*) as places of cultural production where flows of interaction take place, and are networked both globally and locally. Ian Condry, *Hip-Hop Japan: Rap and the Paths of Cultural Globalization* (Durham: Duke University Press, 2006), 19.

NOTES   213

11. Jason Ng, "Connecting Asia-Pacific Hip-hop: The Role of the Cross-Cultural Intermediary," PhD dissertation, Monash University (2019), 1–2.
12. Afterthoughts on "A Shut Door: 'Japanese Hip-Hop Has Sectioned Itself Off,'" *The Microscopic Giant* blog (16 August 2018), http://themicrogiant.com/afterthoughts-on-a-shut-door-japanese-hip-hop-has-sectioned-itself-off/.
13. Dexter L. Thomas, "Niggers and Japs: The Formula behind Japanese Hip-Hop's Racism," *Social Identities* 22.2 (2016): 210–11.
14. Qtd. in. Tracey Jones, "A Shut Door: 'Japanese Hip-Hop Has Sectioned Itself Off,'" *Tokyo Weekender*, 24 July 2018, https://www.tokyoweekender.com/2018/07/a-shut-door-japanese-hip-hop-has-sectioned-itself-off/.
15. Halifu Osumare, *The Hiplife in Ghana: West African Indigenization of Hip-Hop* (New York: Palgrave Macmillan, 2012), 178.
16. Kamau Brathwaite, "Jah," *The Arrivants: A New World Trilogy* (Oxford: Oxford University Press, 1967), 162–64.
17. Osumare 1–2.
18. Osumare 78.
19. James G. Spady, H. Sami Alim, and Samir Meghelli, *Tha Global Cipha: Hip Hop Culture and Consciousness* (Philadelphia: Black History Museum Publishers, 2006), 34–35.
20. Spady, Alim, and Meghelli 11, 34–35.
21. Freestyle Sessions, which began in Southern California in 1997, are a series of events held year-round in different parts of the world organized by Cross1.
22. MZK was the dance offshoot of the Universal Zulu Nation (UZN), an organization started in the 1970s by one of Hip Hop's first DJs, Afrika Bambaataa. MZK was revived in 2000 by b-boy Ness4 (aka Alien Ness), evidently under permission from Bambaataa himself. This is according to MZK history, as recorded by Alien Ness on his blog. http://alienness.blogspot.com/2010/10/zulu-kingz-were-created-on-same-day.html (accessed 30 October 2016).
23. See "Freestyle Sessions 10 Final Gambler vs Zulu Kings (HQ) Part1," https://www.youtube.com/watch?v=iClzsCmxYxY (accessed 6 March 2018).
24. Though the original document is undated, personal communication with its author dated it approximately 1998. Krazy Kujo, "Power Moves vs. Styles," http://www.hiphop-network.com/articles/bboyarticles/powervsstylebykujo.asp (accessed 8 March 2010).
25. In a 2006 interview, Krazy Kujo stated that the debate was moot: both power and style are proven to be essential aspects of b-boying. He suggests that the true terms of the debate are progressives versus conservatives—those who favor innovation and those who do not. Yet, as b-boy Poe One has said to me and others many times, "There is no old school or new school. There's only true school." He believes that regardless of where breakers draw their inspiration, they must maintain a b-boying "approach," an unspecified sense of essence, style, and attitude indicative of b-boying culture. Poe One's point is that innovation is limitless, but the approach should retain something "true," or perhaps foundational, in its practice.
26. Images of all kinds helped to amplify breaking's global reach. In addition to popular films, tours, music videos, and the circulation of what dance scholar Mary

Fogarty identifies as "video magazines," VHS tapes and eventually DVDs of battles, crew anniversaries, and breaking events sold and circulated in these underground scenes, bringing Hip Hop to brand-new but spatially far-flung aspiring participants. Recorded videos tended to capture and best showcase power moves, what I think of as visual "soundbites" that prioritized the spectacle over—and perhaps even as a strategic *representation* of—the shared groove experienced kinesthetically in a live context. Mary Fogarty, "'What Ever Happened to Breakdancing?': Transnational B-Boy/B-Girl Networks, Underground Video Magazines, and Imagined *Affinities*," MA thesis, Brook University (2006).

27. This, in fact, is how the documentary *The Freshest Kids* narrativizes b-boying's growth and spread across the country. In contrast, East Coast breakers attempt to counter this narrative by arguing that power moves have always been a part of the dance, and that even in the early 1970s there were b-boys who were known for it. Few contest that in the mid-1980s, West Coast crews seemed to focus on breaking's power moves.

28. I recall an 8 October 2006 conversation I had in London with a group of British breakers just after the UK B-Boy Championships. We were discussing the results of the final crew battles. A young man and I both agreed that the American crew, Massive Monkeys, should have made it to the finals. During the course of our conversation, it came up that the French crew—Pokémon, who eventually won the title—had really strong toprocks. I added that Massive Monkey's toprocking was equally great, if not better. A British b-girl named Genesis responded, "Well yeah but they're Americans." I had to ask, "So you get special points if you're not American and can toprock but no acknowledgment if you are American?" to which Genesis and a b-boy named Chris laughingly replied with a resounding "Yes!" Though they laughed, they were not really joking.

29. Joseph G. Schloss, *Foundation: B-Boys, B-Girls, and Hip-Hop Culture in New York* (New York: Oxford University Press, 2009), 13.

30. Schloss 12.

31. The contradictory desire for and concern about the global life of Hip Hop has produced what I've called a kind of moral panic from below. Rokafella is among those breakers that express a collective anxiety about the globalization of a culture born in poor- and working-class communities of color, especially those of African descent. I draw on the language of moral panic, not to diminish what they say, but because this part of the breaking community often employs the language of moral panics—people taking over, people stealing culture—in order to address anxieties about breaking culture becoming increasingly diffuse, and their own erasure in histories of Hip Hop. These fears stem logically from histories of cultural appropriation that diminish the significance of Black people in contemporary incarnations of rock and jazz music, signaling the immanence of history repeating itself by way of the neoliberal currents that circulate Hip Hop dances without concern for technique, history, etc. Yet it is a kind of panic that ultimately goes unseen because of *who* maintains that anxiety. It represents a social problem only to those whose interests have already been marginalized. This situation is further complicated by the economic ramifications of the global circulation of Hip Hop, which facilitates opportunities to work as artists,

opportunities that otherwise wouldn't exist. The panic from below goes unacknowledged, but its ramifications continue to resonate. What will become of breaking in its global context? Will it still be recognizable as such in the years to come? This idea developed out of an unpublished and ultimately lost paper—due to a motherboard crash—partially recovered and given at the Global Moral Panics Symposium held at Indiana University, 10–11 October, 2014.

32. Gena Caponi, ed., *Signifyin(g), Sanctifyin', and Slam Dunking: A Reader in African American Expressive Culture* (Amherst: University of Massachusetts Press, 1999), 5, 11.
33. *Estilo Hip Hop*, Dir. Vee Bravo and Loira Limbal (2009).
34. His examples include exchanges like, "Are you scared of playing with me? Do you have the guts to run at me? Do you have the bladder to attack me?" *Mongolian Bling*, dir. Benj Binks (2012).
35. Q Rock, phone interview, 19 January 2012.
36. Q Rock, phone interview, 19 January 2012.
37. Q Rock, phone interview, 19 January 2012.
38. Frostalino, personal interview, 19 January 2012.
39. Frostalino, personal interview, 19 January 2012.
40. This echoes the experiences of Norwegian b-boy Dark Marc, who cites a similar relationship to his father, a jazz musician, who taught him to appreciate qualities that later prepared him to appreciate Hip Hop. For a fuller discussion of Dark Mark's experiences, see Imani Kai Johnson, "Black Culture without Black People: Hip Hop and Dance beyond Appropriation Discourse," *Are We Entertained? New Essays on Black Popular Culture in the 21st Century*, ed. Simone Drake, David Ikard, and Dwan Simmons (Durham: Duke University Press, 2019), 191–206.
41. This is an inexact transcript of detailed, nearly verbatim notes taken during a Skype interview. Hanifa Queen, personal interview, 22 May 2007.
42. Profo Won, personal interview, 19 May 2009.
43. Profo Won, personal interview, 19 May 2009.
44. Brenda Dixon Gottschild, *Black Dancing Body: A Geography from Coon to Cool* (New York: Palgrave Macmillan, 2003), 104, 147–48, 188.
45. The difference in valuation comes to bear on how the isolation of that region is meaningful: "The Africanist value placed on the democratic autonomy of body parts stands in contrast to the Europeanist value on unity and line (meaning straight line) working toward one objective." Gottschild 25, 147.
46. Gottschild 188.
47. Profo Won, personal interview, 19 May 2009.
48. Profo Won, personal interview, 19 May 2009.
49. She writes, "Avoidance of the appearance of homosexuality is central to normative masculine embodiment." Maxine Leeds Craig, *Sorry I Don't Dance: Why Men Refuse to Move* (Oxford: Oxford University Press, 2014), 7.
50. Craig 16.
51. Profo Won, personal interview, 19 May 2009.
52. Profo Won, personal interview, 19 May 2009.

53. Brenda Dixon Gottschild, *Digging the Africanist Presence in American Performance: Dance and Other Contexts* (Westport, CT: Praeger, 1996), 3–4.
54. In addition to the circle, Caponi lists six other qualities in common across various "African rituals," each of which also resonates with breaking cyphers. They include: "*(1) rhythmic and metric complexity; (2) individual improvisation and stylization; (3) dialogic interactions or call and response; (4) active engagement of the whole person and the whole community; (5) social commentary or competition through indirection and satire; (6) development of a group consciousness or sensibility—the invisible conductor.*" Gena Dagel Caponi, "Introduction: The Case for an African American Aesthetic," *Signifyin(g), Sanctifyin', & Slam Dunking: A Reader in African American Expressive Culture*, ed. Gena Dagel Caponi (Amherst: University of Massachusetts Press, 1999), 5, 9–10.
55. Dorinne Kondo, *Worldmaking: Race, Performance, and the Work of Creativity* (Durham: Duke University Press, 2018), 29.
56. Kondo 54.
57. Kondo 44.
58. Caponi 9–10.
59. Caponi 11.
60. Caponi 11.
61. "For [John Miller] Chernoff this rhythmic center constitutes an 'additional rhythm' that drummers feel and hear with their inner ears, but do not play. For A.M. Jones this is 'metronome sense,' and for Richard Waterman, 'a subjective beat.' Abraham Adzenyah, of the University of Ghana Dance Ensemble and Wesleyan University, terms it the 'hidden rhythm,' while for John Blacking it is the 'rhythm of an *invisible conductor*.'" Caponi 11.
62. Rickey Vincent, *Funk: The Music, the People, and the Rhythm of the One* (New York: St. Martin's Griffin, 1996), 37.
63. Vincent 37.
64. Kariamu Welsh Asante, "Commonalities in African Dance," *African Culture: The Rhythms of Unity*, ed. Molefi Asante and Kariamu Welsh Asante (Trenton, NJ: African World Press, 1985), 77–78.
65. Welsh Asante 77–78.
66. Ralph Ellison, *Invisible Man* (New York: Signet, 1947), 499.
67. Ellison 503.
68. My emphasis. Fred Moten, *In the Break: The Aesthetics of the Black Radical Tradition* (Minneapolis: University of Minnesota Press, 2003), 73.
69. Moten 63–64.
70. W.E.B. Du Bois, *The Souls of Black Folk* (New York: Bantam Books, 1903), 3.
71. That is why Du Bois names it a double-edged sword, a gift and a burden, a privileged awareness and a surreptitious kind of foresight constantly under surveillance. Du Bois 3, 5, 7.
72. See chapter 1 for more on Poe One's experiences of the extraphenomenal.

73. Thomas F. DeFrantz, "Unchecked Popularity: Neoliberal Circulations of Black Social Dance," *Neoliberalism and Global Theatres*, ed. L. D. Nielsen et al. (New York: Palgrave Macmillan, 2012), 128, 130. My emphasis.
74. I originally came to this bell hooks discussion by way of a mix by DJ Lynnée Denise titled "Soulful Critical Thought: bell hooks and the Making of a DJ Scholar," one of several of her mixes that I played extensively as I revised the manuscript. https://www.podomatic.com/podcasts/djlynneedenise/episodes/2014-04-20T10_38_19-07_00 (accessed 20 November 2020). Transcripts of the original talk can be found here: bell hooks and Sut Jhally, dir., *bell hooks: Cultural Criticism and Transformation*, transcript of the film (Northampton, MA: Media Education Foundation, 1997), 22.
75. DeFrantz 130.
76. Thank you Dorinne Kondo for bringing me to this essential concept. Gayatri Spivak, "Can the Subaltern Speak?," *Marxism and the Interpretation of Culture*, ed. Cary Nelson and Lawrence Grossberg (Urbana: University of Illinois Press, 1988), 291; Michel Foucault, "Two Lectures," *Power/Knowledge: Selected Interviews and Other Writings, 1972–1977*, ed. Colin Gordon, trans. Colin Gordon, Leo Marshall John Mepham, and Kate Soper (New York: Pantheon Books, 1972), 78–108.
77. David Harvey, *A Brief History of Neoliberalism* (Oxford: Oxford University Press, 2005), 7.
78. DeFrantz writes, "Unexamined, 'freedom' appears to be desirable for all. Encouraged by late twentieth-century calls toward a freedom to move as one wants to, black dance is engaged by a global public with little understanding of its aesthetic histories or varied social contexts within black communities." DeFrantz 130.
79. Kondo 28.
80. Rokafella, personal interview, 17 September 2006.
81. Rokafella, personal interview, 17 September 2006.
82. Rokafella, personal interview, 17 September 2006.
83. Rokafella, personal interview, 17 September 2006.
84. Rokafella, personal interview, 17 September 2006.
85. Howard Winant, "The Dark Matter: Race and Racism in the 21st Century," *Critical Sociology* 41.2 (2014): 10.
86. Cornel West, "Black Culture and Postmodernism," *Remaking History* ed. Barbara Kruger and Phil Mariani (Seattle: Bay Press, 1989), 93.
87. Rokafella, personal interview, 17 September 2006.
88. Such work includes her participation in the book *We B-Girlz*, which documents b-girls and their interests and concerns around the world. She also organized the "B-Girl Sit Downs," a series of formal group discussions within Hip Hop communities across the US on the impact of gender differences on participation in the culture, supported by a grant from the Ford Foundation. Her documentary *All the Ladies Say* profiles members of Collective 7—a crew formed with six other women Hip Hop practitioners. *All the Ladies Say*, dir. Ana "Rokafella" Garcia (New York: Third World Newsreel, 2010).
89. Sujatha Fernandes, *Close to the Edge: In Search of the Global Hip Hop Generation* (London: Verso, 2011), 185–86.

90. Fernandes 187.
91. Fernandes articulates why coalition politics matter in a book on social movements, stating that "a functioning substantive democracy may depend on the ability of social movements to build broad-based coalitions, especially across the rural-urban divide. (237). Sujatha Fernandes, *Who Can Stop the Drums? Urban Social Movements in Chávez's Venezuela* (Durham: Duke University Press, 2010).
92. The film references his video for "Holler If You Hear Me." *Slinghsot Hip Hop*, dir. Jacqueline Reem Salloum (2008).
93. Angela Y. Davis, *Freedom Is a Constant Struggle: Ferguson, Palestine, and the Foundations of a Movement*, ed. Frank Barat (Chicago: Haymarket Books, 2016), 39.
94. Davis 139–40.

Coda

1. As of October 15, 2021 this Facebook post was shared over 550 times, first in 2016 and again in summer 2020. The original post can be found here: https://www.facebook.com/AlphaTrion.RftA/posts/10102821531879517.
2. Marcela A. Fuentes, "Performance, Politics, Protest," *What Is Performance Studies?*, ed. Diana Taylor and Marcos Steuernagel (Durham: Duke University Press, 2015), e-ISBN: 978-0-8223-7407-7. Also available as an online journal, https://scalar.usc.edu/nehvectors/wips/performance-politics-and-protest.
3. This site can be better understood as an online, blog-formatted extension of his master's thesis; grimes's citations are hyperlinks, with other links on each page ultimately connect back to preceding and subsequent blog posts, not necessarily in chronological order but in varied directions, undermining a linear approach to reading as the order of the entries almost ceases to matter. See http://www.socialdancemedia.blogspot.com.
4. d. Sabela grimes, "Predictably Unprecedented: Old Shuffles in the New Paradigm," Hip-Hop Studies Conference: Writing and Representing Hip-Hop in the Academy, University of California Berkeley, 18 April 2009; d. Sabela grimes, "Predictably Unprecedented," http://socialdancemedia.blogspot.com/2008/08/predictably-unprecedented.html (accessed 6 March 2018).
5. grimes, "Old Shuffles in The New Paradigm."
6. grimes, "Old Shuffles in The New Paradigm."
7. d. Sabela grimes, "Street Scholar Sampler," 28 August 2008, http://socialdancemedia.blogspot.com/2008/08/street-scholar-sampler.html.
8. grimes, "Street Scholar Sampler."
9. André Zachary, "Blk Haptics—Africanist Aesthetics + Feedback in Performance Technology," UCR Colloquium Series "Towards Antiracist Futures of Dance in the Post-pandemic Academy," lecture via Zoom, 6 May 2021.
10. https://flash---art.com/article/arthur-jafa-face-it-the-affective-proximity-of-imagery/.

11. For unspoken reasons, Jafa uses air quotes around the word "curate."
12. See "bell hooks and Arthur Jafa Discuss Transgression in Public Spaces at the New School," https://www.youtube.com/watch?v=fe-7ILSKSog (accessed 26 September 2021).
13. hooks and Jafa.
14. Others have employed this term in studies of live stimuli and the real-world proximity of bodies encountering them. Kate Brown, "'Black People Figured Out How to Make Culture in Freefall': Arthur Jafa on the Creative Power of Melancholy," https://news.artnet.com/art-world/arthur-jafa-julia-stoschek-collection-1227422 (accessed 6 March 2018).
15. Arthur Jafa and Tina Campt, "Love Is the Message, the Plan Is Death," *e-flux journal* 81 (April 2017): 3, 5.
16. Jafa and Campt 6.
17. Jafa and Campt 6.
18. Katrina Hazzard-Gordon, *Jookin': The Rise of Social Dance Formations in African-American Culture* (Philadelphia: Temple University Press, 1990), 20.
19. *The American Heritage Dictionary*, 3rd ed. (Boston: Houghton Mifflin, 1993).
20. Aria Dean, "Worry the Image," *Art in America*, 26 May 2021, https://www.artnews.com/art-in-america/features/worry-the-image-63266/.
21. Chanda Prescod-Weinstein, *The Disordered Cosmos: A Journey into Dark Matter, Spacetime, and Dreams Deferred* (New York: Bold Type Books, 2021).
22. As it stands, I do not know if I have said too much. An elder Black scholar and ordained minister who studies Black spiritualities beyond Christianity whispered to me once after a talk I gave on chapter 1, "You reveal a lot." She said it matter-of-factly, though it did feel a bit cryptic, like a heads-up to proceed cautiously. Or perhaps it was just a reminder of a responsibility. I have never been absolutely clear on what she meant or where her concern was most situated, but I never forgot it.

Selected Bibliography

Books, Articles, and Dissertations

Abeni, Cleis. "Improvisation in African-American Vernacular Dancing." *Dance Research Journal* 33.2 (2001): 40–53.

Abrahams, Roger D. *The Man-of-Words in the West Indies*. Baltimore: John Hopkins University Press, 1983.

Abrahams, Roger D. *Singing the Master: The Emergence of African-American Culture in the Plantation South*. New York: Penguin, 1992.

Alien Ness. *The Art of Battling: Understanding Judged Bboy Battles*. Self-published, 2007.

Alim, H. Samy. *Roc the Mic Right: The Language of Hip Hop Culture*. New York: Routledge, 2006.

Alim, H. Samy. "Translocal Style Communities: Hip Hop Youth as Cultural Theorists of Style, Language, and Globalization." *Pragmatics* 19.1 (2009): 103–127.

Aprahamian, Serouj. "Going Off: The Untold Story of Breaking's Birth." PhD dissertation, York University, 2021.

Aprahamian, Serouj. "'There Were Females That Danced Too': Uncovering the Role of Women in Breaking History." *Dance Research Journal* 52.2 (2020): 41–58.

Banerji, Anurima. *Dancing Odissi: Paratopic Performances of Gender and State Enactments*. London: Seagull Books, 2019.

Barton, Halbert. "The Challenges of Puerto Rican Bomba." *Caribbean Dance: From Abakuá to Zouk*. Edited by Susanna Sloat. Gainesville: University Press of Florida, 2002, 183–96.

Bragin, Naomi. "Black Power of Hip Hop Dance: On Kinesthetic Politics." PhD dissertation, University of California, Berkeley, 2015.

Bragin, Naomi. "Techniques of Black Male Re/Dress: Corporeal Drag and Kinesthetic Politics in the Rebirth of Waacking/Punkin'." *Women and Performance* 24.1 (2014): 61–78.

Brathwaite, Kamau. *The Arrivants: A New World Trilogy*. Oxford: Oxford University Press, 1967.

Brown, Benita. "The Òrìṣà Paradigm: An Overview of African-Derived Mythology, Folklore, and Kinesthetic Dance Performatives." *Myth Performance in the African Diasporas: Ritual, Theatre, and Dance*. Edited by Benita Brown, Dannabang Kuwabong, and Christopher Olsen. Lanham, MD: Scarecrow Press, 2014, 53–70.

Browning, Barbara. *Samba: Resistance in Motion*. Bloomington: Indiana University Press, 1995.

Caponi, Gina, et al. *Signifyin(g), Sanctifyin', and Slam Dunking: A Reader in African American Expressive Culture*. Amherst: University of Massachusetts Press, 1999.

Carroll, Sean. *Dark Matter, Dark Energy: The Dark Side of the Universe, Parts I and II*. Chantilly, VA: Teaching Company, 2007.

Chang, Jeff. *Can't Stop Won't Stop: A History of the Hip-Hop Generation*. New York: St. Martin's Press, 2005.

Chew, Matthew Ming-tak and Sophie Pui Sim Mo. "Towards a Chinese Hip-hop Feminism and a Feminist Reassessment of Hip-hop with Breakdance: B-Girling in Hong Kong, Taiwan and China." *Asian Studies Review* 43.3 (2019): 455–74.

Christian, Barbara. "The Race for Theory." *Cultural Critique* 6 (1987): 51–63.

Concepción, Alma. "The Challenges of Puerto Rican Bomba." *Caribbean Dance: From Abakuá to Zouk*. Edited by Susanna Sloat. Gainesville: University Press of Florida, 2002, 168–69.

Cooper, Martha and Nika Kramer. *We Be*Girlz*. New York: powerHouse Books, 2005.

Cox, Aimee Meredith. *Shapeshifters: Black Girls and the Choreography of Citizenship*. Durham: Duke University Press, 2015.

Craig, Maxine Leeds. *Sorry I Don't Dance: Why Men Refuse to Move*. Oxford: Oxford University Press, 2014.

Crawley, Ashon T. *Blackpentecostal Breath: The Aesthetics of Possibility*. New York: Fordham University Press, 2017.

Daniel, Yvonne. *Dancing Wisdom: Embodied Knowledge, in Haitian Vodou, Cuban Yoruba, and Bahian Candomblé*. Urbana: University of Illinois Press, 2004.

Davis, Angela Y. *Freedom Is a Constant Struggle: Ferguson, Palestine, and the Foundations of a Movement*. Edited by Frank Barat. Chicago: Haymarket Books, 2016.

DeFrantz, Thomas F. "The Black Beat Made Visible: Hip Hop Dance and Body Power." *Of the Presence of the Body: Essays on Dance and Performance Theory*. Edited by André Lepecki. Middletown, CT: Wesleyan University Press, 2004: 64–81.

DeFrantz, Thomas F. "Hip-Hop Habitus v.2.0." *Black Performance Theory*. Edited by Thomas F. DeFrantz and Anita Gonzalez. Durham: Duke University Press, 2014: 223–242.

DeFrantz, Thomas F. "Unchecked Popularity: Neoliberal Circulations of Black Social Dance." *Neoliberalism and Global Theatres: Performance Permutations*. Edited by Lara D. Nielsen and Patricia Ybarra. New York: Palgrave Macmillan, 2012, 128–42.

Desch-Obi, Thomas. "Combat and the Crossing of Kalunga." *Central Africans and the Cultural Transformations in the American Diaspora*. Edited by Linda Heywood. Cambridge: Cambridge University Press, 2001: 353–370.

Desch-Obi, Thomas. *Fighting for Honor: The Story of African Martial Arts in the Atlantic World*. Charleston: University of South Carolina Press, 2008.

Du Bois, W.E.B. *The Souls of Black Folk*. New York: Bantam Books, 1903.

Du Bois, W.E.B. "Sociology Hesitant." *boundary 2* 27.3 (Fall 2000 [1905]): 37–44.

Dumas, Henry. "Will the Circle Be Unbroken?" *Echo Tree: The Collected Short Fiction of Henry Dumas*. Edited by Eugene B. Redmond. Minneapolis: Coffee House Press, 2003, 104–15.

Edwards, Brent Hayes. *The Practice of Diaspora: Literature, Translation, and the Rise of Black Internationalism*. Cambridge: Harvard University Press, 2003.

Ellison, Ralph. *Invisible Man*. New York: Signet, 1947.

Fanon, Frantz. *The Wretched of the Earth*. Trans. by Constance Farrington. New York: Grove Press, 2005.

Fernandes, Sujatha. *Close to the Edge: In Search of the Global Hip Hop Generation*. New York: Verso, 2011.

Flores, Juan. *The Diaspora Strikes Back: Caribeño Tales of Learning and Turning*. New York: Routledge, 2009.

Fogarty, Mary. "Breaking Bad: New B-girls." *Dance Current*, March–April 2015, 34–45.
Fogarty, Mary. "'Each One Teach One': B-Boying and Ageing." *Ageing and Youth Cultures: Music, Style and Identity*. Edited by Andy Bennett and Paul Hodkinson. London: Bloomsbury, 2012, 53–65.
Fogarty, Mary. "'What Ever Happened to Breakdancing?': Transnational B-Boy/B-Girl Networks, Underground Video Magazines, and Imagined Affinities." MA thesis, Brock University, 2006.
Foucault, Michel. *Power/Knowledge: Selected Interviews and Other Writings, 1972–1977*. Edited by Colin Gordon, translated by Colin Gordon, Leo Marshall John Mepham, and Kate Soper. New York: Pantheon Books, 1972.
Fricke, Jim and Charlie Ahearn, eds. *Yes Yes Y'all: Oral History of Hip-Hop's First Decade*. Oxford: Perseus Press, 2002.
Gates, Henry Louis. "The 'Blackness of Blackness': A Critique of the Sign and the Signifying Monkey." *Critical Inquiry* 9.4 (June 1983): 685–723.
Gates, Henry Louis. *The Signifying Monkey: A Theory of African-American Literary Criticism*. Oxford: Oxford University Press, 1989.
Gaunt, Kyra D. *The Games Black Girls Play: Learning the Ropes from Double-Dutch to Hip-Hop*. New York: New York University Press, 2006.
Geurts, Kathryn Linn. *Culture and the Senses: Bodily Ways of Knowing in an African Community*. Berkeley: University of California Press, 2002.
Glissant, Édouard. *Poetics of Relation*. Translated by Betsy Wing. Ann Arbor: University of Michigan Press, 1997.
Godreau, Isar P. "Folkloric 'Others': *Blanqueamiento* and the Celebration of Blackness as an Exception in Puerto Rico." *Globalization and Race: Transformations in the Cultural Production of Blackness*. Edited by Kamari Maxine Clarke and Deborah A. Thomas. Durham: Duke University Press, 2006, 171–87.
Gomez, Michael A. *Exchanging Our Country Marks: The Transformation of African Identities in the Colonial and Antebellum South*. Chapel Hill: University of North Carolina Press, 1998.
Gonzalez, Evelyn. *The Bronx*. New York: Columbia University Press, 2004.
Gottschild, Brenda Dixon. *The Black Dancing Body: A Geography from Coon to Cool*. New York: Palgrave Macmillan, 2005.
Gottschild, Brenda Dixon. "Crossroads, Continuities, and Contradictions: The Afro-Euro-Caribbean Triangle." *Caribbean Dance from Abakuá to Zouk: How Movement Shapes Identity*. Edited by Susanna Sloat. Gainesville: University Press of Florida, 2002, 3–10.
Gottschild, Brenda Dixon. *Digging the Africanist Presence in American Performance: Dance and Other Contexts*. Westport, CT: Praeger, 1996.
Gunn, Rachel. "'Don't Worry, It's Just a Girl!': Negotiating and Challenging Gendered Assumptions in Sydney's Breakdancing Scene." *Journal of World Popular Music* 3.1 (2016): 54–74.
Gunn, Rachel and John Scannell. "Overcoming the Hip-Hop Habitus." *Shifting Sounds: Musical Flows*, edited by Oli Wilson and Sara Attfield, special issue of *Journal of World Popular Music* 3.1 (2012): 53–61.
Hager, Steven. *Hip Hop: The Illustrated History of Break Dancing, Rap Music, and Graffiti*. New York: St. Martin's Press, 1984.
Halberstam, Jack. *Female Masculinity*. Durham: Duke University Press, 1998.

Hall, Stuart. "Negotiating Caribbean Identities." *Postcolonial Discourses: An Anthology*. Edited by Gregory Castle. Oxford: Blackwell Publishers, 2001, 280–92.

Hartman, Saidiya V. *Scenes of Subjection: Terror, Slavery and Self-Making in Nineteenth Century America*. New York: Oxford University Press, 1997.

Hartman, Saidiya V. *Wayward Lives, Beautiful Experiments: Intimate Histories of Riotous Black Girls, Troublesome Women, and Queer Radicals*. New York: Norton, 2019.

Harvey, David. *A Brief History of Neoliberalism*. Oxford: Oxford University Press, 2005.

Hazzard-Donald, Katrina. "Dance in Hip Hop Culture." *Droppin' Science: Critical Essays in Rap Music and Hip Hop Culture*. Edited by William Eric Perkins. Philadelphia: Temple University Press, 1996, 220–35.

Hazzard-Gordon, Katrina. *Jookin': The Rise of Black Social Dance Formations in African-American Dance*. Philadelphia: Temple University Press, 1992.

Hewitt, Andrew. *Social Choreography: Ideology as Performance in Dance and Everyday*. Durham: Duke University Press, 2005.

hooks, bell. "An Aesthetic of Blackness: Strange and Oppositional." *Lenox Avenue* 1.1, 1995: 65–72.

Hurston, Zora Neale. "Characteristics of Negro Expression." *"Sweat": Written by Zora Neale Hurston*. Edited by Cheryl A. Wall. New Brunswick, NJ: Rutgers University Press, 1997, 55–72.

Ibrahim, Awad. *The Rhizomes of Blackness: A Critical Ethnography of Hip-Hop Language, Identity, and the Politics of Becoming*. New York: Peter Lang, 2014.

Jafa, Arthur and Tina Campt. "Love Is the Message, the Plan Is Death." *e-flux journal* 81 (April 2017): 1–10.

Johnson, Imani Kai. "Black Culture without Black People: Hip Hop Dance beyond Appropriation Discourse." *Are You Entertained? Black Popular Culture in the Twenty-First Century*. Edited by Simone C. Drake and Dwan K. Henderson. Durham: Duke University Press, 2020: 191–206.

Johnson, Imani Kai. "From Blues Women to B-Girls: Performing Badass Femininity." *Women and Performance: A Journal of Feminist Theory*, Special issue "All Hail the Queenz," edited by Jessica N. Pabón and Shanté Paradigm Smalls, 24.1 (2014): 15–28.

Johnson, Imani Kai. "Music Meant to Make You Move: Considering the Aural-Kinesthetic." *Sounding Off!* Blog. 18 June 2012. http://soundstudiesblog.com/2012/06/18/music-meant-to-make-you-move-considering-the-aural-kinesthetic/.

Jones, LeRoi. *Blues People: Negro Music in White America*. New York: Harper Perennial, 1963.

Katz, Mark. *Groove Music: The Art and Culture of the Hip-Hop DJ*. Oxford: Oxford University Press, 2012.

Kelley, Robin D. G. *Yo' Mama's Disfunktional! Fighting the Culture Wars in Urban America*. Boston: Beacon Press, 1997.

Kondo, Dorrine. *Worldmaking: Race, Performance, and the Work of Creativity*. Durham: Duke University Press, 2018.

KRS-ONE. "The Milk and the Meat: An Essay on Christ." *Bronx Biannual* 1 (June 2006): 145–58.

Lepecki, André. "Inscribing Dance." *Of the Presence of the Body: Essays on Dance and Performance Theory*. Edited by André Lepecki. Middletown, CT: Wesleyan University Press, 2004, 124–39.

Lewis, Earl. "To Turn on a Pivot: Writing African Americans into a History of Overlapping Diasporas." *American Historical Review* 100.3 (1995): 765–787.

Lewis, John Lowell. *Ring of Liberation: Deceptive Discourse in Brazilian Capoeira*. Chicago: University of Chicago Press, 1992.

Malone, Jacqui. *Steppin' on the Blues: The Visible Rhythms of African American Dance*. Urbana: University of Illinois Press, 1996.

Martin, Randy. "A Precarious Dance, a Derivative Sociality." *TDR: The Drama Review* 56.4 (2012): 62–77.

Morgan, Marcyliena. *The Real Hip Hop: Battling for Knowledge, Power, and Respect in the LA Underground*. Durham: Duke University Press, 2009.

Moten, Fred. *In the Break: The Aesthetics of the Black Radical Tradition*. Minneapolis: University of Minnesota Press, 2003.

Nketia, J. H. Kwabena. *The Music of Africa*. New York: Norton, 1974.

Osumare, Halifu. *The Hiplife in Ghana West African Indigenization of Hip-Hop*. New York: Palgrave Macmillan, 2012.

Pabón-Colón, Jessica Nydia. *Graffiti Grrlz: Performing Feminism in the Hip Hop Diaspora*. New York: New York University Press, 2018.

Pabón-Colón, Jessica Nydia. "Writing', Breakin', Beatboxin': Strategically Performing 'Women' in Hip-Hop." *Signs* 43.1 (2017): 175–200.

Perry, Imani. *Prophets of the Hood: Politics and Poetics of Hip Hop*. Durham: Duke University Press, 2004.

Power-Sotomayor, Jade "Corporeal Sounding: Listening to Bomba, Listening to Puertorriqueñxs." *Performance Matters* 6.2 (2020): 43–59.

Prescod-Weinstein, Chanda. *The Disordered Cosmos: A Journey into Dark Matter, Spacetime, and Dreams Deferred*. New York: Bold Type Books, 2021.

Rivera, Raquel Z. "New York Afro-Puerto Rican and Afro-Dominican Roots Music: Liberation Mythologies and Overlapping Diasporas." *Black Music Research Journal* 32.2 (Fall 2012): 3–24.

Roberts, John Storm. *Black Music of Two Worlds: Africa, Caribbean, Latin, and African-America Traditions*. Belmont, CA: Wadsworth, 1998.

Robinson, Cedric. *Black Marxism: The Making of the Black Radical Tradition*. Chapel Hill: University of North Carolina Press, 2000.

Rosa, Cristina F. *Brazilian Bodies and Their Choreographies of Identification*. London: Palgrave Macmillan, 2015.

Rose, Tricia. *Black Noise: Rap Music and Black Culture in Contemporary America*. Hanover, NH: Wesleyan University Press, 1994.

Schippers, Mimi. "Recovering the Feminine Other: Masculinity, Femininity, and Gender Hegemony." *Theory and Society* 36.1 (2007): 85–102.

Schloss, Joseph G. *Foundation: B-Boys, B-Girls, and Hip-Hop Culture in New York*. Oxford: Oxford University Press, 2009.

Schloss, Joseph G. *Making Beats: The Art of Sample-Based Hip-Hop*. Middletown, CT: Wesleyan University Press, 2004.

Schloss, Joseph G. "'Like Old Folk Songs Handed Down from Generation to Generation': History, Canon, and Community in B-Boy Culture." *Ethnomusicology* 50.3 (2006): 411–32.

Schwegler, Armin. "Black Ritual Insulting in the Americas: On the Art of 'Vociferar' (Colombia), 'Vacilar' (Ecuador) and 'Snapping', 'Sounding' or 'Playing the Dozens' (U.S.A.)." *Indiana* 24 (2007): 107–155.

Smith, Ernie Adolphus. "The Evolution and Continuing Presence of the African Oral Tradition in Black America." PhD dissertation, University of California, Irvine, 1975.

Snead, James. "On Repetition in Black Culture." *Black American Literature Forum* 15.4 (Winter 1981): 146–154.
Spady, James G., H. Samy Alim, and Samir Meghelli. *The Global Cipha: Hip Hop Culture and Consciousness*. Philadelphia: Black History Museum Publishers, 2006.
Spivak, Gayatri. "Can the Subaltern Speak?" *Marxism and the Interpretation of Culture*. Edited by Cary Nelson and Lawrence Grossberg. Urbana: University of Illinois Press, 1988: 271–313.
Stuckey, Sterling. *Slave Culture: Nationalist Theory and the Foundations of Black America*. New York: Oxford University Press, 1987.
Taylor, Diana. *The Archive and the Repertoire: Performing Cultural Memory in the Americas*. Durham: Duke University Press, 2003.
Thompson, Robert Farris. "An Aesthetic of the Cool: West African Dance." *African Forum* 2 (1966): 85–102.
Thompson, Robert Farris. *Flash of the Spirit: African and Afro-American Art and Philosophy*. New York: Vintage Books, 1983.
Thompson, Robert Farris. "Hip Hop 101." *Droppin' Science: Critical Essays in Rap Music and Hip Hop Culture*. Edited by William Eric Perkins. Philadelphia: Temple University Press, 1996, 211–19.
Toop, David. *Rap Attack #3: African Rap to Global Hip Hop*. 3rd ed. London: Serpent's Tail, 2000.
Tsing, Anna L. *Friction: An Ethnography of Global Connection*. Princeton: Princeton University Press, 2005.
Tsing, Anna L. "The Global Situation." *The Anthropology of Globalization: A Reader*. Edited by Jonathan Xavier Inda and Renato Rosaldo. Oxford: Blackwell Publishing, 2002.
Vega, Marta Moreno. "The Ancestral Sacred Creative Impulse of Africa and the African Diaspora: Asé, the Nexus of the Black Global Aesthetic." *Lenox Avenue* 5 (1999): 45–57.
Vincent, Rickey. *Funk: The Music, the People, and the Rhythm of the One*. New York: St. Martin's Griffin, 1996.
Welsh-Asante, Kariamu. *The African Aesthetic: Keeper of the Tradition*. Westport, CT: Praeger, 1994.
West, Cornel. "Black Culture and Postmodernism." *Remaking History*. Edited by Barbara Kruger and Phil Mariani. Seattle, WA, Bay Press, 1989: 87–96.
Wilson, Olly. "The Association of Movement and Music as a Manifestation of a Black Conceptual Approach to Music-Making." *More Than Dancing: Essays on Afro-American Music and Musicians*. Edited by Irene V. Jackson. Westport, CT: Praeger, 1985: 9–23.

Films

All the Ladies Say. Directed by Ana "Rokafella" Garcia, New York: Third World Newsreel, 2010.
City of God. Directed by Fernando Meirelles and Katia Lund, O2 Filmes, 2004.
Estilo Hip Hop. Directed by Vee Bravo and Loira Lamball, performances by Eli Efi, Guerrillero Okulto, and Magia, 2006.
Everything Remains Raw: Hip Hop's Folkloric Lineage. Directed by Moncell "Ill Kosby" Durden, 2010.
Flashdance. Directed by Adrian Lyne, Paramount Pictures, 1983.

Flyin' Cut Sleeves. Directed by Henry Chalfant and Rita Recher, Mvd Visual, 1993.
Freshest Kids: A History of the B-Boy. Directed by Israel, performances by Crazy Legs, Trac2, Kool Herc, and Popmaster Fable, QD3 Entertainment, 2002.
Mongolian Bling. Directed by Benj Binks, Flying Fish Films, 2012.
Redder Than Red: The Story of B-Girl Bubbles. Directed by Martha Cooper and Nika Kramer, We B*Girlz Productionz!, 2005.
Rock Dance History: The Untold Story of Up-Rocking. Directed by Jorge "Popmaster Fabel" Pabón, 2011, http://www.youtube.com/watch?v=AR_MULaVMg0.
Shake the Dust. Directed by Adam Sjöberg, Loose Luggage Media, 2014.
Style Wars. Directed by Tony Silver, Public Art Films, 1983.
Wild Style. Directed by Charlie Ahearn, Wild Style, 1983.

Interviews and Correspondence

Aby. Personal Interview. 18 March 2007.
Anna of Fraggle Rock Crew. Personal Interview. 16 March 2007.
Aruna. Personal Interview. 1 July 2007.
Baby Love. Personal Interview. 29 June 2007.
Black Pearl. Personal Interview. 21 Oct 2006.
Brooklyn Terry. Personal Interview. 13 October 2006.
Cartoon. Personal Interview. 28 September 2006.
Charl. Personal Interview. 21 October 2006.
Chuco. Personal Correspondence. 29 August 2006.
Dark Marc. Personal Interview. 11 August 2006.
David of Subway Entertainment. Personal Interview. 27 September 2006.
DJ Flex. Personal Interview. 16 March 2007.
DJ Renegade. Personal Interview. 18 February 2008.
Emiko. Personal Interview. 18 September 2006.
Float. Personal Interview. 28 May 2007.
Frostalino. Personal Interview. 19 January 2012.
Genesis. Personal Correspondence. 26 July 2006.
Hanifa Queen. Personal Interview. 22 May 2007.
Hanifa Queen. Personal Correspondence. 31 May 2007.
Hannibal. Personal Interview. 27 July 2007.
Icey Ice. Personal Interview. 18 March 2007.
Ill Kosby. Personal Correspondence. 12 March 2008.
Jaekwon. Personal Interview. 17 August 2012.
Jihad. Personal Interview. 2 April 2004.
Kid Glyde. Personal Interview. 13 August 2006.
King Kotee. Personal Interview. 15 April 2009.
K-Mel. Personal Interview. 31 August 2007.
Krazy Kujo. Personal Interview, 4 September 2006.
Kwikstep. Personal Interview 26 May 2007.
Kwikstep. Personal Interview. 8 August 2007.
Kwikstep and Trac2. Interview co-conducted with Moncell Durden. 26 May 2007.
Lady Champ. Personal Interview. 1 July 2007.
Leanski. Personal Correspondence. June 29 2006.

Lil' Cesar. Personal Interview. 19 February 2005.
Lil' Cesar. Personal Interview. 3 April 2005.
Macca. Personal Interview. 10 June 2006.
Machine. Personal Interview. 30 August 2007.
Megatron and Shallow. Personal Interview. 24 June 2006.
Miss Little. Personal Interview. 27 November 2006.
Ness4. Personal Interview. 9 August 2006.
Pete Nasty. Personal Interview 25 June 2006.
Pia. Personal Interview. 17 August 2012.
Poe One. Personal Interview. 3 January 2007.
Poe One. Personal Interview. 6 March 2007.
Poe One. Personal Interview. 17 July 2007.
Popmaster Fabel. Personal Correspondence. 23 May 2005.
Profo Won. Personal Interview. 19 May 2009.
Q Rock. Personal Interview. 19 January 2012.
Rokafella. Personal Interview. 17 September 2006.
Rome-1. Personal Correspondence. 13 September 2006.
Severe. Personal Interview. 29 June 2007.
Silky Jones. Personal Interview. 10 August 2006.
Slinga. Personal Interview. 14 August 2006.
Trac2. Personal Correspondence. 28 July 2006.
Trac2. Personal Interview 26 May 2007.
Triple7. Personal Interview, 3 Oct 2006.
Viazeen. Personal Interview. 7 July 2007.
Viazeen. Personal Interview. 5 July 2009.
YNot. Personal Interview. 13 November 2006.

Index

For the benefit of digital users, indexed terms that span two pages (e.g., 52–53) may, on occasion, appear on only one of those pages.

Tables and figures are indicated by *t* and *f* following the page number

Abeni, Cleis, 14–15, 66, 67, 200n.56
Abrahams, Roger D., 34, 109, 205n.42
Aby, 21–22, 31, 40, 41–43, 47–49, 49f, 64, 77, 192n.75
   on TBB/TBG, 77–81
active spectatorship, ix, 1, 31
Advocates for Children (AFC), 197n.27
Adzenyah, Abraham, 216n.61
aesthetics
   of battling, 137–39
   of Black radical tradition, 2–3, 177n.2
   of breaking, xiii–xiv
   of Hip Hop, 14–15
   See also Africanist aesthetics
affective proximity, 168–69, 219n.14
Africanist aesthetics, xiii–xiv, 1, 4, 17–21
   antiblackness and, 57
   aural kinesthetics as, 17–18
   balance and, 170
   blackness and, 53–54
   blurring of audience and performer, 88–90
   of breaking, 31–32, 52–53, 63, 156
   capitalism and, 17
   of capoeira, 31–32
   the collective and, 79, 153
   of cyphering, 17–18, 18t, 52, 56, 142–43, 161, 164
   of dance, 147
   of dark matter, 18–21, 171
   diaspora and, 17–18, 132, 135
   diasporic circles and, 30–52, 88, 199n.45
   digital media and, 164–67
   erasure of, 153–54
   foundation and, 142–43
   gender and, 101
   of Hip Hop, xiii–xiv, 1, 23, 164–65
   innovation and, 215n.32
   invisibilizing of, 1–2, 17–19, 21–22, 52–55
   isolations, 83–84
   liberation and, 101, 171
   online, 171
   originality and, 22, 105, 112–13, 114–24
   rituals of derision, 22, 105–14
   the sacred and the profane, blurring of, 107–8, 113–14
   sampling, 91
   of sexualized burns, 207n.57
   sociality of, 122
   survival and, 101, 171
Afrofuturism, 19–20
Afropessimism, 185–86n.63
Ahearn, Charlie, 5–7
Akomfrah, John, 168–69
Alim, H. Samy, 3, 32, 34, 132, 134–35
All Ladies Say (film), 160–61, 217n.88
antiblackness, xiii–xiv
   Africanist aesthetics and, 57
   Black dance and, 153–55
   confronting, 171
   dance, 153–55
   erasure and, xiii–xiv, 17–18
   global circulation of, 1–2
A-Plus, 106
Aprahamian, Serouj, 180n.18, 202n.6
   on burning, 105–6, 107
Ardit, 95–96
Aruna, 100–1, 201n.3
aural kinesthetics, 15–16, 67, 183n.43, 183n.48, 196n.14
   as Africanist aesthetic, 17–18

babalao, 89–90, 200n.69
Baby Love, 22, 64, 77, 85, 91–92, 200n.59
badass / badass-ness, 105, 122, 124–26
badass femininity, 104
  of blues women, 101, 109–10
  breaking and, 99–100, 101, 114–15, 210n.87
  limitations of, 104–5
Bailey, Marlon, 104
Bambaata, Afrika, 87, 213n.22
Banerji, Anurima, 66, 67
Barton, Halbert, 38
battles, ix, 4, 5–7, 6f, 14f
  burns in, 105–14, 117, 136–37
  gender and, 74, 96–97, 99–101
  improvisation in, 137, 138–39, 140
  judging of, 137–39
  outlaw culture and, 72, 92–93
  rituals of derision in, 108
  social choreography of, 73–74
  in South Bronx, 63
  See also breaking; burns; cyphers
battling
  aesthetic standards of, 138–39
  difference and, 135–43
  four principles of, 74–77
  gender and, 74, 206–7n.55
  illusionism, 74, 76–77
  nomadism, 74, 75–77, 87, 198n.36
  politics of, 66
  strategizing, 74, 75, 76–77
  survivalism, 74–75, 76–77
  See also breaking; cyphering
Bayarmagnai, 143–44, 215n.34
b-boy
  as gendered term, 103
B-Boy All Stars Block Party, 59–62, 61f, 63
"b-boying," 8–9, 10, 180n.18
Beat Street (film), xiii, 59, 82
belonging
  Hip Hop, 73–74, 132–33
  neighborhood, 73–74
b-girls, 22, 79–81, 85–86, 91–92, 102f, 125f
  femininity and, 100–1, 201–2n.5
  gender and, 99–101
  masculinity and, 101, 103, 201–2n.5
Bing, Benj, 143–44
Blacking, John, 216n.61

blackness
  Africanist aesthetics and, 53–54
  Black social dance and, 169–70
  breaking and, 57, 156, 157–58
  commodification of, 154
  cyphering and, xiv, 146
  dance and, 47, 169–70
  dark matter as metaphor for, 19, 20–21, 185–86n.63
  gender and, 101
  Hip Hop and, xiv
  performance of, 16
  physics and, 21
  Puerto Rico and, 56–57
Black Pearl, 22, 99, 118–23
Black radical tradition
  aesthetics of, 2–3, 177n.2
  cyphering and, 177n.2
Black studies
  dark matter in, 20–21, 186–87n.70
Black United Front, 198–99n.44
blue notes (worried notes), 170–71
blues women, 101, 109–10
bomba, 30–31, 32, 35, 55, 56–57, 189n.15, 191–92n.55
  spiritual dimensions of, 38–39
Bragin, Naomi, 67, 82, 84, 203n.13
Braithwaite, Kamau, 134–35
Bravo, Vee, 143–44
breakdancing
  as umbrella term, 9–10
  See also breaking
Breakin' (film), xiii, 9–10
Breakin' 2: Electric Boogaloo (film), xiii, 9–10
breaking, x, 8–11, 177n.1
  aesthetics of, xiii–xiv
  as African diasporic tradition, 155–57
  African influences on, 52–53
  Africanist aesthetics of, 31–32, 52–53, 63, 156
  badass femininity and, 99–100, 101, 114–15, 210n.87
  "b-boying," 8–9, 10, 180n.18
  blackness and, 57, 156, 157–58
  body critiques, 119–20, 210n.87, 210n.89
  "breakdancing" and, 9–10

capoeira, likeness to, 31–32, 188n.12, 189–90n.27
cultural appropriation and, 154
as culture, 1
diaspora and, 188n.12
difference and, 131–32, 155–60
extraphenomenal capacities of, 39, 40–52, 107–8
foundation, 141–43
four elements of, 74, 198n.35
freedom and, 120, 121–22, 148, 161
gender and, 74, 100, 110, 115–18
gender expectations of, 100
identity and, 91–92, 121–24, 153
legacy of NGE, 13
martial arts and, 55–56, 193n.87
mastery of, 116
misogyny and, 97, 100
old school v. new school, 136–38, 139–40, 141, 213n.25
originality and, 112–13, 114–24
origins of, 9
power v. style, 136–41, 157, 213–14nn.26–27
social choreography of, 92–93
sociality of, 29–30, 118
the South Bronx and, 22, 63–64
See also cyphering; cyphers
Bronx, the
See South Bronx
Bronx Boys/Girls Rocking Crew, The (TBB/TBG), 77–81, 180n.20
Brooklyn Terry, 133–34
Brothers, Nicholas, 9
Brown, Benita, 39, 73, 191–92n.55
Brown, James, 9, 118
Brown, Trisha, 87
Browning, Barbara, 36
Buddha Stretch, 132–33, 212n.9
burns, 105–14, 136–37, 204n.26, 204n.28, 204n.30
  Africanist aesthetics of, 207n.57
  sexualized, 111–14, 206n.54, 206–7nn.55–57, 208n.64
Butler, Judith, 186n.69, 208n.64

call and response, 31–34
  in circle practices, 30–31, 199n.45
  in cyphers, 131
  spiritual dynamics of, 34
Campbell, Don "Campbellock," 180–81n.28
Campt, Tina, 169
candomblé, 35, 36
capoeira, 30–31, 47, 55, 56, 191–92n.55
  Africanist aesthetics of, 31–32
  call and response in, 33–34
  capoeira Angola, 33, 36, 189n.23, 190n.30, 190n.34, 190n.36
  likeness to breaking, 31–32, 188n.12, 189–90n.27
  origins of, 194n.93
  rodas of, 30–31, 33–35, 36
  spiritual dimensions of, 35, 38–39
  styles of, 190n.34
Caponi, Gena, 88, 148–49, 199n.45, 215n.32, 216n.54
  on the hidden rhythm, 149–51, 216n.61
Cartoon (popper), 22, 59, 61–62, 61*f*, 64, 77, 82–85, 86–85, 90, 91–92, 199n.47
Cham, Jorge, 185n.60
Chambers, Michael "Boogaloo Shrimp," 9–10
Chang, Jeff, 197n.25
Chernoff, John Miller, 216n.61
Chew, Ming-tak, 100–1, 104, 210n.87
choreography
  as improvisation, 66–67
  politics of, 65–66
  ritual and, 67
choreography, social, 64–67, 72
  of battles, 73–74
  of breaking, 92–93
  of Bronx breakers, 72–77, 78
  improvisation and, 67
choreosonic, the, 16, 18*t*, 32–33, 37, 183–84n.50
Christian, Barbara, 3
Chyna (b-girl), 99–100
circle practices, 164, 194n.99
  Africanist aesthetics of, 30–52, 88, 199n.45
  call and response in, 30–31, 199n.45
  diasporic, 21–22, 30–52, 88, 191n.42, 199n.45

circle practices (*cont.*)
   extra-phenomenal qualities of, 34–39, 191–92n.55
   improvisation in, 199n.45
   principles of, 199n.45
   ring shouts, 16, 30–31, 34, 35, 36–38, 55, 56, 190–91nn.40–46
   rodas, 30–31, 33–35, 36
   as worldmaking practices, 34
   See also cyphers; ritual
City of God (film), 71–72
Clinton, George, 150
coalitional politics, 22–23
Collective 7, 217n.88
Committee Against Fort Apache (CAFA), 198–99n.44
Condry, Ian, 133
corporeal orature, 17–18, 18*t*, 118–19, 183n.48
Cosell, Howard, 197n.25
COVID-19, 171
Cox, Aimee Meredith, 65–66, 67, 91, 196n.8
Craig, Maxine Leeds, 147, 215n.49
Crawley, Ashon, 16, 183–84n.50, 198–99n.44
   centrifugitivity, 37–38, 209n.76
   otherwise possibilities, 117, 191n.44, 209n.76
   on ring shouts, 37, 191n.42, 191n.46
   See also choreosonic, the
Crazy Legs, 178–79n.11, 206n.54
crews
   Bronx Boys/Girls Rocking Crew, 77–81, 180n.20
   gender and, 79–81, 85–86
   violence and, 79, 81
cyphering, ix–xii, xiv, 11–16, 177n.1, 177n.2
   Africanist aesthetics of, 17–18, 18*t*, 52, 56, 142–43, 161, 164
   blackness and, xiv, 146
   Black radical tradition and, 177n.2
   Black sociality of, S7
   circling back, 143–44
   as collective experience, 13, 182n.38
   as diasporic, 161
   digital media and, 164–69
   epistemology and, 4
   as escape, 42–44
   in Europe, 211–12n.1
   extra-phenomenal capacities of, 20–22, 29, 40–52, 148, 187–88n.2
   fighting at, xii
   freedom and, 18*t*, 46–47, 48–49, 50–51, 52, 148
   highs in, 40–44
   judging of, 137–39
   in outlaw culture, 68, 196n.19
   political potentiality of, 161–63
   as "real," 44–45
   as ritual, 13–15, 48–49, 67, 144–48, 181n.33
   as spiritual experience, 44–47, 48–49, 52, 57
   stealing away and, 43–44, 52
   time and, 47–52
   See also battling; breaking; cyphers
cyphers, xiii, 14*f*, 49*f*
   aesthetic standards of, 138–39
   b-girl cyphers, 22
   bridging cultures, 144–48
   call and response in, 131
   as collective experience, 13, 153, 182n.38
   community and, 62
   dark matter of, 57, 171
   defined, 1, 11–12
   as diasporic, 63
   epistemology and, 4
   hitter's circles, 128–29
   hungry dancers, 27, 187n.2
   non-cypher circles, 127–29, 128*f*
   online, 166–69, 171
   origins of term, 12–13
   possibilities of, 148–50
   as ritual, 13–15, 181n.33
   as ritual points of connection, 144–48
   sociality of, 114–15, 116–17
   social media and, 23
   social relationship to state, 67
   whiteness and, 104
   See also battles; breaking; cyphering

dance
   Africanist aesthetics of, 147
   antiblackness and, 153–55
   blackness and, 47

the body in, 147–48, 215n.45
  as communicative phenomenon, 39
  as kinesthetic form, 15
  masculinity and, 147
  physics and, 20
  politics and, 65
  as ritual, 12
  sexuality and, 147, 215n.49
dance, Black
  antiblackness and, 153–55
  blackness and, 169–70
  as commodity, 153–54
  racial politics of, 158–59
  See also breaking
dancehall, 134–35
Daniel, Yvonne, 12
Dark Marc, 29–30, 211–12n.1, 215n.40
dark matter
  Africanist aesthetics of, 18–21, 171
  in Black studies, 20–21, 186–87n.70
  of cyphers, 57, 171
  defined, 18–19, 185n.60
  diaspora and, 20
  as metaphor for blackness, 19, 20–21, 185–86n.63
  speculative possibilities of, 19–21, 185–86n.63, 186n.69
Davis, Angela, 162–63
Dean, Aria, 170–71
DeFrantz, Thomas, 17–18, 114–15, 124–26, 183n.48, 211n.93
  on antiblackness and dance, 153–55
Deleuze, Gilles, 115, 117, 123–24
Desch-Obi, Thomas, 35, 36, 56, 110, 189–90n.27, 190n.36, 194n.93, 206n.51
diaspora, 52–57
  Africanist aesthetics and, 17–18, 30–52, 88, 132, 135, 199n.45
  articulation and, 55, 193n.84
  breaking and, 188n.12
  circle practices of, 21–22, 30–52, 88, 191n.42, 199n.45
  cyphering and, 63, 161
  dark matter and, 20
  femininity and, 110
  Hip Hop and, 134–35
  hiplife, 134
  masculinity and, 110

Dickey, Lucinda, 9–10
difference
  Africanist aesthetics and, 131–32
  battling and, 135–43
  breaking and, 131–32, 155–60
  Hip Hop and, 139–40, 144–48, 155–60, 161–62
  national, 155–56
  racial, 139–40, 155–60
discrimination, 1–2
dispossession, 70–71
double consciousness, 152, 216n.71
Du Bois, W. E. B., 152, 153, 216n.71
Dumas, Henry, 19–20
Durden, Moncell "Ill Kosby," 8–9, 52–53, 70, 180–81n.28, 193n.80
Durkheim, Émile, 186n.69

Edwards, Brent Hayes, 55, 132, 193n.84
Electric Boogie Fat, 82–83
Ellison, Ralph, 151–52, 153
Emiko, 22, 29–30, 112–14, 121, 123, 124, 208nn.62–63
epistemology
  Africanist, 178n.4
  cyphers and, 4
  Hip Hop, 3
  performance as, 4
erasure
  of Africanist aesthetics, 153–54
  antiblackness and, xiii–xiv, 17–18
  global Hip Hop and, 142, 214–15n.31
  jazz and, 214–15n.31
  pop culture and, 153
  rock 'n' roll and, 142, 214–15n.31
Eshun, Kodwo, 182–83n.40
Estilo Hip Hop (film), 143–44
ethnography, 4
Evans, Monica, 68

Fancy Dancing, 144–45
Fastin, Kari, 207–8n.60
femininity, 22
  b-girls and, 100–1, 201–2n.5
  diaspora and, 110
  Hip Hop and, 102–3, 123
  See also badass femininity; b-girls; gender

Fernandes, Sujatha, 161–63
Flashdance (film), 9–10
Float, 21–22, 31, 40, 42–44
Flores, Juan, 55, 212n.6
Fogarty, Mary, 103–4, 115–16, 210n.89, 213–14n.26
Fort Apache: The Bronx (film), 198–99n.44
Foucault, Michel, 154
foundation, 141–43, 165*f*
   Africanist aesthetics of, 142–43
   sociality of, 149
Freestyle Session, 135, 213n.21
Frostalino, 22–23, 145, 146
Fuentes, Marcela A., 166
funk
   the one, 149–50

Gamblerz Crew, 135–40
Gaunt, Kyra, 15–16, 203n.13
genba, 133, 212n.10
gender, 102–5
   Africanist aesthetics of, 101
   battles and, 74, 96–97, 99–101, 206–7n.55
   b-boy/b-girl terminology, 103
   "b-boying" and, 8–9
   "b-boys" and, 74
   b-girls and, 99–101
   blackness and, 101
   breaking and, 74, 100, 110, 115–18
   breaking crews and, 79–81, 85–86
   crews and, 85–86
   femininity, 22, 100–1, 102–3, 110, 123, 201–2n.5
   graffiti and, 203n.13
   Hip Hop and, 160, 203n.13
   masculinity, 101–4, 110, 147, 201–2n.5, 203n.15
   performativity, 208n.64
   See also badass femininity; b-girls
Genesis, 214n.28
Glissant, Édouard, 117–18
global, the, 212n.2
   See also Hip Hop, global
Godreau, Isar, 56–57
Gomez, Michael, 36–37, 190–91n.40
Gonzalez, Evelyn, 69–70
González, Lydia Milagros, 38

"Good Times," 198–99n.44
Gottschild, Brenda Dixon, 1–2, 17–18, 54–55, 57, 88, 177–78n.2, 211n.93
   on Africanisms, 194n.99
   on circles, 30
   on dance and the body, 147, 215n.45
   on improvisation, 114–15
   on isolations, 83–84, 200n.53
graffiti, 180n.25
   gender and, 203n.13
Grand Wizzard Theodore, 60
grimes, d. Sabela, 166–67, 218nn.3–4
Guattari, Félix, 115, 117, 123–24
Guerrillero, 143–44
Gunn, Rachael, 111–12, 115–16, 206n.52, 207n.56, 208n.62, 208n.64, 210n.87

Hall, Stuart, 52, 193n.78, 193n.84, 211n.92
Hanifa Queen, 22–23, 93, 123, 124, 145–46
Harris, Travis, 118
Hartman, Saidiya, 43–44, 109–10, 192n.61, 205–6n.47
Hazzard-Gordon, Katrina, 170
Hewitt, Andrew, 65–66, 67
Hill, Marc Lamont, 3
Hip Hop
   aesthetics of, 14–15
   Africanist aesthetics of, xiii–xiv, 1, 23, 164–65
   Africanist elements of, 188n.12
   belonging and, 73–74, 132–33
   blackness and, xiv
   cultural influence of, xiii
   diaspora and, 134–35
   early representations of, 4, 178–79n.11
   epistemology, 3
   femininity and, 102–3, 123
   freedom and, 124–26, 154–55
   gender and, 160, 203n.13
   history and, 158–61
   masculinity and, 102–4, 203n.15
   media exposure of, 140–41, 213–14n.26
   mind/body split and, 182–83n.40
   multiculturalism and, 57
   national difference and, 155–56
   NGE discourse in, 13, 182n.37
   origins of, 63
   outlaw aesthetics of, 107–8, 160

political potentiality of, 155–63
racial difference and, 155–60
rap and, 8, 179n.17
as resistance, 158
ritual practice of, 3
sociality of, 117, 123–24
social media and, 128*f*
soulfulness and, 156–58
worldmaking and, 149
Hip Hop, global, 131–35, 143–44, 143*f*, 161–62, 211–12n.1
  African, 134–35
  Africanist aesthetics of, xiii–xiv, 1, 23, 164–65
  Asian, 100–1, 104–5, 123, 133–34, 136, 158
  China, 100–1, 104–5
  cultural appropriation and, 154, 159
  difference, bridging of, 144–48, 161–62
  difference, ethnoracial, 139–40
  erasure and, 142, 214–15n.31
  European, 158, 214n.28
  Japan, 123, 133–34
  power moves and, 140–41
  race and, 159
  racism and, 139
  South Korean, 136
  worldmaking and, 149
Hip Hop studies
  the global in, 133
hiplife, 134
Hodges-Persley, Nicole, 91
hooks, bell, 17, 168–69

Ibrahim, Awad, 123–24
illusionism
  battling and, 74, 76–77
  in popping, 81–84, 87
improvisation, 114–15
  in battles, 137, 138–39, 140
  choreography as, 66–67
  in circle practices, 199n.45
  popping and, 82
International Battle of the Year (IBOTY), 95, 127, 128*f*, 131, 143*f*, 211–12n.1
intersectionality of struggles, 162–63
Invisible Man (Ellison), 151–52

Jaekwon, 31, 40, 51, 211–12n.1
Jafa, Arthur, 168–71
James, Ansley Joy, 207n.57
Jay-Z, 29
jazz, 1–2, 214–15n.31
Jazzy Jay, 87
Jones, A. M., 216n.61
Jones, Tracy, 133–34

kalunga line, 35–36, 189–90n.27, 190n.30
Kelley, Robin, 38–39, 205n.42
Khabeer, Su'ad Abdul, 3
Kid Glyde, 59, 62
kinesthetic, social, 87, 88–89, 200n.65
kinetic orality, 15–16, 183n.48
Kiprana, 95–97
knowledge, embodied, 12, 181n.30
Kondo, Dorinne, 149–50, 154–55, 217n.76
Kool Herc, 9, 180n.22
Kramer, Nika, 100–1
Krazy Kujo, 29–30, 56, 140, 213n.25
KRS-One, 45–46
KR3Ts (Keep Rising to the Top), 59, 195n.1
Krush Groove (film), xiii
kung fu movies
  influence on breaking, 55, 193n.87
Kwikstep, 22, 64, 77, 89–90, 91–92, 209n.84

Lady Rock, 85–86, 200n.59
Langnes, Tonja, 207–8n.60
Lanternari, Vittorio, 178n.4
LaSalle, Alex, 38–39
Lee, Bruce, 55–56
Lewis, Earl, 212n.6
Lewis, J. Lowell, 34–35, 38, 190n.30
Lil' Cesar, 140–41, 178–79n.11
Limbal, Loira, 143–44
locking
  origins of, 180–81n.28
Loose Boots, 82–83

Machine (b-boy), 29–30
Mackey, Nathaniel, 29, 187–88n.2
Malone, Jacqui, 14–15, 83–84, 200n.53
marronage, 38–39, 178n.4
Martin, Randy, 87–89, 200n.65

Martinez, Brina (Mama Zulu), 206–7n.55
masculinity, 102–3
   b-girls and, 101, 103, 201–2n.5
   dance and, 147
   diaspora and, 110
   Hip Hop and, 102–4, 203n.15
Massive Monkey, 214n.28
Megatron, 8–9
Meghilli, Samir, 134–35
Merleau-Ponty, Maurice, 186n.69
Mighty Zulu Kingz (MZK), 135–40, 213n.22
Miss Little, 40, 47
Mo, Sophie Pui Sim, 100–1, 104, 210n.87
Mongolian Bling (film), 143–44
Morgan, Joan, 202n.10
Moten, Fred, 2–3, 152, 153, 177n.2
   on Mackey, 187–88n.2
Mr. Wiggles, 64, 70–72, 82–83, 87
Muhammad, Elijah, 181–82n.34
Mullin, Gerald, 178n.4
multiculturalism
   Hip Hop and, 57

Nation of Gods and Earths (NGE), 13
Nation of Islam, 13, 181–82n.34
neoliberalism, 154–55
   Black dance forms and, 153–54
Ness4 (Alien Ness), 27, 29–30, 105–6, 136, 187n.2, 206–7n.55, 213n.22
Nicholas Brothers, 9, 53
Nketia, H. Kwabena, 15
nomadism, 84–85, 87–92, 205–6n.47
   battling and, 74, 75–77, 87, 198n.36
   popping and, 81–82

on the one, 149–51
oral history, 4
Osumare, Halifu, 1–2, 134
outlaw culture, 22, 64
   battles and, 72, 92–93
   cyphering in, 68, 196n.19
   Hip Hop as, 69, 71–72, 76–77, 107–8, 160
   in South Bronx, 68–72

Pabón-Colón, Jessica, 3, 74, 119–20, 202n.10, 203n.13, 203n.15
Papo Luv, 106

Park, MiRi "Seoulsonyk," 207–8n.60
Pauly G, 82–83
Payne, Daniel Alexander, 56
Pellerin, Eric, 193n.87
performance, 4
   of blackness, 16
   as epistemology, 4
   of gender, 100
performance, dance, 12
performativity
   of gender, 208n.64
Perry, Imani, 68–69, 75
Phase 2, 9
phenomenology, 186n.69
Pia, 21–22, 31, 40, 49–51, 192n.75
Poe One, ix, 21–22, 26f, 31, 40, 44–47, 150–51, 153, 177n.1, 213n.25
Pokémon (b-boy), 214n.28
Popmaster Fabel, 87, 102–3, 106
popping, 64, 199n.47
   differences from breaking, 82
   illusionism in, 81–84, 87
   improvisation and, 82
   nomadism and, 81–82
   origins of, 180–81n.28, 195n.4
   relationship to Hip Hop, 195n.4
Popin' Pete, 87, 198n.41
Power-Sotomayor, Jade, 32–33
Prescod-Weinstein, Chanda, 185–86n.63
Profo Won, 22–23, 146–48

Q Rock, 22–23, 144–45, 146
Quiñones, Adolfo "Shabadoo," 9–10

Raboteau, Albert, 190–91n.40
race
   difference and, 139–40, 155–60
   Hip Hop and, 155–60
   style and, 157
racialization
   visibility and, 21
racial politics
   of Black dance, 158–59
racism, 1–2
   Africanist practices, suppression of, 56
   discrimination, 1–2
   global Hip Hop and, 139
"Rapper's Delight," 198–99n.44

reggaeton, 134–35
repertoire, 4
   v. archive, 179n.14
resistance
   Hip Hop as, 158
   marginality and, 68–69
rhythm
   finding the rhythmic center, 149–53
ring shouts, 16, 30–31, 34, 36–38, 55, 56, 190–91nn.40–46
   yowa cross and, 35
ritual
   choreography and, 67
   cyphering as, 13–15, 48–49, 67, 144–48, 181n.33
   dance, 12
   rituals of derision, 31, 105–14, 205n.38
   space and, 1
   time and, 1
   See also circle practices; rituals of derision
rituals of derision, 31, 105, 205n.38, 205n.41
   Africanist aesthetics and, 22, 105–14
   burns, 105–8, 110, 111–14, 204n.26, 204n.28, 204n.30
Rivera, Raquel Z., 38–39
Robinson, Cedric, 2–3, 16, 178nn.4–5
Rob Nasty, 146
rock dance (uprocking), 106, 204n.29
rocking, 9, 73, 180n.20, 180n.23
rock 'n' roll, 1–2
   erasure and, 142, 214–15n.31
Rodriguez, Peaches, 59, 61–62
Rokafella, 22–23, 115–16, 155–61, 214–15n.31
   All Ladies Say, 217n.88
   B-Girl Sit-Downs, 160–61, 217n.88
Rosa, Christina, 33, 189n.19, 189n.23
Rose, Tricia, 14–15, 210n.87
   on sampling, 91

samba, 189n.19
sampling, 90–91
Scannell, John, 115–16
Schippers, Mimi, 105, 203–4n.19
   identity and, 91

Schloss, Joseph, 14–15, 63–64, 179n.17, 188n.12, 189–90n.27
   on Africanist aesthetics, 91
   on foundation, 141
Schwegler, Armin, 108
segregation, 1–2
Shakes, 87
Shallow, 8–9
Sharma, Nitasha, 3
Silky Jones, 21–22, 31, 40–44
Smith, Ernie Adolphus, 205n.41
Smurf (b-boy), 26–27, 168
Snead, James, 91
social choreography
   See choreography, social
social death, 48–49
sociality
   Africanist aesthetics of, 122
   of breaking, 29–30, 118
   the collective and, 148–49
   of cyphers, 114–15, 116–17
   of foundation, 149
   of Hip Hop, 117, 123–24
   in rodas, 35
Solomon, "Boogaloo Sam," 87, 180–81n.28, 195n.4
Sommer, Sally, 186n.69
soulfulness
   diasporic aesthetics of, 161
   Hip Hop and, 156–58
South Bronx, 64–65, 80*f*
   battles in, 63
   breaking and, 22, 63–64
   limited archive of, 63–64
   1970s deterioration, 69–71, 197nn.25–26
   outlaw culture in, 68–72
   urban renewal in, 196–97n.24
Spady, James, 134–35
Speedy Gonzales, 96, 201n.1
Spillers, Hortense, 101
Spivak, Gayatri, 154
Spy, 73, 76
Stallings, L. H., 107–8
Star, Veronica, 59, 62
stealing away, 43–44, 52, 192n.61
storytelling, 7–8
strategizing, 77–82
   battling and, 74, 75, 76–77

Stuckey, Sterling, 36–37
Style Wars (film), 9–10
survivalism, 77–82
    Africanist aesthetics and, 101, 171
    battling and, 74–75, 76–77

tap, 53
Taylor, Diana, 4, 179n.14
Thomas, Dexter, 133–34
Thompson, Robert Farris, 36, 190n.33
Three Stooges, The, 26–27, 187n.1
Trac2, 8–9, 22, 64, 72–77, 180n.23, 198nn.35–36
Triple7, 31, 40, 45–46, 192n.67
Tsing, Anna L., 131–32, 212n.2
Turner, Victor, 186n.69

US Battle of the Year (BOTY), ix, 25, 26*f*

Vega, Marta Moreno, 186n.69
Vendetta, 106
Viazeen, 25, 54, 150–51
Vincent, Rickey, 150
violence
    breaking crews and, 79, 81
    hierarchy and, 79
    state, 75
    systemic, 70–71
Vizenor, Gerald, 75

Walker, Alice, xiv
Washington, Booker T., 152
Waterman, Richard, 216n.61
"welfare hotels," 70, 197n.27
Welsh, Kariamu, 151
West, Cornel, 15–16, 159
whiteness
    Americanness and, 1–2
    cyphers and, 104
    in Hewitt, 65–66
Whitey's Lindy Hoppers, 168
Wild Style (film), 9–10
Wilson, Olly, 15, 183n.45
Winant, Howard, 159
worldmaking, 34, 149–50, 154–55

Young City Girls (crew), 85–86
yowa cross, 35–37

Zachary, André, 167
Zulu Killers, xii
Zulu Kings, xii